Ricoeur and Castoriadis in Discussion

SOCIAL IMAGINARIES

SOCIAL
IMAGINARIES

Series Editors

Suzi Adams, Paul Blokker, Natalie J. Doyle,
John W. M. Krummel, and Jeremy C. A. Smith

This ground-breaking series aims to investigate social imaginaries from theoretical, comparative, historical, and interdisciplinary perspectives. Its objective is to foster challenging research on the burgeoning but heterogeneous field of social imaginaries, on the one hand, and the related field of the creative imagination, on the other. The series seeks to publish rigorous and innovative research that reflects the international, multiregional, and interdisciplinary scope across these fields.

Titles in the Series

Ricoeur and Castoriadis in Discussion, edited by Suzi Adams
Productive Imagination, edited by Saulius Geniusas and Dmitri Nikulin
(forthcoming)
Stretching the Limits of Productive Imagination, edited by Saulius Geniusas
(forthcoming)

Ricoeur and Castoriadis in Discussion

On Human Creation, Historical Novelty, and the Social Imaginary

Edited by
Suzi Adams

ROWMAN & LITTLEFIELD
——INTERNATIONAL——
London • New York

Published by Rowman & Littlefield International Ltd.
Unit A, Whitacre Mews, 26–34 Stannary Street, London SE11 4AB
www.rowmaninternational.com

Rowman & Littlefield International Ltd. is an affiliate of Rowman & Littlefield
4501 Forbes Boulevard, Suite 200, Lanham, Maryland 20706, USA
With additional offices in Boulder, New York, Toronto (Canada), and Plymouth (UK)
www.rowman.com

Originally published in French as Dialogue sur l'imagination sociale

British Library Cataloguing in Publication Data
A catalogue record for this book is available from the British Library

ISBN: HB 978-1-7866-0134-6
       PB 978-1-7866-0135-3

Library of Congress Cataloging-in-Publication Data Is Available

ISBN: 978-1-78660-134-6 (cloth: alk. paper)
ISBN: 978-1-78660-135-3 (pbk: alk. paper)
ISBN: 978-1-78660-136-0 (electronic)

™
⊖ The paper used in this publication meets the minimum requirements of American
National Standard for Information Sciences—Permanence of Paper for Printed Library
Materials, ANSI/NISO Z39.48-1992.

Printed in the United States of America

Contents

Acknowledgements   vii

Editor's Foreword   ix
Suzi Adams

Note to the French Edition   xiii
Johann Michel

Preface: Situating Castoriadis and Ricoeur   xv
Johann P. Arnason

Preface to the French Edition   xxxiii
Johann Michel
(translated by Scott Davidson)

**PART I: RICOEUR AND CASTORIADIS
RADIO DIALOGUE**   **1**

1 Dialogue on History and the Social Imaginary   3
Paul Ricoeur and Cornelius Castoriadis
(translated by Scott Davidson)

PART II: ESSAYS   **21**

2 On the Cusp: Ricoeur and Castoriadis at the Boundary   23
George H. Taylor

3 Castoriadis and Ricoeur on Meaning and
      History: Contrasts and Convergences   49
      Johann P. Arnason

4 Ricoeur and Castoriadis: The Productive Imagination
      between Mediation and Origin   77
      Jean-Luc Amalric

5 Castoriadis and Ricoeur on the Hermeneutic Spiral and
      the Meaning of History: Creation, Interpretation, Critique   111
      Suzi Adams

6 The Social Imaginary as Engine of History
      in Ricoeur and Castoriadis   139
      François Dosse
      (translated by Natalie J. Doyle)

Biographical Notes on Paul Ricoeur and Cornelius Castoriadis   171

Index   175

About the Contributors   185

Acknowledgements

It took a veritable village to bring the Ricoeur–Castoriadis dialogue to publication. I would like to express my gratitude to Johann Arnason and George Taylor for their wise counsel through the many months of complex negotiations and concrete formulation of the project. I would like to thank the Castoriadis heirs and the Ricoeur literary executors, and the *École des hautes études en sciences sociales* (EHESS) Press for granting their permission for the English-language publication of the dialogue. I would also like to thank Johann Michel for his behind-the-scenes advocacy with the EHESS. The translators – Scott Davidson and Natalie Doyle – were beyond generous with their time and expertise; thank you very much! Additionally, I would like to acknowledge Scott's translation of the Castoriadis and Ricoeur biographical notes and the note to the French edition, which have been incorporated into the English publication. George Sarantoulias and Erin Carlisle provided vital editorial assistance; thank you both! I would also like to thank the authors for their respective contributions, as well as for their comments on aspects of the project at various stages. It is an enduring delight to be part of the Social Imaginaries Collective, and I would like to thank Paul Blokker, Natalie Doyle, John Krummel, and Jeremy Smith for their support of the project. I would like to thank the Newgen team for their skilful production of the book. Finally, I would like to extend a big thank you to Sarah Campbell and her colleagues at Rowman & Littlefield International. Sarah has been tireless in her dedication to the book project (and ensuing book series), and her editorial advice and expertise have been invaluable.

Editor's Foreword

Suzi Adams

The radio discussion between Paul Ricoeur and Cornelius Castoriadis took place in March 1985. It is the only direct encounter between these two great thinkers of the imagination and human creativity. While each was familiar with – and occasionally referred to – the other's work, they were not interlocutors in any systematic way. This makes the radio dialogue especially valuable. The dialogue itself is relatively short and sometimes fiery. The fault lines are clear to see. Where, for example, Castoriadis defends an approach to creation *ex nihilo* that rejects an interpretative dimension, Ricoeur repudiates the idea of absolute novelty in favour of a more measured and hermeneutic perspective on human creativity. But as the supplementary essays in this volume clearly demonstrate, critical comparison between Ricoeur and Castoriadis's intellectual projects provides fertile ground for further philosophical, sociopolitical, and historical reflection.

The dialogue is, however, peppered with some persistent misunderstandings. At one point, Castoriadis notes that they seem to be speaking 'at cross purposes'. This can be attributed – at least in part – to the various seminar series that each had given in the years prior to the radio encounter, but which were not published at that time and thus remained unknown to the other. This is especially important in Ricoeur's case, who gave two series of lectures in Chicago in 1975: the first on ideology and utopia as the social imaginary and the second on the more properly philosophical aspects of the imagination. In Castoriadis's case, his seminars on ancient Greece, delivered at the EHESS in 1982–1983, were a significant source for his views in the radio discussion.

It is an honour to present the English-language publication of the Ricoeur–Castoriadis radio discussion. The French edition was published as *Dialogue sur l'histoire et l'imaginaire social* in 2016. It comprised the Ricoeur–Castoriadis dialogue proper and a substantive preface by distinguished Ricoeur scholar, Johann Michel (who, in collaboration with Pascal Vernay, also edited the publication). The English version offers a translation of both the radio dialogue and Michel's preface. It also includes a preface written especially for this edition by eminent Castoriadis scholar, Johann P. Arnason. Each preface offers a thoughtful contextualisation of the Ricoeur–Castoriadis encounter, but it does so from a different vantage point. Additionally, the English-language publication features supplementary essays by Ricoeur and Castoriadis scholars. Four of these – by George H. Taylor, Johann P. Arnason, Jean-Luc Amalric, and Suzi Adams – were commissioned especially for this volume and engage directly with the themes of the radio dialogue. The final essay by François Dosse, who has written intellectual biographies on both Ricoeur and Castoriadis, takes a broader perspective.

The first essay, by George Taylor, focuses on Ricoeur and Castoriadis's shared interest in the social imaginary, but notes their divergent emphasis on the creative and productive imagination, and the implications that this difference holds for their approaches to historical novelty. Taylor argues, however, that Ricoeur's earlier work on the imagination, such as that found in the imagination lectures and the ideology and utopia lectures, demonstrates a different approach to the question of creativity that brings him closer to Castoriadis's perspective. Johann Arnason's contribution takes a different approach. He not only notes common ground between the two thinkers, but highlights points of possible conflict from which each thinker retreats. Taking up the themes of historical novelty and continuity/discontinuity in history, Arnason argues that their shared concern with questions of meaning, historical reactivation, and creation does not result in discussion of historical processes, which, as historical novelty unfolds over time, would be important to incorporate. Jean-Luc Amalric's essay focuses on the role that the imagination plays in each thinker's approach to human creativity. In Castoriadis's thought, it features as origin, whereas in Ricoeur's hermeneutical approach, it has a mediating function. Amalric takes the interrelated themes of 'creation', 'production', and 'institution' to build his argument that, although there is indeed common ground, the two thinkers diverge significantly regarding the *method* of accessing the imagination, as well as their approach to its ontological/ hermeneutical *status* for the human condition. In her contribution, Suzi Adams emphasises the underdetermined quality of meaning that allows a potential bridge to be built between Castoriadis's 'creation *ex nihilo*' and Ricoeur's articulation of production as 'from something to something'. In her reconstruction of the problematic of historical continuity and discontinuity in the radio discussion, Adams expands the scope of reference to reveal an implicit dialogue on the hermeneutic spiral, which she argues needs to be rethought in relation to creation, interpretation, and critique. The book concludes with an essay by François Dosse. Dosse focuses on the overall intellectual trajectories of Ricoeur and Castoriadis, rather than on the radio encounter. Taking a wider – and more historical – scope, Dosse traces the shifting implications of the imagination and imaginary in Ricoeur's and Castoriadis's respective projects. He argues that, despite their many differences (philosophical, political, and otherwise), there is genuine convergence in the pivotal place that the imaginary holds for the human condition, as the motor of history.

Finally, on a more personal note, I visited the Castoriadis Archives in Paris in 2003, as part of my doctoral research. During my sojourn there, I stumbled across an unedited transcript of the Ricoeur–Castoriadis radio dialogue. Its intellectual significance was immediately apparent, and I was fortunate enough to be able to refer to it in my thesis and subsequent monograph. It is thus an honour to have the opportunity to edit the English edition of the dialogue's publication, and thereby make it available to a broad audience. It is, in fact, a double pleasure, for the publication of this book simultaneously launches the 'Social Imaginaries' book series with Rowman & Littlefield International, which is a sister project to the *Social Imaginaries* journal. These projects are edited by the Social Imaginaries Collective.

Note to the French Edition

Johann Michel

Dialogue on History and the Social Imagination is the posthumous title given to the conversation from the show *Le Bon Plaisir* (on *France Culture*) on 9 March 1985, to which Paul Ricoeur invited Cornelius Castoriadis. Excerpts from this conversation have been preserved in the archives of the *Institut National de l'Audiovisuel*. However, Zoé Castoriadis also created a transcript based on the recording of their exchange. It is valuable even though it remains a fragmented and first-hand document. So we decided to cross this source with extracts from the audio broadcast and the typescripted excerpts stored at *France Culture* (which are also held in the archives of the Fonds Ricoeur).

The transmission from the living word to its fixation in writing, however, required a complete rewriting of the text in successive steps (no less than eight versions were developed) with the help of the talents of both 'Ricoeurian' and 'Castoriadian' experts accustomed to the words of the respective authors: Catherine Goldenstein, Pascal Vernay, Olivier Fressard, and myself. Without losing sight of the fact that it was first a broadcasted conversation and the limitations inherent in this kind of operation, we hope that this document meets the high standards of our philosophers. For their support, we thank the editorial board of the Fonds Ricoeur and the heirs of Castoriadis for their permission to publish this conversation. We also thank the press of the EHESS and Emmanuel Désveaux for publishing this work in the series 'Audiographie'.

Preface

Situating Castoriadis and Ricoeur

Johann P. Arnason

POLITICAL CONNECTIONS

Comparing the philosophical trajectories of Cornelius Castoriadis and Paul Ricoeur, or exploring real and possible points of contact between them, might seem a far-fetched idea. The intellectual coordinates of the two thinkers are very different. Ricoeur pursued a philosophical vocation throughout his active life and developed his ideas through academic debates; not that he ignored political issues or avoided political statements, but his basic philosophical arguments were never constitutively linked to a political project. It is true that his project underwent major shifts, and if there is an underlying unity, it can only be understood as an itinerary, involving multiple refocusing of problems and responses to intellectual challenges. None of the landmarks in this story was primarily related to politics. This is not to deny the significance of his political thought. The essay on the 'political paradox' (Ricoeur 1965), written in response to the Hungarian Revolution of 1956, deserves particular mention. What Ricoeur identifies as a paradox is the double role of the state, as a monopoliser of violence and an agency of rational regulation; the argument is a sustained critique of Marxist failure to recognise the autonomy of the political, but it can also be read as a critical reflection on the Weberian conception of the state (although there is no direct engagement with Weber, neither here nor elsewhere in Ricoeur's work). Among later writings, the critique of Rawlsian liberalism and the attempt to place the political philosophy of recognition in a broader context (Ricoeur 2005, his last major work) are of major importance, but they neither reflected nor foreshadowed any fundamental reorientation.

Castoriadis was from early on a political activist with revolutionary views, although his version of revolutionary Marxism was always distinguished by broader intellectual horizons than the more orthodox readings. His earliest writings attest to familiarity with Hegel and Weber, and the untranslated 1948 essay on the phenomenology of proletarian consciousness (Castoriadis 1973) is probably the most Hegelian text ever written by a Marxist; but in the 1940s and 1950s, he was, above all else, defending and developing a political project. The radical rethinking that he undertook at the beginning of the 1960s was prompted by an all-round dissatisfaction with Marxism as a guide to political action. This called for a new vision of history, and the resulting critique of historical materialism remains, as the present author has argued elsewhere (Arnason 2012), the most comprehensive and convincing of its kind. But to break new ground in the understanding of history, Castoriadis had to engage in a wide-ranging exploration of philosophical horizons, questioning basic traditional assumptions and identifying points of new beginning; this took him far beyond the political sphere, and the transformation of his thought after 1960 coincided with a reluctant withdrawal from political engagement. He retained the hope that his version of radical philosophy would find a political expression, but after the de facto termination of *Socialisme ou Barbarie* in the mid-1960s, he was never involved in an organised group, although it seems clear that he repeatedly considered such possibilities, not least in connection with the events of May 1968.

VIEWS ON RELIGION

Another marked contrast between the two thinkers has to do with their attitude to and understanding of religion. Here the comparison becomes very asymmetric. It is worth noting that neither Castoriadis nor Ricoeur is discussed in Camille Tarot's important book on French theories of religion (Tarot 2008), probably for opposite reasons: Castoriadis seems too dismissive, Ricoeur too committed to a particular religion. But as will be seen, both deserve closer consideration.

Castoriadis's conception of religion, succinctly formulated in one short text (Castoriadis 1993), is essentially a complement to his theory of self-instituting society, and as he notes, it begins with the acknowledgement of a Durkheimian insight: the crucial and foundational role of religion in the formation of human societies. It serves to 'tie together the origin of the world and the origin of society' (Castoriadis 1993, 6). The starting point is, in other words, 'the religious core of the institution of all known societies, with two incomplete exceptions, Greece and the modern Western world' (Castoriadis 1993, 5). Castoriadis also follows Durkheim in identifying the sacred as the central element of religious beliefs and practices. But the next step parts ways with the Durkheimian perspective. Durkheim saw the sacred as a self-projection of society onto environment, making it possible to grasp the world as a totality; for Castoriadis, the sacred is a transfiguration of the unfathomable and indeterminate expanse that surrounds the human domain. A transcending and threatening horizon is covered over by a more meaning-laden image of transcendence, which thus becomes the centre of cosmic and social order. At the same time, the social constitution of the sacred results in a denial of self-instituting capacity and subordination to imagined supra-social instances. Religion is thus understood exclusively as an instituting force, and more precisely as a mainstay of heteronomous institutions. Castoriadis notes that this analysis does not consider the question of sects, nor of religions that emerged – as did early Christianity and early Buddhism – at a distance from dominant institutions but were later adapted to them. An obvious though unstated corollary is that no note is taken of the possible role of such religions in moves towards autonomy. And on another level, this view of religion disregards the traditions of mysticism.

Castoriadis's verdict on religion is, in short, uncompromisingly definitive: It belongs to the world of heteronomy, it can be judged from outside and found wanting, and the critical perspective needed to do so can be derived from a rethought ontology of the social-historical. An ongoing dialogue with religion is not envisaged, and not required for the argument at issue. It might be questioned whether Castoriadis maintained this view throughout his later work. For one thing, his seminars on ancient Greek thought and history suggest a more nuanced view: If rational theology was an enduring concern of Greek philosophy, the latter was by the same token engaged in a dialogue with religion, but that did not prevent it from becoming a paradigm of radical questioning.

In Ricoeur's work, religion has a much more significant role, too complex to be discussed in detail here, but some main points should be mentioned. Ricoeur's approach to historical themes is marked by his allegiance to a particular religious tradition and his distinctive conception of its message. A Christian and more specifically Protestant conviction, coupled with an unusually strong emphasis on the lasting and necessary complementarity of Judaism and Christianity, imposes certain choices and directions on thought in this field. We should therefore start with a brief glance at Ricoeur's way of demarcating faith from reflection (or conviction from critique, to use the title of a particularly revealing work [Ricoeur 1998]). François Dosse (2012, 25–6) quotes Ricoeur's statement, late in life, to the effect that he had maintained a commitment to the 'Christianity of philosophers', but not argued as a Christian philosopher. This may be taken as a key to his self-understanding, and it seems true that he never tried to build philosophical conclusions on theological premises; but we can nevertheless ask whether the distinction retained the same meaning throughout all phases of his work, and whether some major conceptual shifts did not blur or move the boundary between philosophical Christianity and Christian philosophy. If, as seems generally agreed, Christian existentialism was Ricoeur's original frame of reference, the two perspectives were perhaps not as clearly distinguished as he would later have it; nor is it obvious that subsequent changes were all and only in the spirit of stricter separation.

We may gain further insight from another statement, referring to complementary fields rather than mutually exclusive alternatives. In a book-length conversation with François Azouvi and Marc de Launay, first published in 1995 and covering his entire work to date, Ricoeur describes his intellectual situation, from early on, as 'at the crossroads of two currents of thought that have not been reconciled – philosophical critique and religious hermeneutics' (Ricoeur 1998, 28). The reference to crossing as well as to tension suggests a complex relationship, and further clarification must draw on other sources. The identification of philosophical analysis with critique reflects a particular affiliation with Kant, whose work Ricoeur consistently regarded as the keystone of modern thought (and therefore also as the most important mutually acceptable guide to a dialogue between analytical and continental philosophy). Not that this implied a devaluation of post-Kantian insights; Ricoeur's definition of himself as a 'post-Hegelian Kantian' signals both an opening to and a distance from German idealism, and Jean Greisch's suggestion that he might just as well have used the term 'post-Husserlian' underlines the role of phenomenology in the reorientation of the critical approach.

Even so, there is no doubt about Kant's exceptional significance or Ricoeur's understanding of the philosophical tradition. It is therefore striking that he should – at a late stage – single out Kant's work on 'religion within the bounds of mere reason' as an example of religious hermeneutics moving beyond the limits of philosophical critique. In fact, his reading of Kant might suggest that 'religion at the borders of mere reason' would have been a better title. The engagement with religion is an exemplary case of philosophy exploring patterns of meaning outside its jurisdiction and without binding claims on acceptance, but relevant to basic philosophical aspirations. It is not enough to enlist religion as a motivating auxiliary to practical reason; its own internal meaning must be clarified. That is not a matter of bringing religion into the orbit of critical philosophy, as Kant's *Critique of Judgment* did with art and living nature. Rather, the philosophical project – as formulated by Kant and rearticulated by Ricoeur – enters into contact with another realm of meaning, through the medium of hermeneutics. Three reasons are given for taking this view (Ricoeur 1995, 75–6). Kant deals with religion as a historical reality, made up of representation, belief, and institution, not – unlike nature and the good will – as a fact 'whose objectivity would be completed by universality'. Second, the focus is on the factual situation of the free will, and thus on an 'existential historicity' outside the realm of transcendental reflection. Finally, the treatise on religion confronts the question of justifying hope, not to be settled in the same terms as the questions of limits of knowledge and imperatives of action.

Ricoeur's interpretation of Kant's treatise on religion was first published in 1992. Three years later, in the conversation with Azouvi and de Launay (Ricoeur 1998), he recapitulates the road taken by his religious hermeneutics in more explicit terms. He acknowledges the strong influence of Mircea Eliade (whom he ranks alongside Gabriel Marcel as an intellectually inspiring friend), and a glance at Ricoeur's writings on hermeneutics in the 1950s will confirm this. The landmark essay on symbols as a guide to thought (Ricoeur 1959) lists Eliade as the first of several authoritative thinkers in that field, and his work on symbols of the sacred figures alongside the interpretation of dreams and of poetic symbolism. But the conversation also reveals the main reasons for growing reservations about Eliade's approach. For Ricoeur, the most fundamental problem seems to have been the notion of a radical autonomy of the religious dimension, inseparable from the mirage of immanent comprehension (through immersion in the phenomenon to be understood), as well as from the project of a universal and self-sufficient history of religion. All this was summed up in a single-minded focus on the contrast between the sacred and the profane, which Ricoeur describes, somewhat puzzlingly, as an 'almost ideological obsession'.

Ricoeur's critical turn against Eliade began, as he describes it, with the last-mentioned aspect. He toned down the excessive emphasis on the sacred and stressed the plurality of symbolisms; following his own account (Ricoeur 1998, 54), he eventually came to think that the very idea of the symbol – or a symbolic dimension – as a direct focus of interpretation was misguided, and that the more accessible phenomenon of metaphor should be in the foreground. This shift indicates a radicalisation of Ricoeur's linguistic turn. But at the same time, the debate with Eliade led to a reorientation within the field of religious studies. Against Eliade's insistence on beginning with a recovery of archaic and oriental sources, long forgotten by European believers and scholars alike, Ricoeur argues for a self-reflection of Judaic and Christian traditions (he underlines the importance of both), in his view necessary to pave the way for more comparative interpretations. This reflexive step explains his suggestion that the opposition of saint and sinner might be more significant than that of sacred and profane. But the most fundamental result of the hermeneutical return to foundations is a new twist to the idea of revelation. Ricoeur's comments in the conversation with Azouvi and de Launay seem to mark the borderline situation where religious hermeneutics moves beyond philosophical critique without taking a confessional stand. A key formulation refers to a 'a ground of questioning that was ultimately more resistant, more profound, and that comes from farther back than critique itself', and goes on to invoke a 'giving of meaning', constituting 'constitute me both as a receptive and a critical subject' (Ricoeur 1998, 146). That is as far as the clarification of religious meaning can go, and it does not obliterate the difference between critique and conviction; nor does it rationalise or domesticate the idea of God. Ricoeur maintains that this notion has no place in philosophical discourse. On the other hand, his differentiated understanding of revelation (especially in Ricoeur 2010) seems potentially very suggestive for comparative religious studies. A comprehensive overview of biblical genres highlights the 'play of contrasts between narrative and prophecy, then between history and legislation, then between legislation and wisdom, finally between wisdom and lyricism' (Ricoeur 2010, 228).

THE RAMIFICATIONS OF HERMENEUTICS

For Ricoeur, the philosophical lesson of these thoughts on revelation is an acceptance of 'dependence without heteronomy' (Ricoeur 2010, 268), a notion also applicable in regard to poetic creation, and referring to an opening of the imagination rather than a submission of the will. More generally speaking, dependence without heteronomy becomes a kind of common denominator for philosophy's dialogue with extra-philosophical sources of meaning. This articulation of receptivity should be seen in connection with other aspects of the hermeneutical pluralism in Ricoeur's work. On the basic level of location within traditions, he links up with philosophical hermeneutics as a distinctively modern accompaniment to critical philosophy, but characterised by a continuing divergence of paradigms rather than an ongoing elaboration or clarification of shared ideas. Schleiermacher, Dilthey, Heidegger, and Gadamer represent different ways of re-centring philosophical reflection around meaning, understanding, and interpretive visions of the human condition; their affinities are marked enough to define a current in modern thought, but do not add up to any mainstream version of hermeneutics. For Ricoeur, this pluralism prefigures a fundamental point: '[T]he hermeneutical field is an essentially conflictual field' (Ricoeur 1990, 19). The centrality of conflict manifests itself on multiple levels, from the elementary polysemy of natural language (important for the analysis of metaphor) to the interpretive disputes inherent in the reception of art and the alternative readings of philosophical traditions. Ricoeur's insistence on the inexhaustible resources of past philosophical systems is one of his main arguments against Heidegger's attempt to close the book on metaphysics, but the possibility of ever new interpretations also implies a continuing conflict.

The idea of conflict as a general feature of the hermeneutical field is qualified by a more specific notion of polarity, most emphatically formulated in Ricoeur's book on Freud, and thus particularly salient in the middle phase of his thought. His now well-known distinction between a hermeneutic of suspicion and a hermeneutic of recovery contrasts two fundamentally opposed formations of meaning. Reductionist modes of interpretation convert manifest meanings into an expression or disguise of underlying forces, with varying emphasis on interest, power, or more elementary infra-social factors. The opposite approach aims at a more adequate understanding and a reappropriation of neglected or forgotten meaning. This stark confrontation reflects the particular thematic focus of the book: Freud's metapsychology, more precisely Freud's own understanding of a new and elusive problematic, represents the hermeneutic of suspicion at its most distant from cultural meaning; conversely, the hermeneutic of recovery is most closely linked to a transcultural symbolism of the sacred, conceived in a way clearly close to Eliade's.

Against this background, Ricoeur's later elaboration of hermeneutical perspectives may be seen as a multifaceted but unfinished effort to find the proper balance between the pluralistic and the bipolar vision of the field. The growing emphasis on language, and on linguisticality as a precondition of human thought and action, shifts attention to the common ground of the two alternative hermeneutics, as well as to conflicts arising at this level, without involving an option for either recovery or suspicion. Further differentiations and complications emerge on both sides. Although Ricoeur never engaged with Marx to the same extent as with Freud, his work on ideology and utopia did discuss Marx and the Marxist tradition at some length, and the result appears as a combination of the hermeneutic of suspicion with the hermeneutic of recovery. The analysis of Marxian approaches to social consciousness examines their credentials as an exercise in the hermeneutic of suspicion, but an adequate understanding of their themes depends on the acceptance of meaning as a constitutive element of social being, and this is clearly a case of the hermeneutic of recovery overcoming reductionism. And as we have seen, Ricoeur's idea of religious hermeneutics developed new aspects. The focus on Judaic and Christian religiosity entails a specific hermeneutic of revelation, with the clear implication that other traditions would call for other accentuations of the hermeneutical stance.

This ongoing differentiation raises questions about locating other thinkers in the hermeneutical universe of discourse, and for present purposes, that applies to Castoriadis. There is no doubt that such a reading would run counter to his self-understanding; he rejected hermeneutical approaches on the grounds that they overemphasised the interpretation of meaning in various forms and contexts, at the expense of the creativity which he attributes to meaning in the social-historical realm. Ricoeur's sustained analysis of imagination and meaning, with particular reference to metaphor as linguistic innovation, shows that a hermeneutical perspective does not preclude interest in creation. Conversely, it can – as I will try to show – be argued that a hermeneutical logic is essential to Castoriadis's line of thought, and that his reflections on specific issues reveal some affinity with Ricoeur's distinction between the hermeneutic of suspicion and the hermeneutic of recovery. A first indication of reasons for a hermeneutical turn can be seen in the thoroughgoing emphasis on meaning, fundamental for Castoriadis's whole critique of historical materialism. But there is more to be said about particular steps of the unfolding argument.

The discussion of the revolutionary project (Castoriadis 1987 [1975], 71–114) is a key aspect of the transition from heterodox Marxism to a militantly non-Marxist conception of history and society, documented in the first part of *The Imaginary Institution of Society*, and deserves closer examination than it has so far received. It would not seem far-fetched to describe the line taken in this chapter as a critique of revolutionary reason, in a roughly Kantian sense: Against under-reflected and at the same time overambitious visions of revolution, Castoriadis wanted to establish a rational project, in full awareness of legitimate aspirations as well as of basic limits. But the argument proceeds in such a way that we can also speak of a hermeneutical clarification, beginning with the elementary point that the revolutionary project is described on the basis of canonical texts that make up the Marxist–Leninist tradition (including its Trotskyist offshoot, which Castoriadis knew particularly well). More importantly, the critique can be divided into four successive steps, all hermeneutical in character but not in the same sense. Here I will reconstruct them in a slightly different order from Castoriadis's presentation.

The first move is, necessarily, a critique of pretensions to ground the revolutionary project in a comprehensive theory of history and society. This part of the argument combines a hermeneutic of suspicion with a hermeneutic of recovery. The ideas of a total rationality and a correspondingly complete theory are called in question, shown to be untenable in principle and self-destructive in practice (notably in the Marxist–Leninist version); the objections to such constructs apply *a fortiori* to the determinist view that prevailed in dominant currents of

Marxism, and here we encounter the added problem that determinism excludes the autonomous action presupposed by the revolutionary ambitions of the same theory. But the very refutation of these misguided notions discloses aspects of historical experience that have also been, at least tentatively, acknowledged by undercurrents in the Marxist tradition. History is a realm of open horizons, changing perspectives, and innovative action; to quote a formulation that foreshadows much of Castoriadis's later work, it is 'the domain of creation' (Castoriadis 1987 [1975], 44–5). Here the hermeneutic of recovery is at work, and its implications become clearer with the second step. The revolutionary project is a strategic starting point for reflection on ways to advance our understanding of human action, but Castoriadis also draws on other examples, from psychoanalytical therapy to the creation of works, and his line of interpretation links up with the classical concepts of *praxis* and *poiesis* (although only the former is explicitly invoked, and Castoriadis's own preferred term is 'doing', *faire*). Creative work, whether aesthetic, intellectual, or institutional, involves a broadening of horizons and an unfolding of meanings beyond the orientations present at the outset. The clarification of the revolutionary project, against authoritarian misconceptions, highlights a point also important for the self-understanding of psychoanalysis as an intervention in the human condition and indicated in the most general terms by the concept of *praxis*: the autonomy of the other as a presupposition and ever-renewed goal of action, neither a mere means nor a definite end. Last but not least, this conception of human doing emphasises the ongoing transformation of its subject.

The third step of Castoriadis's hermeneutical operation is a de-mythologising one, directed against the dominant vision of communism. His target is, more precisely, a cluster of loosely defined notions, relating to the social changes to be achieved through revolution. They suggest a stateless society that has not only abolished classes, but also overcome the division of labour and dispensed with markets; the idea of a leap from the realm of necessity to the realm of freedom sums up these exaggerated expectations. On the anthropological level, the image of the future centres on a 'total human being', in full control of history and society. It might be objected that Marx's writings show a distinct shift from highly utopian to more realistic perspectives on communism, but it is also true that this change was never explicitly theorised, the results remained inconclusive, and later experience showed that utopian extremes could be reactivated. For Castoriadis, the ideas in question (he describes them as mythical, but never uses the concept of political religion) suggest a transparent society that 'would discover, formulate and realise the collective will without passing through institutions, and whose institutions would never be a problem' (Castoriadis 1987 [1975], 111), and he regards this phantasm as comparable to the illusions of absolute knowledge or a complete elimination of the unconscious.

The de-mythologising detour paves the way for a final round. Castoriadis characterises the human relationship to the social-historical dimension as a matter of 'inherence', a mixture of 'interiority and exteriority, of participation and exclusion' (Castoriadis 1987 [1975], 111); the condition of inherence does not exclude advances of reflection and liberty, but the ideology that cannot accept 'finitude, limitation and lack' (Castoriadis 1987 [1975], 112) is in denial of social-historical reality. In light of later developments, it is easily recognisable as the common denominator of communist and capitalist utopias. Castoriadis argued for a revolutionary alternative to both, and tried to show that workers' self-management was the kind of institutional innovation most likely to result in all-round radical change. Given the transformations of capitalism, political culture, and ideological patterns, this perspective now seems a good deal less plausible than in the 1960s. But here it is not the viability of political strategies that concerns us. The point to note is that the all-round rethinking involved in Castoriadis's break with Marxism gave rise to the central problematic of his whole later work: the question of interrelations between social-historical being and the human subject.

There will be more to say on the ontology of the social-historical. But to conclude the present part of the discussion, the hermeneutical context of Castoriadis's ontological turn should be considered from one more angle. He introduces his key ontological theme – social-historical creativity – through confrontation with alternative images of society. The first chapter in the second part of *The Imaginary Institution of Society* (Castoriadis 1987 [1975], 167–220) begins with a critique of established but, on closer view, untenable models that have served as frameworks for the interpretation of human societies. Two exemplary cases are considered, conceptions that reduce social-historical being respectively to organic or logical patterns. The former has a long tradition, and is also the shared foundation of modern functionalist theories, while the focus on the latter reflects the exceptionally strong influence of Lévi-Strauss's structural anthropology on French social thought during the 1960s. Conversely, the somewhat surprising absence of the individualist image, often criticised in passing elsewhere in Castoriadis's work, can be explained by the limited appeal of such ideas in a tradition still marked by rival interpretations of the Durkheimian legacy. If the fallacy of the organic and logical paradigms consisted in assimilating the social-historical domain to models drawn from elsewhere, the individualist perspective mistakes a specific and derivative part of that domain – the instituted individual – for a key to the whole. It is the contrast with these misdirected approaches that brings out the implications of Castoriadis's effort to elucidate the questions of society and history, conceived as aspects of one and the same problematic. The meaning of social-historical creativity is clarified in direct contest with the preconceptions that have blocked its understanding. This constellation exemplifies the hermeneutical field of conflicting interpretations, as defined by Ricoeur.

HUMAN ACTION AND ITS ONTOLOGICAL HORIZONS

A brief recapitulation will help to situate the final step in our comparison of Castoriadis and Ricoeur. The question of religion, incomparably more important for Ricoeur than for Castoriadis, was discussed at some length, and with a view to underlining the distance between the two thinkers. But Ricoeur's continuing reflections on religious texts and traditions – as one of the non-philosophical sources of philosophy – was clearly also crucial for the elaboration of a multifaceted hermeneutical framework, which can in turn be seen as a latent common ground between Ricoeur and Castoriadis. It remains to be examined whether their affinity leads to convergences of a more specific kind, and whether significant contrasts reappear within that more narrowly demarcated field.

Ricoeur often referred to philosophical anthropology as the thematic centre of his work, and critical interpreters have argued that broader horizons and advancing insights in this field are the main reasons for differences between his earlier and later writings. The idea of a 'capable human being' has been singled out as an emerging and overarching theme (Clément 2006); *Fallible Man* (Ricoeur 1987 [1960]) and *Oneself as Another* (Ricoeur 1992 [1990]) can be seen as the opening and concluding stages of an anthropological project (e.g. Sugimura 1995). But the last-mentioned work ends with a chapter on possible ontological prolongations of the argument. The ontological project, very tentatively formulated, grows out of Ricoeur's analysis of the self and the other. These two poles of a dialectical relationship (Ricoeur strongly emphasises that term) cannot be adequately understood without thematising their mode of being, and that brings into play the more general question of being. Despite this opening of ontological horizons, Ricoeur's suggestions remain on the cautious side; they are fundamentally different from Heidegger's variations on the question of being, and more akin to the elementary ontologies that have emerged in the orbit of analytical philosophy. Identity and otherness, persons, things, and events are the categories to be considered. On the other hand, the ontological frame of reference serves to avoid what Ricoeur calls the 'closed semantism' of mainstream analytical philosophy, its inability to account 'for human action as actually *happening* in the world' (1992, 301; emphasis in original).[1] Here the connection between a philosophy of action and a philosophical perspective is particularly pronounced, and in the same paragraph, Ricoeur speaks of linking philosophical thought to effective doing, using the same word as Castoriadis (*faire*).

It is clear from the preface to *The Imaginary Institution of Society*, as well as from the concluding passages of the second part, that Castoriadis's rethinking of social-historical being was to be accompanied by a similar elucidation of human doing; the posthumously published fragment on 'the imaginary as such' (Castoriadis 2015) stresses the need for interconnected analyses of representing and doing, but the unfinished argument also shows that Castoriadis found the former theme (which in fact became the cornerstone of his social ontology) much easier to tackle than the second. Notwithstanding declarations of intent and various insightful observations, doing remained an underdeveloped theme in his later work. In contrast to Ricoeur, Castoriadis had started out from a more emphatic conception of the possibilities open to human action (on the level of the revolutionary project), but made less progress with conceptualising the elementary patterns of action. One way to develop his reflections in that vein would be to explore points of contact with Ricoeur's thought.

On the other hand, Castoriadis's ventures into general ontology were more ambitious than those of Ricoeur. His proposal to revive the Greek notion of *physis*, understood as a world in creative becoming, did not develop into anything comparable to the work on society and history, but his reflections on the philosophical implications of the natural sciences, with particular emphasis on discontinuities between their respective domains of enquiry, reveal the outlines of a strongly anti-reductionist programme. Even so, the contrast between the two thinkers should not be exaggerated. There are at least two indications of shared assumptions and cautionary perspectives. Both Castoriadis and Ricoeur refer explicitly to Aristotle's thesis on the multiple modes of being. For Ricoeur, this is primarily a matter of distinguishing between the meanings attributable to the diverse aspects of the self and the others (including the difference between reality and potentiality, inherent in the concept of the capable actor); what Castoriadis had in mind was a more comprehensive spectrum of regional ontologies, ranging from cosmo-logical hypotheses through more solidly anchored analyses of living beings to the elucidation of society, history and the psyche. But in both cases, the reminder of polysemy serves to warn against premature theo-rising, and another shared theme adds emphasis to that. Ricoeur (1990) stressed the fragmentary character of the ontology that he could envis-age. The fundamental reason for this reservation was his understanding of reflexive philosophy, enriched by phenomenology and hermeneutics, as an enduringly problematic clarification of 'the broken cogito', the self-awareness that remains an indispensable and unbypassable starting point but can no longer be mistaken for a certain foundation. This con-text of reference – not a transcendental ground, an ever-renewed horizon of questioning – is perhaps Ricoeur's most significant link to the trad-ition that began with Kant and continued with Fichte; it rules out any definitive or comprehensive ontological turn. When Castoriadis referred to a 'world in fragments' (first in a working title for a text on philosophy and science, and then in the book title chosen for a collection of essays), he was drawing on a different framework, but with some comparable implications. The fragmented view of the world is, first and foremost, due to the limited grip of human thought on an understructured and ever-emerging reality, but also due to tensions between identitarian thought, rooted in basic social institutions, and more or less articulated attempts to overcome its limits; last but not least, it has to do with the fragmented state of contemporary culture and society, where dominant modes of thought have disintegrated but not been replaced by adequate alternatives. The resulting constellation is incompatible with any sys-tematic ontology.

SHARED PROBLEMATICS

The above reflections have identified some common ground between Castoriadis and Ricoeur; further aspects will be explored below, with direct reference to their conversation. Here I will only add a brief comment on a less obvious but not uninteresting affinity. Johann Michel concludes his very thorough study of Ricoeur's philosophy with the suggestion that it combines a traditionalist, a modernist, and a post-modernist paradigm. The first posits an 'already given meaning' as a founding ground, the second affirms the primacy of the human subject, and the third centres on a rejection of the very idea of foundation (Michel 2006, 470). There is no doubt that the three problematics – the precedence of meaning, the question of the subject and the critique of foundations – are present and interconnected in Ricoeur's work. It is much less clear that we can identify them with the three paradigms mentioned by Michel. Acknowledging the precedence of meaning (in other words: a universe of meaning neither produced, nor mastered, nor exhausted by a subject) does not *eo ipso* entail a traditionalist position; rather, this theme is rediscovered by modern thought (most momentously by its romantic currents), and put in a new perspective that highlights the self-questioning capacity, the comparative understanding, and the internal interpretive conflicts of traditions. Ricoeur's approach to traditions, including his special relationship to Judeo-Christian sources and his pluralistic attitude to past philosophical systems, clearly belongs in this context. The modern character of subject-centred philosophies is not in dispute; Ricoeur's version is, as we have seen, particularly sensitive to the complexity, openness, and interpretive ambiguity of the subjective dimension. As for the critique of foundationalism, there is nothing postmodern about it. The anti-foundationalist turn is a recurrent trend in modern thought; to mention only some key twentieth-century cases, it is evident in the shift from the early to the late philosophy of Wittgenstein, in the Popperian critique of positivism, and in the post-transcendental turn of phenomenology, most clearly exemplified by Merleau-Ponty's work. If postmodernism gave a new twist to this theme, it was an effort to convert reasoned critique into an 'anything goes' style. Ricoeur's critique of foundationalism, unmistakably present from early on and enriched through phenomenological and hermeneutical insights, certainly owed nothing to postmodernist influences.

The three problematics, not to be identified with separate paradigms, also seem represented in Castoriadis's work. His account of meaning as an irreducible dimension rests on two complementary sources, the representational flux of the unconscious and the collective unconscious web of social imaginary significations. Nobody would think of describing this approach as traditionalist, but it is worth noting that it allows for specific traditional references. As Castoriadis's seminars on ancient Greece show, his Greek affiliation was not only based on philosophical and political breakthroughs to autonomy. He reconstructs a Greek 'grasp of the world', going back to the archaic period that preceded classical developments of rational interrogation and self-government. This distinctive image of and attitude to the world centres on a vision of partial order against a chaotic background, without any ultimate divine authority and therefore compatible with a certain autonomy of mortal human beings existing and acting within it. Castoriadis regards the Homeric epics as the most representative expression of these archaic notions, but the underlying framework is a distinctive pattern of the mythical imaginary. If we confront this analysis with Castoriadis's theory of religion, it seems obvious that he saw archaic Greece as a case of mythical thought breaking through the core structure of religion: the 'simulacrum' of the sacred as a protective screen against a chaotic world. This is a very strong claim, and would deserve clearer formulation, but it remains implicit. While it is not being suggested that his invocation of Greek beginnings is of the same order as Ricoeur's commitment to biblical traditions, a certain affinity should be noted. In his debate with Lévi-Strauss, Ricoeur had argued against overgeneralised theories of myth and maintained that, when myth becomes a vehicle of revelation, new ground is broken and new approaches are needed. Castoriadis appears to be claiming that Greek mythology entered upon a new path, thus becoming a prelude and an enduring stimulus to philosophical reflection (rather than the stark opposite suggested by the traditional contrast between *mythos* and *logos*), as well as a cultural quarry for various genres.

Castoriadis's reframing of the modern question of the subject is directly related to his two perspectives on meaning. He sees the subject as a changing and self-transforming product of interaction between the social-historical and the psyche; the most fundamental link between the two levels is the imagination, but reflection, 'definable as the effort to

break closure' (Castoriadis 1997, 271), is the precondition for autono-
mising moves in both directions, in relation to the psyche as well as to
the institutional architecture of society. Castoriadis's main complaint
against philosophies of the subject is that they have tried to screen
out the constitutive contexts, and as a result lapsed into egology. That
verdict does not do justice to differences between major figures and
paradigms in this tradition, but the combined horizons of the social-
historical and the psyche do transform the whole problematic. And they
are conceived in such a way that philosophical reflection becomes a
questioning without end. That is Castoriadis's way of rejecting foundationalism, certainly no closer to postmodernism than Ricoeur's views
were. The survey of the three problematics has thus revealed further
contrasts and resemblances between the two thinkers, and these issues
will be revisited in light of the exchange between them.

NOTE

1. A more literal translation would be: 'for human acting as an effective
arrival in the world'.

REFERENCES

Arnason, Johann P. 2012. 'Castoriadis im Kontext: Genese und Anspruch eines
metaphilosophischen Projekts'. In *Das Imaginäre im Sozialen. Zur Sozialtheorie
von Cornelius Castoriadis.* Edited by Harald Wolf, 39–62. Göttingen: Wallstein.
Castoriadis, Cornelius. 1973. 'Phénoménologie de la conscience prolétari-
enne'. In *La société bureaucratique, v. 1: Les rapports de production en
Russie,* 115–29. Paris: Union Générale d'Éditions.
———. 1987 [1975]. *The Imaginary Institution of Society.* Translated by
Kathleen Blamey. Cambridge, MA: Massachusetts Institute of Technology
Press.
———. 1993. 'Institution of Society and Religion'. *Thesis Eleven* 35: 1–17.
———. 1997. *World in Fragments: Writings on Politics, Society, Psychoanalysis,
and the Imagination.* Stanford, CA: Stanford University Press.
———. 2015. 'The Imaginary as Such'. Translated by Johann P. Arnason,
Social Imaginaries 1:1: 59–69.
Clément, Bruno. 2006. *L'homme capable: Autour de Paul Ricoeur.* Paris: Presses
Universitaires de France.

Dosse, François. 2012. *Paul Ricoeur: Un philosophe dans son siècle*. Paris: Armand Colin.

Michel, Johann. 2006. *Paul Ricoeur: Une philosophie de l'agir humain*. Paris: Cerf.

Ricoeur, Paul. 1959. 'Le symbole donne à penser'. *Esprit* 27:7/8: 60–76.

———. 1965. 'The Political Paradox'. In *History and Truth*. Translated by Charles A. Kelby, 247–70. Evanston, IL: Northwestern University Press.

———. 1987 [1960]. *Fallible Man*. New York: Fordham University Press.

———. 1990. 'De la volonté à l'acte: Entretien avec Carlos Oliveira'. In *'Temps et récit' de Paul Ricoeur en débat*. Edited by Christian Bouchindhomme and Rainer Rochlitz, 17–36. Paris: Cerf.

———. 1992 [1990]. *Oneself as Another*. Chicago, IL: Chicago University Press.

———. 1995. 'A Philosophical Hermeneutics of Religion: Kant'. In *Figuring the Sacred. Religion, Narrative and Imagination*, 75–92. Minneapolis, MN: Fortress Press.

———. 1998. *Critique and Conviction*. Translated by Kathleen Blamey. Cambridge, UK: Polity Press.

———. 2005. *The Course of Recognition*. Cambridge, MA: Harvard University Press.

———. 2010. 'Herméneutique de l'idée de revelation'. In *Écrits et Conférences, t. 1: Herméneutique*. Paris: Seuil.

Sugimura, Yasuhiko. 1995. 'L'homme, médiation imparfaite. De *L'homme faillible* à l'herméneutique du soi'. In *Paul Ricoeur – L'herméneutique à l'école de la phénoménologie*. Edited by Jean Greisch, 195–218. Paris: Beauchesne.

Tarot, Camille. 2008. *Le symbolique et le sacré. Théories de la religion*. Paris: La Découverte.

Preface to the French Edition

Johann Michel

Everything seems to be opposite and opposed, in some sense, between Castoriadis and Ricoeur: two different temperaments, two different styles, two different philosophies. One could readily say that Castoriadis is 'forward' and incisive; he has a very affirmative style that does not make concessions to his opponents. One could easily describe Ricoeur by the art of the detour and the negotiation between opposites, by a type of argumentation that is more aporetic than affirmative. While this description might be pertinent regarding their respective writings, it is less so, for Ricoeur at least, when philosophy is heard in living dialogue. It suffices to re-read or replay Ricoeur's exchanges with some of his contemporaries – Claude Lévi-Strauss, Jean-Pierre Changeux, to name but a few – to be persuaded of this point. The Ricoeur who is described sometimes as ecumenical and sometimes as timid gives way to a Ricoeur who is not aggressive but sometimes very biting and who does not let go of his arguments. And that is one of the interests of this dialogue between Ricoeur and Castoriadis in which the incisive speech of the former has nothing to envy of the latter.

At the time of this interview, in March 1985, Ricoeur was 72 years old. He had already released the first two volumes of *Time and Narrative* and was preparing to publish the third volume a few months later. The reflection on history is at the heart of this trilogy that contributed to his international renown. Ten years earlier, Castoriadis (who was 63 years old at the time of this conversation) published his masterpiece – *The Imaginary Institution of Society* – in which the social and political imagination, as well as history, occupies a crucial role. It was also in 1975 that Ricoeur taught his famous course on ideology and utopia at the University of Chicago, which was later published in English by Columbia University Press (Ricoeur 1986) in 1986 (before being translated into French by Seuil in 1997) (Ricoeur 1997).

So, it must be recognised that in the ten-year span between 1975 and 1985, Castoriadis and Ricoeur worked on research topics that were very close, but that were rarely explored in the academic community of the time. It is therefore no coincidence that Castoriadis had sought out Ricoeur for his thesis project (that never ended) precisely on the question of the social-historical imagination, nor that Ricoeur invited Castoriadis to this episode of *Le Bon Plaisir* on *France Culture*, nor that he pays homage at the beginning of the conversation to *The Imaginary Institution of Society*. There is a very revealing slip of the tongue by Ricoeur (who speaks about the 'imaginary *production* of society' in reference to Castoriadis's work) which sets in motion the conversation whose unity revolves entirely around one question: Is it possible to create the new historically? Whence the importance that both men grant to the symbolic or imaginary function as a collective faculty for producing social changes. This clearly connects the imaginary and history.

The particular tone of this exchange should be emphasised. Like billiard balls, the replies of Ricoeur and Castoriadis sometimes only intersect, sometimes collide, and sometimes eventually converge in order to immediately diverge more. Though it is 'lively', the exchange never loses its friendly character, even at the time of its greatest differences. As readers of each other's work, they have never hidden their mutual intellectual respect.[1] Even though the risk of a living exchange is dispersion, it is rather remarkable that the same problem punctuates the conversation from beginning to end: Can one speak of historical *creation* or does every new human *production* proceed from already existing historical configurations? While the issue is, after all, fairly standard in the theory of history, the interest of the conversation is the battery of arguments and examples (drawn from literary and artistic history, from the history of science, social and political history, the history of philosophy, etc.) that are brought up in support of their remarks. Instead of taking place in a void, the controversy is nourished by new elements that open philosophy outside of itself. This enterprise is facilitated by the fact that dialogue with the social sciences is a central motif of Ricoeur's philosophy, while the many disciplinary caps worn by Castoriadis (philosopher, psychoanalyst, economist, etc.) make him a unique mind of his time.

The regular reader of their work will not be surprised to know that it is up to Castoriadis, in this game of roles and verbal jousts, to defend the thesis of historical *creation* relentlessly (in a purely anthropological sense, it should be recalled). This is understood as the possibility of creating new 'forms' (institutional, artistic, political, scientific, etc.) which are not already foreshadowed in the existing order, which are not a mere effect of already existing forms, and which are not already contained in some sort of predetermined plan.

This thesis, taken in its most radical sense, is simply unacceptable to Ricoeur, who prefers to speak of *production* rather than *creation*. The point is not to say that everything is already prefigured but to attest that new human productions do not proceed from something non-existent but are always inscribed in a dialectic between innovation and sedimentation. If there is a discontinuity or innovation on some levels of human existence (scientific and technical for example), they do not affect all the other levels (whence Ricoeur's opposition on this point to Foucault's *The Archaeology of Knowledge* [1972]), especially not what he calls in the conversation the 'basso continuo' of human communities. In response to this objection, Castoriadis seems to concede Ricoeur's thesis that the 'discontinuity of meaning' can be accompanied to a certain extent by the 'continuity of existence'. The key, in Castoriadis's eyes, is the question of meaning and more specifically of creative social and political imaginaries, that is to say, those that are truly *instituting*. In fact, this is not a concession at all or else it is expressed ironically, because for Castoriadis, the existence of human societies is given from the outset in meaning. Therefore, to admit radical ruptures of meaning is at the same time to admit radical transformations of existence, even if Castoriadis readily recognises that these ruptures do not affect all of the levels of the existence of human communities at once (thus the Athenian democratic revolution was not accompanied by any substantial technical progress).

Ricoeur's allergy towards the thesis of a human historical *creation* does not point to a theological substitute (which would be incompatible with the radical atheism of Castoriadis), as if only God could claim the title of creator (of a world *ex nihilo*). Aside from the fact that Ricoeur would harbour serious doubts about the theological thesis of an 'absolute beginning',[2] this idea is never brandished in support of his arguments.[3] Such a theological reading would be all the more reductive insofar as the philosopher draws his argumentative resources from the 'new history' as well as from the hermeneutic tradition, each of which refuse any stance of radical uprooting from things that have already been said and inscribe all understanding in a pre-understanding. It is the hermeneutic primacy of the *pre-* which prevents Ricoeur from crossing the Rubicon of historical *creation*. Notably, it is the always prior existence of language, whose pre-existing rules prevent Ricoeur from subscribing to the idea that a new form could arise from some kind of formless chaos. His favourite model is derived from the hermeneutic theory of the text in virtue of which we proceed from interpretations and successive reinterpretations based on an already existing configuration. The weight of the central concept of *retroaction* follows from this; it helps to make living beings the reservoirs of already existing meanings. By the retroaction of 'our new creations on the old moments, we can deliver possibilities that had been prevented'. This is not simply to say that the past continues to haunt the present, but that the opening of new productions liberates at the same time the buried potential of the past.

Although he is not wed to all the prerequisites of structuralism – his heated dialogue with Lévi-Strauss can testify to that[4] – Ricoeur has never hidden his interest in structural analyses (all the while expressing his criticism of an all-encompassing and rigid structuralism) in order to objectify our 'historical societies' (as opposed to 'totemic societies').[5] So there is a sense in characterising Ricoeur's enterprise as a post-structuralist hermeneutics. By contrast, despite the influence of Lacan, Castoriadis only expressed distrust and resistance regarding the various forms of structuralism, due to the primacy accorded to synchrony over diachrony and due to its insistence on thinking change only in terms of the differential gap, in short, due to structuralism's inability to think creation as a true *instituting* imaginary. The few moments at which Castoriadis and Ricoeur seem to converge the most, and almost to be surprised by it, are in their opposition to a purely structuralist conception of language and history. So, in response to Castoriadis's assertion that 'each new form that emerges is not the result of a combination of pre-existing forms, even if it does retain a certain reference to the past', Ricoeur agrees by exclaiming, 'But then we are both on the same side!' as if they at least shared in this struggle: the idea that structures are never frozen and saturated but that they carry a still unemployed meaning. This shared struggle, however, is not yet an agreement between the two.

There are other readings, other influences, and especially other historical experiences that largely explain Castoriadis's profound attachment to the thesis of historical *creation*. These historical experiences, which appear repeatedly in his work and in this conversation, are the birth of mathematics in ancient Greece as well as the emergence of new unforeseen political forms, such as the Paris Commune. That is not to say that these 'new forms' fall from the sky or result from genius, but that one could not understand their unexpressed and radically innovative character if one sought to deduce them from already existing forms.

While the debate between Ricoeur and Castoriadis in this conversation certainly contains an epistemological dimension concerning history – against the backdrop of a discussion on the question of discontinuity and historical creation – it is at the same time animated by a practical, praxeological, political concern. In a sense, the stakes of this controversy have less to do with the conditions of the possibility of historical science than with the conditions of the possibility of human action in given historical circumstances. It is ultimately the problem of praxis that stirs up our two authors more than questions of pure epistemology. In addition to the interconnection of history and the imaginary, it can thus be opportune to put this conversation into perspective with a third network that reconfigures the preceding remarks. Let us call it the political, to express it in other terms than praxis, whose Marxian sense has been imposed on this term.

There is very little direct concern with Marx over the course of ·this conversation. Yet, it is against a Marxist version of history that Castoriadis's philosophy largely takes shape, and his reaction is echoed in Ricoeur's work itself. Their shared adversary can be called historicism, and Marxism is one variety of it, in the narrow sense that Popper and Arendt give to it. It is unacceptable (and in a sense this makes the dialogue between Ricoeur and Castoriadis possible, even though they disagree) to think that history is governed by immutable laws unveiled by materialist science. The flaw of 'Marxist science' is not only epistemological (in its curious mixture between the scientific atmosphere of the nineteeth-century atmosphere and the Hegelian philosophy of history which nurtured the work of Marx) insofar as it spreads a layer of explanatory principles from the natural sciences over human history. Its flaw is also political inasmuch as this science turns individuals and groups into puppets on a historic stage that are governed by anonymous forces. For Ricoeur and Castoriadis, the postulate that historical phenomena obey a blind necessity spawned by the cunning of reason remains unacceptable.

This indictment of historical totalisation plays out in Ricoeur, moreover, with a struggle against the philosopher 'who always comes out of some closet', to repeat an expression that he uses in *Time and Narrative* to distance himself from the philosopher of Jena. Historical philosophy's claim to absolute knowledge is indeed what leads Ricoeur to renounce Hegel. But on this historicist level, Marx and Hegel might both come out of the same closet whose door both Ricoeur and Castoriadis would like to close. For, to spin another metaphor, this time with Castoriadis, Marx has only changed the 'costume' of Hegelian rationalism, in which what was ' "spiritualist" in Hegel, is "materialist" in Marx' (Castoriadis 1987 [1975], 54). The offspring of this rejection of Hegelian and Marxist historicism is nothing other than the space left open to the possibility of constructing a historical action whose sense and degree of self-determination still remain to be defined. And indeed, it is this shared conviction that allows us to understand the moments where Ricoeur and Castoriadis converge the most during this 1985 exchange, that is to the say, with respect to the plea in favour of historical innovation.

The *political overdetermination* of their respective historical epistemologies is reinforced by their critique of totalitarianism. It is nothing new, at least after Arendt and Popper, to observe as well as to denounce the complicity between the attempt, which is more ideological than scientific, to provide a pseudo-rationalistic totalisation of the historical process and the totalitarian experiences of the twentieth century. Not that Ricoeur and Castoriadis turn Hegel and Marx, even less Plato, into the 'enemies of open societies'. This would be an overly simplistic reduction of such immense works. Or, as Castoriadis says, in his 'provisional assessment' of Marxism, with a hint of provocation, 'Marx, for example, is a great economist even when he is wrong, while François Perroux is only a windbag, even when he is not mistaken' (Castoriadis 1987 [1975], 33).

Although the use of the word 'totalitarianism' does occur later in Ricoeur's work[6] in connection with his study of Arendt's work, one can still consider his pioneering article, 'The Political Paradox' (Ricoeur 1965), which was published at the time when Soviet tanks seized Budapest, as a critique of Soviet totalitarianism, under the prism of a broader reflection on the autonomy (denied by Marxism) of the political in relation to the economic infrastructure. The critique of Soviet regimes and their successors is certainly less radical than the one found in Castoriadis during the same time period. Whereas the co-founder of *Socialisme ou Barbarie* condemns without reservation the regimes that have deliberately stolen and violated the sovereignty of the people, the contributor to the journal *Esprit* still hopes, after the period of Stalinism, to reform the so-called socialist regimes (while maintaining the principle of collective ownership of the means of production) through greater political liberalisation and control over the State, following a path that is reminiscent of 'socialism with a human face'. For Castoriadis, these regimes, even after de-Stalinisation, are completely unreformable and are incompatible with the project of economic self-management and political self-government.

Beyond this divergence, there is one analysis that Ricoeur and Castoriadis share: the refusal to reduce and to base politics on economics. When Ricoeur shows that the abolition of private property did not change political alienation in the Soviet Union, when he says that there is an evil belonging to the political (which consists of the abuse of power), he fundamentally rejoins Castoriadis in his analysis of the autonomisation of the Soviet bureaucratic class.

Marxism is, in the eyes of both Ricoeur and Castoriadis, a third common adversary in terms of the primacy given to productive forces (and especially to the weight of technology) in the analysis of the historical process and its transformations (in virtue of the contradiction between productive forces and the relations of production). The first Marxist flaw consists of transposing the same schemas of analysis on to other societies than the modern capitalist society. In other words, technical and technological transformations are important for understanding the changes of the modern world, but they are largely devoid of any meaning that would explain, for example, the upheavals of ancient societies. Considerable cultural, social, and political transformations can occur over a long duration on the same technological level. This observation applies, on an ethnological level, for so-called primitive societies:

> The idea that the meaning of life consists in the accumulation and conservation of wealth would be madness for the Kwakiutl Indians, who amass wealth *in order* to destroy it (...). Myopic Marxists laugh when one cites these examples, which they consider to be ethnological curiosities. But the real ethnographic curiosities are precisely these 'revolutionaries,' who

have set up the capitalist mentality as an eternal content of human nature considered everywhere the same and whom, while gabbing on interminably about colonialism and underdeveloped countries, overlook in their reasoning two-thirds of the population of the globe. (Castoriadis 1987 [1975], 26)

The second flaw of this materialism consists of presupposing that one can gain access to a fundamental technical-economic reality that is freed from any symbolic components (which are then referred to the cluster of superstructures). One shared teaching that can be found in all of Castoriadis's work as well as in Ricoeur's is that all social reality is already mediated symbolically. The idea of a pure economic reality known as a non-symbolic or pre-symbolic infrastructure is a pure chimera; the imagination is not added, whether to deform or mask it, on to techno-economic reality. It is already constitutive of it:

> Unless social life has a symbolic structure, there is no way to understand how we live, do things and project these activities in ideas, no way to understand how reality can become an idea or how real life can produce illusions; these would all be simply mystical and incomprehensible events. This symbolic structure can be perverted, precisely by class interests and so on as Marx has shown, but if there were not a symbolic function already at work in the most primitive kind of action, I could not understand, for my part, how reality could produce shadows of this kind. (Ricoeur 1986, 8)

It is on the basis of this shared analysis that Ricoeur and Castoriadis converge the most and that their dialogue is most fecund, insofar as it is based largely on the same anthropological root. While, for Marx, the human is first a *Homo faber* and *Homo laborans*, the human is, for Castoriadis and Ricoeur, first a *Homo loquax*. Not only as a speaking human being, but as a human who exchanges, imagines, invents, and transmits signs, meaning, symbols, texts, and stories. Ricoeur first learned about this anthropological root from the hermeneutic tradition that is focused on symbols and myths. It was further enriched by his passage through Freudian psychoanalysis, which he approached precisely from the side of the hermeneutical sciences.

Castoriadis inherits this anthropological root directly from the psychoanalysis that he theorised and practiced, *especially* when, under the influence of Lacan, he considered the unconscious to be structured like a language. It is this anthropological root that allows Ricoeur, as much as Castoriadis, to challenge the techno-centric materialism of Marxism (which considers the symbolic and imaginary sphere as a kind of varnish that distorts reality) and thus to rehabilitate the strictly symbolic and imaginary component of actions and institutions. What Ricoeur calls the integrative (and thus positive) function of ideology, echoing the cultural anthropology of Clifford Geertz, connects perfectly with what Castoriadis calls 'a second-order symbolism': 'Institutions cannot be reduced to the symbolic but they can exist only in the symbolic; they are impossible outside of a second-order symbolism; for each institution constitutes a particular symbolic network. A given economic organisation, a system of law, an instituted power structure, a religion – all exist socially as sanctioned symbolic systems' (Castoriadis 1987 [1975], 117).

There are, therefore, three fields of adversity (which mutually reinforce one another) against which Ricoeur and Castoriadis are fully in agreement: historicism, totalitarianism, and technocentrism. In other words, they agree completely about the defence of historical action in its symbolic and imaginary dimension. But this convergence, as fundamental as it is, does not yet make for a shared philosophy. It would not enable one to understand why the two thinkers run into recurrent disagreements in their 1985 conversation.

Even though it does not appear explicitly in their exchange, a first point of disagreement manifests itself at the very heart of their respective theories of the social and political imaginary. While Ricoeur and Castoriadis both claim, against the Marxist vulgate, the positive function of a constitutive imagination of action and institutions, they differ on the status of the other components of the imagination. Ricoeur acknowledges the pertinence of Marx's use of ideology, which he calls ideology-dissimilation (of class relations), but at the cost of a very personal appropriation of it. On the one hand, the recognition of this negative function of ideology, as we have seen, presupposes in turn the recognition of an undistorted constituting imaginary that is incompatible with the Marxism of Marx and his successors.[7] On the other hand, the epistemological basis of this ideology-dissimilation is the opposite of what is found in Marxism since, along with Max Weber, Ricoeur seeks to think the status of this function, namely the gap between the 'claim' of an authority and the 'belief' in its legitimacy. Ricoeur leads Weber's discovery to its culmination:

> First, can we not say that the problem of ideology concerns precisely this supplement, this gap between claim and belief, the fact that there must be something more in the belief than can be rationally understood in terms of interests, whether emotional, customary, or rational? Second, is it not the function of ideology to fill in this credibility gap? If this is the case, then third do we not need to elaborate a concept of surplus-value, now linked not so much to work as to power? (Ricoeur 1986, 201)

Ricoeur's stroke of genius is to rediscover Marx through Weber (this is the reason why we can speak of a post-Weberian Marxism to describe his iconoclastic approach). Indeed, there is a kind of analogy between, on the one side, economic surplus value understood as the difference between the wage of the worker and the market value of the sold product and, on the other side, political surplus value understood as the difference between the status accorded to the claim and that granted to the belief.

At stake here is the hermeneutics of suspicion in its Ricoeurian form. Ricoeur did not only coin the phrase 'masters of suspicion' that has flourished. There is a radicality in the Ricoeur of the 1960s which distances him from the warm clichés by which he is sometimes described today. There is a recovery, albeit tinged with critique, of the strategy of suspicion carried out by these three masters: Marx, Nietzsche, and Freud. First, *Freud and Philosophy: On Interpretation* is Ricoeur's great explanation of Freudian psychoanalysis, whose merits are justified as the unveiling of false consciousness. Second, the last part of *The Conflict of Interpretations* provides his explanation of Nietzschean anti-morality, whose pertinence is partially justified as a tracking down of false idols, bad conscience, and a life governed by the law. Finally, *Ideology and Utopia* is Ricoeur's great explanation of Marx and Marxisms from whom he resumes, albeit in a very unorthodox way, the critique of ideology as distortion.

If it can occur to Castoriadis, with more than a touch of irony, to say that Marxism has become an ideology in the sense that Marx defined it,[8] he also refuses to think the imaginary on the epistemological foundation of Marxism. The reason for this is due to his refusal to dissociate (in contrast with Ricoeur's approach) 'the method' (the causal and mechanistic approach to the superstructure and infrastructure) from 'the content' (ideology as dissimilation-distortion). Of course, Castoriadis does not hesitate to admit that there are pathological imaginaries, but it is essentially with the resources of psychoanalysis that he seeks to objectify them. They are objectified as 'the discourse of the other' by transposing the social-historical mechanism of alienation on to the individual scale:

> This is because alienation, social heteronomy, does not appear simply as the 'discourse of the other'—although the latter plays an essential role here as a determining factor and as a content of the unconscious and consciousness of the mass of individuals. The other, however, disappears in collective anonymity, in the impersonal nature of the 'economic mechanisms of the market' or in the 'rationality of the Plan', of the law of a few presented as the law as such. (Castoriadis 1987 [1975], 109)

Ricoeur, still for the sake of interpretive orthodoxy, could recognise himself in this repetition of the Freudian, and even Lacanian, gesture, all the while coordinating it with the Marxist strategy of suspicion. We have seen this with the reappropriation of 'the mirror stage' (see above). But one should also mention his dialogue with the 'early Habermas', who sees in the Freudian model a 'depth hermeneutics' that is able to unmask the distortions of language in public space and, correlatively, through the model of the cure, provides a way to attain an ideal communication that is exempt from distortions:

> In his attempt to link Marx and Freud, Habermas argues that the notion of alienation in Marx has its correlative concept in desymbolisation, and he follows Lorenzer in affirming that psychoanalysis is the process by which we go from desymbolisation toward resymbolisation through the intermediate stage of transference. As we shall see, Habermas maintains that critical social science parallels psychoanalysis in this regard and is itself a process incorporating explanation within a larger interpretive model. (Ricoeur 1986, 230)

It is also on the basis of this approach that Ricoeur hopes to put ideology in its pathological form at a distance in favour of utopia. The positive function of utopia, in contrast with that which gets lost in illusion, consists of shaking up the given order and subverting the existing world by proposing new horizons of expectation to societies, without necessarily realising all of their potential. Here we return to the concept of *retroaction* that is evoked in the conversation. What is essential is the

Preface to the French Edition

utopian ability to preserve a distance from social reality. To the extent that ideology is what preserves, or in its 'pathological' sense conceals, the social order, one can better understand why utopia is presented at the outset as a critique of ideologies.

Ricoeur seeks to replace the conceptual opposition (inherited from Marx) between science and ideology with a dialectic between ideology and utopia. In other words, a discourse on ideology, without being ideological itself, is only possible from the point of view of a utopian discourse. Ideology can only be recognised through the utopian possibilities which unmask it, the ideal of an unlimited and unconstrained communication in the Habermasian sense can fulfil this utopian function for Ricoeur.

Castoriadis cannot consent to this perspective, because he ceaselessly criticises the notion of utopia, not only as a flight from reality, but also in the Habermasian sense that is given to it by Ricoeur:

> Habermas took the term up again more recently, because after the total ruin of Marxism and Marxism-Leninism, it seems to legitimate some vague criticism of the current regime by talking about a utopian socialist transformation, with a whiff of 'pre-Marxism'. Actually, it's quite the opposite. No one can understand (except a neo-Kantian philosopher) how it is possible to criticise what is on the basis of what cannot be. (Castoriadis 2010, 3)

That is to say that the notion of utopia is mystifying (ultimately in a Marxist sense). And that is the whole issue for Castoriadis's distinction between *utopia* and the *project*: While utopia is akin to a 'sort of polar star' forever inaccessible and unsuited for action, the project (of autonomy) has not only already been realised in the course of history (the Greek *polis*, the Paris Commune, the Soviets, the workers councils, etc.), but can (and should) still be achieved here and now through the 'lucid activity of individuals and of peoples, through their understanding, their will, and their imagination'.

Castoriadis ultimately rejects utopia, because he adheres to the revolutionary project (of a radical transformation of society in the sense of autonomy). Conversely, we could say that Ricoeur adheres to utopias because he is not (or is no longer) revolutionary. If the question of the revolutionary project does not explicitly come up in the 1985 conversation between the two men, it is however this issue that continually passes through their disagreement about the historical conditions of human action. It is a *political overdetermination* that once again underlies their epistemological disagreement. The perspective of the instituting social imaginary that Castoriadis wishes for – as the production of radically new meanings that do not proceed from an order of meaning that is already there – is inseparable from his revolutionary project that is oriented towards autonomy. Conversely, for Ricoeur, the fact of showing that new meanings, new social configurations, cannot be created from nothing, that institutions always proceed from already existing institutions, is inseparable from his political reformism and his mistrust towards a project of radical transformation of society in defiance of what already exists. This distrust was mostly acquired by Ricoeur through his contact with the hermeneutic tradition and his political thinking, especially from his reading of Arendt (the revolutions of the blank slate lead to catastrophe: terror, totalitarianism, etc.). This is also the reason why Ricoeur seeks precisely to put ideology and utopia into a dialectic; this dialectic is not unlike the one found in Koselleck (who is discussed in the conversation) (see chapter 1, p. 12)[9] between 'the space of experience' and 'the horizon of expectation' (Koselleck 2004). On the one hand, as we have seen, utopia allows for subversion and taking a distance from a petrified ideological order. On the other hand, when utopia becomes an excuse to escape and loses its function of distanciation, ideology is justified in its positive function of integration and the space of experience. Through its integrative function, ideology allows for a distinction between a utopia of possibilities and a chimerical utopia. While ideology, in its positive sense, bends the phantasmagorical tendency of utopia, conversely, utopia, in its positive function, allows for a putting at a distance of the conservative and dissimulating tendency of ideology, by offering other possibilities of existence.

Castoriadis cannot recognise himself in this dialectic that disregards the actual and radical transformation of the historical process. To put something at a distance is not yet to transform it. But the great originality of Castoriadis, especially in the historical context in which he writes and militates, consists in maintaining a revolutionary project (up to the end of his life) that is purified of Marxism (even though for a long time Marxism believed that it had a legitimate monopoly over the revolutionary project). While Castoriadis did have a Marxist moment as a youth in his revolutionary development, he was certainly, along with his comrades in *Socialisme ou Barbarie*, a pioneer in a critical approach that did not make any concessions to Soviet totalitarian regimes or to Marxism itself. We know the meaning of his alternative: 'Starting from revolutionary Marxism, we have arrived at the point where we have to choose between remaining Marxist and remaining revolutionaries' (Castoriadis 1987 [1975], 14).[10] Certainly, Castoriadis's anti-Marxism is not simplistic. Not just because he does not cease to praise the immense work that he puts under his critical lens, but also because Castoriadis nourishes a certain interest for the young Marx (the same as Ricoeur), whose philosophy of history is based on the suppression of the actually existing state through the emancipation and self-organisation of the workers. Castoriadis can recognise himself in a Marx who focuses his reflection on the creation, by the masses, of new forms of social and political action (in situations they have not produced), such as the Paris Commune. But this project will remain on an intuitive level in Marx according to Castoriadis, and will be stifled by a 'second element' of historical philosophy that gets lost in the determinism of productive forces and scientific historicism that are decidedly incompatible with a revolutionary project. Hence, it is necessary to break with Marxism in order to remain revolutionary.

By contrast, one could say that Ricoeur retained elements of Marxism while rejecting any revolutionary project, whereas Castoriadis ended up rejecting Marxism in order to remain revolutionary. But then again, things are more complex and need to be situated historically. Something that is not well known is that Ricoeur did go through a period during his youth (in the 1930s) that was both Marxist and revolutionary. Engaged very early on the left (a card-carrying member of the Section Française de l'International Ouvrière), a supporter of the Popular Front and of the young Spanish Republic, Ricoeur wrote articles in *Etre* and especially in the extreme-left journal *Terre Nouvelle* (which had anarcho-Communist leanings).[11] The originality, even the incongruous character of this commitment, as François Dosse points out, is that it is accompanied at the same time by Christian beliefs such as the slogan 'For Christ, vote red'.

One can also find in Ricoeur's militant articles of the 1950s–1960s, especially those published in *Esprit*, including the 'The Political Paradox', more than just a residue of the Marxist critique of the capitalist system as an economy of waste and of the exploitation of man by man. But at the same time, his revolutionary verve is lost in favour of a pedagogy of reform of the so-called Socialist regimes, as we have seen, without however denying his sympathy for the 1968 student movement (though he did strongly reject its subsequent radicalisation by the Maoists). There will still persist some (non-revolutionary) elements of Marxism in the 1970s, at the time when he gave his lectures on ideology and utopia at the University of Chicago. This attests to the fact that he did not break with critical theory (which clearly leaned towards the Habermasian side then). It is only in the 1990s that references to Marx will become more discreet at the moment when he encounters the work of John Rawls. This turn carries with it a clear justification of the market economy but still retains a strong rejection of econom-ism, *especially* the neo-liberal kind, along with an attachment that always led him towards the principles of social justice and his sympathy for the most progressive political utopias. In spite of their membership to the complex web of the 'anti-totalitarian left', there thus remains a contrast between Ricoeur and a Castoriadis who remained deeply attached, up to the end of his life, to the revolutionary project in a society that seems to have mourned the very idea of a (new) revolution, in the name of discrediting Marxism itself.

—Translated by Scott Davidson

NOTES

1. Castoriadis thus states in his book *World in Fragments*: 'My obvious and central differences with Paul Ricoeur do not, of course, stand in the way of my admiration for the richness and solidity of his critical analysis of the main inherited philosophical conceptions regarding time' (438). It should also be noted that several years before this conversation, Ricoeur wrote a letter of recommendation in favour of Castoriadis's candidacy as the director of studies at the EHESS in 1980.

2. I thank Olivier Abel and Jean-Louis Schlegel for asking me to clarify this point.

3. It is symptomatic that in the course of their discussion, Ricoeur considers it to be a myth (of deriving a form from something absolutely formless) how Castoriadis himself describes new forms of historic creation, in thinking human language as a human 'self-creation'.

4. See Ricoeur (1963). A summary of the debate is available on the Fonds Ricoeur website: www.fondsricoeur.fr/uploads/medias/articles_pr/prcluadel-evistraussesprit63.PDF.

5. It is in terms of the relation between structuralism and post-structuralism that I developed a first confrontation between Ricoeur and Castoriadis in Michel (2014).

6. See, in particular, the collection of conversations in Ricoeur (1998).

7. One can ask, however, whether ideology-integration can be stripped of all pathological features. Ricoeur reconnects this positive function with a quasi-narcissistic component of groups in a Lacanian psychoanalytic sense (the 'mirror stage') in which symbolic mediations contribute to the display of an idealised image of the group.

8. Castoriadis defines ideology in the following way: '[A] set of ideas that relate to a reality not in order to shed light on it and to change it, but in order to veil it and to justify it in the imaginary, which permits people to say one thing and do another, to appear as other than they are' (Castoriadis 1987 [1975], 11).

9. Hereafter, the references to the dialogue proper appear as single page numbers.

10. See also the summary by Caumières (2013).

11. For these biographical details, see Dosse (1997, 49–51).

REFERENCES

Arendt, Hannah. 1951. *The Origins of Totalitarianism*. New York: Schocken Books.

Castoriadis, Cornelius. 1987 [1975]. *The Imaginary Institution of Society*. Translated by Kathleen Blamey. Cambridge, MA: Massachusetts Institute of Technology Press.

———. 1997. *World in Fragments: Writings on Politics, Society, Psychoanalysis and the Imagination*. Translated and edited by David Ames Curtis. Stanford, CA: Stanford University Press.

———. 2010. *A Society Adrift: Interviews and Debates, 1974–1997*. Translated by Helen Arnold. New York: Fordham University Press.

Caumières, Philippe. 2013. 'Au-delà du marxisme: L'apport de la critique castoriadienne du marxisme'. In *Imaginer avec Castoriadis*. Edited by Aurélien Liarte and Philippe Georges. Paris: Ovadia, pp. 19–40.

Dosse, François. 1997. *Paul Ricoeur: Les sens d'une vie*. Paris: La Découverte.

Foucault, Michel. 1972. *The Archaeology of Knowledge*. Translated by Alan Sheridan. New York: Pantheon Books.

Koselleck, Reinhart. 2004. *Futures Past: On the Semantics of Historical Time*. Translated by Keith Tribe. New York: Columbia University Press.

Michel, Johann. 2014. *Ricoeur and the Post-Structuralists*. Translated by Scott Davidson. London: Rowman & Littlefield International.

Ricoeur, Paul. 1963. ' "La pensée sauvage" et le structuralisme'. *Esprit* 11: 618–19.

———. 1965. 'The Political Paradox'. In *History and Truth*. Translated by Charles A. Kelbley, 247–70. Evanston, IL: Northwestern University Press.

———. 1986. *Lectures on Ideology and Utopia*. Edited by George Taylor. New York: Columbia University Press.

———. 1997. *L'idéologie et l'utopie*. Paris: Seuil.

———. 1998. *Critique and Conviction*. Translated by Kathleen Blamey. New York: Columbia University Press.

Part I

RICOEUR AND CASTORIADIS
RADIO DIALOGUE

Chapter One

Dialogue on History and the Social Imaginary

Paul Ricoeur and Cornelius Castoriadis

Cornelius Castoriadis: Needless to say, how happy I am to speak with you, Paul Ricoeur, and how honoured that you have invited me to speak with you on *Le Bon Plaisir*.[1] You know this quite well, moreover, because I came to see you shortly after 1968 to propose a doctoral thesis topic on the imaginary element, which remains as it was then: elementary and imaginary ...[2]

Paul Ricoeur: You have published more than a few elements. And I have referred many times to the 'imaginary production of society'[3], because this issue of the imaginary foyer of social relations and of social production is, I believe, our shared interest.

C. C. Yes, indeed, but for my part I do not speak of production but of 'institution'. Deliberately, of course. And I wanted to ask you about this, about this word 'production'. This could have the air of a scholastic dispute, but I'm not looking to quarrel with you. Kant, when he speaks of the imagination, calls it 'productive' ...

P. R. That indeed is my lineage.

C. C. He only calls it 'creative' once, in passing, in the third *Critique*. This is surely no accident inasmuch as Kant, in the *Critique of Judgment*, is inspired by eighteenth-century literature and makes many references to English authors. But for me, this term 'production' is too closely linked to Marx, of course, but also to Heidegger.

P. R. Let me make this interjection ... Actually, I return to a pre-Marxian moment of the word, its Fichtean moment. *Produzieren*,[4] that is Fichte.

What drew me to the concept of the productive, rather than the creative imagination, is that I attached something infinitely more primordial to the idea of creation, something that would have a relationship with the order of a foundational sacred, whereas on the human scale, we are always in an institutional order. That is where I encounter a *producing* that is not a *creating*. The word 'production' should be paired with the word 'reproduction', it seems to me. In contrast with an imagination that only reproduces a copy of something that is already there, production is essentially a production of new syntheses and new configurations. This is what got me interested in metaphor on the level of language:[5] We produce new meanings through the intersection of different semantic fields. Now that I'm working on narrative, I see the production of a story in terms of the production of narrative configurations by the plot.[6] That is how I use the word 'produce'.

C. C. We have immediately entered into what, at the same time, unites us and divides us the most. And I would like to take advantage of this pro-gramme to better understand you. You say production, reproduction – and reproduction even when it comes to the combination of things that aren't already there! However, it is impossible for me to think of the *polis*, the Greek city, for example, or philosophy, which emerges in the sixth cen-tury BCE, as mere recombinations of elements that were already there. What institutes the *polis* as a *polis* is a meaning that it creates and through which it creates itself as a *polis*.

P. R. But we never experience production in this form! There you are pre-senting us with the myth of production. Let's set aside the question of the Greek city in order to consider an experience that we can actually have, namely that of a production in the order of language. We do not know any other type of production than regulated productions, which is to say that we do not produce everything in what we produce. I completely agree with you that we cannot speak about 'elements that were already there'. In my current analysis of narratives, I show that there are no prior elements in the sense that the events that are combined and compose the story do not exist as the variables of this story. For example, consider the different ways in which one can tell the events of the French Revolution: The event varies each time according to the story, depending on whether it is taken from the plot of Tocqueville, someone like Augustin Cochin[7] or someone else like Furet.[8] That is why we cannot speak of a combination of pre-established elements, which would be some type of associationist view.

C. C. But that is the structuralist view. Lévi-Strauss wrote it in black and white.

P. R. This is not my view, because it would imply that there are types of atoms that get combined differently ...

C. C. And each society throws the dice.

P. R. That is only the case in a static view, but not a productive one. By a static view, I mean the view that considers a combination as a set of fixed 'elements' which it redesigns, resulting in static structures that are discontinuous with each other. In contrast, in what I call emplotment, a process is set in motion where the 'elements' are reshaped by the lesson learned from an event. An event is determined by its role in the story that one is telling. Something might be an event for one story, but not for the other. In one plot, the storming of the Bastille is not an event; in another plot, it is an origin. Consequently, there are no elements that are somehow fixed in advance. But this is what I maintain: We can only produce according to rules; we do not produce everything that we produce, if only because we already have a language before we can talk. Others have spoken and have established the rules of the game. What we can do is to put them back into what Malraux called 'coherent deformations'.[9] We can proceed by coherent deformations, but this always takes place within a pre-structure, within something already structured that we restructure. That is why we are never in a situation that you would call creation, as if form could be derived from the absolutely formless.

C. C. And that is precisely why the idea of institution, rather than production, is at the centre of my work. The self-institution of society implies that we are always working within what is already established by changing or amending the rules but also by establishing new ones, by creating them. That is our autonomy.

P.R. The idea of absolute novelty is unthinkable. There can only be something new by breaking with the old: pre-established rules exist before us, and we deregulate them in order to regulate otherwise. But this is not a situation ... of the first day of creation.

C.C. That is precisely the whole problem, in the way of thinking about temporality and about being in temporality. According to one view, which is not necessarily yours, everything is predetermined, already logically pre-inscribed in a great book of possibilities. From these essential elements, both physical as well as spiritual or meaningful ones, certain combinations are produced, which allow for other combinations, and so on. But another way to think about temporality is to see the emergence of levels of being. One example that is as empirical as could be: The first living cell on Earth represents something new in relation to the primordial

ocean. Of course, it is not absolutely new; it is regulated; it cannot violate
a number of rules. The same goes for Wagner composing his operas: He
cannot violate certain musical laws, or others concerning his biological
metabolism, or his relations to others, etc. Nonetheless, he offers new
harmonies that before him seemed absurdly dissonant. When the Greeks
created mathematics – and regardless of the pioneering role of the
Babylonians or Egyptians – they created the idea of proof on the basis of
a minimal number of axioms and according to a set of established rules.

P. R. Ah, but I follow you! Earlier we were talking about what is more
near and more distant between us. Here, I find myself very close to
you. I never cease to plead in favour of the concept of an event in
thought: There are events in thought, there are innovations. But here we
have to think dialectically. One can only think about innovation under
some conditions: First, there must have been previous configurations.
This is not at all what you said when you mentioned an order of possibilities that would be immutable, as if we were going to tap into some sort
of great treasure of possibilities. That does not exist. What does exist are
the configurations prior to what we reconfigure – and we proceed in this
way, from configurations to configurations. You just spoke about Greek
rationality, about the Greek miracle ... but you should not go too far!
There was something before ... that was done by tests, by trial and error.
Around Plato, we see from other schools, the school of Eudoxus, how to
find the five regular solids. All of that constitutes small developments that
are cumulative but that emerge precisely from a prior set of failed tests
and fruitless attempts. One sees that the cosmological representation of
Copernicus and Kepler was anticipated ...

C. C. By Eratosthenes.

P. R. One is never in a passage from nothing to something, but from something to something, from one to another – which goes from the configured
to the configured, but never from the formless to form. This is what
I wanted to say by limiting the excesses of a kind of anarchism of reason.
Reason follows after itself, but in a dialectic of innovation and sedimentation. There is the sedimentation of research and thoughts, and of the *said*,
of what has been said before us. It is on the basis of these things that have
already been said that we can say something else. Sometimes we say it
better, but we remain in a sort of continuity of saying that is self-correcting
and cumulative. I do not know if you are close to Michel Foucault, but this
is a debate that can be had about his *Archaeology of Knowledge*[10]: Can we
think of total discontinuity as the leap from one episteme to another? In
Foucault's case, this works well when you take three or four registers such
as language, biological classifications, the economy, currency, etc. But

when there is break in one line, there is continuity in another line. It isn't because we changed an episteme in one of these registers that we would have changed in mathematics or in theology or in the law and especially in continuous existence. Maybe we would no longer be in agreement here, and I would like to discuss this with you because that is the issue with the word 'institute'. It seems to me that, behind all of these ruptures of thought, there is a continual setting which still forms the continuity of human communities. Before the institution, there is a living-together that has a certain continuity, which can be instituted, reinstituted, and constituted by ruptures but against the backdrop of a transmitted and received inheritance, which ensures, if I might say, the 'basso continuo' ...

This analysis gives a certain primacy to the continuity of existence, to the perpetuation of a living-together as the ground for instituting operations, and that allows us to situate the discontinuities of sense against the continuities of existence. There is a relation of sense and existence: It is on the level of sense that there can be ruptures, events, and emergences.

You mentioned biology earlier, but in the end, we no longer have changes of human beings: We are in a biological continuity across generations, which is like the continuity of living beings against the background of the discontinuity of our thoughts. It was in that respect that I wanted to limit the claim (in the English sense of a *claim* in a *truth claim*: a claim of truth, of correctness) of the concept of discontinuity in the creation of institutions.

C. C. If you accept discontinuity on the level of sense but not on the level of existence, that suits me perfectly. If I were polemical, I would say that you are granting me what I need. As for me, ontologically, society as history is sense. And it is on the basis of this level that I can establish a discontinuity between the Sudanese president (Nimeiri) or the Ayatollah Khomeini and us. Otherwise, we are all talking bipeds; we live in established societies anchored in a shared Jewish past, that of the religions of the Book. But the discontinuity, the cut, occurs on the level of sense – and is also accompanied with other cuts, the cutting of the hands and of other members for thieves and fornicators. This is something that we cannot accept and that we should condemn, if we were not caught up in a stupid type of self-accusation. This discontinuity alone is what interests me. As for Foucault, I spoke briefly and very harshly about him: His conception of the human enterprise as a staccato of epistemes unrelated to one another is something that I totally reject.

P. R. But you, what do you say? I limit Foucault's claim precisely by the affirmation of a historical continuity of inheritance.

C. C. What continuity?

P. R. Something like the continuity of life, not necessarily from a biological point of view, but the life of the mind, the properly human life, continuous living and living together – the convivial. In other words, we can only think the notion of interruption on the basis of the idea of continuation. I believe that this is also the definition of time in Spinoza.[11] He said that it was the continuation of existence.

C. C. Of course, but let's try to take a little distance in relation to *our* own history, even if it is what allows us to talk, a condition that is anything but negligible philosophically. While remaining in the course of a Western Greek or European history in the broad sense which begins at least with the Homeric poems, each sense or each new form that emerges is not the result of a combination of pre-existing forms, even if it does retain a certain reference to the past.

P. R. But then we are both on the same side!

C. C. Yes, here we are on the same side. But if I consider the Aztecs, I can no longer say the same thing.

P. R. Me neither!

C. C. And one would have to be a very intrepid Hegelian–Marxist to maintain that the Aztecs were dialectically overcome and surpassed – Derrida would say 'sublated' [*relevés*] – in being massacred by Christopher Columbus![12] There is no longer any continuity there. Or else it is a continuity of another order: No human society can do without making sense of the world. And this *Sinngebung*, as Heidegger calls it, this bestowal of meaning can have little relation, if not trivial, with that of another society.[13]

P. R. I can't see where we differ because I grant that each configuration – be it narrative, metaphorical, political, or institutional – is, as such, new in relation to every other one: It is qualitatively different from any other. I simply objected that a configuration cannot emerge out of nothing. I see humanity actually proceeding through ruptures, discontinuities, but always within the order of configuration. If we have a great continuity, it is indeed the one that you have stated, in which, through the fibre, the root, the Greek trunk, we recognise ourselves within a certain continuity.

C. C. But that is the case for us.

P. R. Yes, it is the case for us, and also for those who we call the other. But can we conceive an absolute alterity? What language reveals, or more precisely what is manifested in language, is not only that translation has been possible, but also that it has been successful. We will never encounter a language which would be absolutely untranslatable ...

C. C. We will not encounter an absolutely translatable text, either, unless it's a series of mathematical formulae.

P. R. To speak about the limits of translation assumes that one has at least been able to begin and to some extent succeed in this operation. Without translation, there would be no humanity but only human species, as with dogs and cats. What makes humanity exist is this translatability in principle that recreates the continuity of meaning within the discontinuity of productions and efforts of configuration.

C. C. There may be another way to see this. Jakobson has taught us that a successful translation in the domain of poetry is not strictly cognitive and that it is in fact a new creation. I think that the whole problem is there. Look, for example, at everything that the seventeenth, eighteenth, and nineteenth centuries were able to produce as historical knowledge about the Old Testament, Hebrew history, and Greek history. This is absolutely mind-boggling, it is sometimes said. But what are we talking about? About Greece? About the Old Testament? No, in fact we are talking about the seventeenth, eighteenth, and nineteenth centuries. Where I distance myself radically from Foucault is that for me there is a Greece, there is an Old Testament, and all our interpretations of them are based on a meaning that serves as the referent for the successive creations of various interpretations. They are not absolutely arbitrary. If someone tells me that the *Iliad* speaks in fact about the battle of Verdun, no discussion or rebuttal is necessary. There is a limit. When the great Gladstone thought that he could establish that the *Iliad* is a theology derived from the Old Testament, he crossed this limit and spoke nonsense. This nonsense might have been necessary to his politico-philosophical–theological attempt, admittedly, but it was nonsense anyway. It can only interest me for what it says about Victorian England. But other interpretations of Greece, from nineteenth-century France and from our time, are interesting and relevant. Why so? This is a big problem.

P. R. In order to identify our dispute better, I would like to start from what we certainly share in common when you say: 'I believe that there is a referent and that there was an Old Testament, a Greece, etc.' What does that mean, if not that the multiple interpretations and reinterpretations of interpretations are other approximations of the same thing. Something that happened in the order of thought was also a collection of events. This collection, recorded in the canonical texts of the Bible or recorded in literary texts, somehow puts us face to face with them. It is a source of the corrections and approximations of all our reconstructions. In other words, our constructions, in the historic case that you yourself have chosen, are intended to be reconstructions. It is a task of restitution in some sense. I take this word in the sense used in painting when we speak about the 'rendering' of a landscape, and the verb 'render' [*rendre*] in both senses of the word. On the one hand, it is necessary to repay a debt, and on the other hand, to do the work of creation, a creation that at the same time confronts an unpayable debt. One can see this struggle in the creator who always makes different paintings when he produces a series – the series of Monet, the haystacks, or ...

C. C. Cézanne's *Apples.*

P. R. Yes, the *Apples* of Cézanne. There is always something different and yet still the same thing. With something on the order of duty: He had to repay his debt somehow, to do justice to something which exists and which precedes him.

C. C. Cézanne, Monet, they are inexhaustible. Obviously, this is not because *The Water Lilies* or the *Apples* are inexhaustible as physical phenomena, but because they are inexhaustible as visible objects and as objects to paint. And I will remain forever in debt towards Greece, on which I chose to work.

P. R. This inexhaustibility is what I call the continuous; it is the greater continuity of being behind the discontinuity of productions.

C. C. That is the difference. I will not call it the continuous, since it is a mode of being. And this is more than a terminological problem. I will always be in debt with respect to ancient Greece, and we will always be, because the meanings that it has created are inexhaustible and constantly give rise to new interpretations ...

P. R. Yes, that is quite right. It is a mode of being. In any case, you're not in favour of these kinds of eruptions or irruptions that would be different from all the others and would never form a series ... ? In my opinion, what characterises a human memory, a cultural memory, is that it can be cumulative; it is not simply additive, as if it somehow erased its own precedents. No, it has a connection with them, and at the same time, they become its antecedents.

C. C. I completely agree, but what you say there is only true for our history, which is the only one that is based on such an accumulation. This is, first of all, because it sought to be this way. Instead of resting on the traditions of the tribe – there was a hero who did this or that – and of repeating them with small, continuous deformations (this is precisely what Lévi-Strauss describes in the four volumes of his *Mythologiques*), it has returned to them and, with Herodotus, gave them another status: What the Ancients valued was pure gossip, that is not the truth, and we want to know the truth. And there again you have a rupture.

P. R. The successive forms in which the past, which you yourself characterised as the inexhaustible, has been revived and reinterpreted themselves contained potential and incompleteness. And through a sort of retroaction of our new creations on the old moments, we can deliver possibilities that had been prevented. That is a fundamental difference from structuralism – and perhaps here we are on the same side: Structures are not saturated. And this unemployed, repressed potential is something that each new creation somehow delivers retroactively. There is probably room there for Freudian concepts like the inhibited and the repressed. It is by the deliverance of the repressed that we establish continuity with our own past, but by means of the discontinuity that you were talking about. This is where the concept of institution ...

C. C. Forgive me for being a bit direct, but you see clearly where these unemployed potentials will lead you, you just as much as Freud before. Ultimately, this comes down to saying that the whole history of humanity was already there at the moment when the first anthropopithecus created the first spark by striking two stones against each other ... This is not an infinite regress, but precisely a finite one. Or an infinite descent, as Fermat or Euclid would say. For me, the potentiality of the human being is, if I can say so, the potentiality of potentiality. We cannot talk in terms of a potential that becomes actual, but we can talk about the creation of new potentials. And there again, it becomes scholastic to say: Of course, all these potentials must be from the outset in an initial potential. The potential to play the piano presupposes the piano, European musical writing, teachers to teach it to students, some separation of music from religious ritual, etc. All of these are created potentials.

P. R. You are not taking account of my main argument at all, namely retroaction. By opening the future, we deliver new potentialities. I don't at all feel locked into a scholastic argument where everything would already be contained in the beginning ... Canguilhem[14] already discussed this conception with regard to seeds that contain seeds, etc. Leibniz himself once held this view, which he called development ...

C. C. But biologists already sought the seed in the seed, to infinity.

P. R. I'm not there at all! I completely reject this idea of *development* [*Entwicklung*], as if everything were wrapped up and all that one had to do were to unfold it. My own historical schema would hold instead that we are always in a dialectical relationship between what Reinhart Koselleck[15] (this German from the Bielefeld school,[16] who worked so extensively on the categories of history) calls a horizon of expectation and a space of experience. One should not go outside of this polarity. This is because we project a horizon of expectation, thus opening the innovation ahead of us, that we can restore continuity with what precedes us, because we read it otherwise ... There's something absolutely unique about historicity: precisely this power to establish the new in the recovery of the received legacy. Once again, this is what I call retroaction. It has nothing to do with the biological theory where we have alternatives between development and evolution ... We are not in biology, but in history.

C. C. Of course, we are in history, and not in biology. But this domain that you call the symbolic is what I call, for my part, the domain of meaning, and this meaning ...

P. R. But I do not want to let myself be led into opposition to the imagination ... And that is why I keep the Kantian imagination that covers what has been broken in two by fantasy and the symbolic.

C. C. The Kantian imagination – but this is a subject to which we should return – remains the imagination of a subject, even as it is taken up by Heidegger in his book on *Kant and The Problem of Metaphysics*.[17] As for myself, I try to conceive a social imaginary, that is to say, a creativity of the socio-historical field, of the socio-historical community as such. And I begin with the beginning, the first principle, the first paradigm: the institution. It presupposes a continuity of living together in human communities. I do not believe that there can be human communities without institutions. We are both readers of Freud: The primordial drives of a being which would not be instructed by the institution is not to live together but 'to kill each other', or to be 'incestuous' with each other. There is thus an institution which is the self-creation of society, and which gives rise to this third region in being, that of an immanent sense, an instituted sense, an incarnate meaning. And when you say that there's no absolute rupture, that one always remains in the rules of language, that is certainly true. But what about language itself? Can it be derived from the mimicry of the apes, as someone who passes for a philosopher does?[18] Can I derive the polysemy of language ...

P. R. That is absolutely not what I am saying. We always speak in a context where it has already been spoken. In this sense, we are already preceded both as individuals and as a collectivity. We don't know a language that comes from the animal cry. We are already in language.

C. C. And we do not know of humanity without language. Therefore, we do not know a humanity which, in a certain way, does not result from an initial self-creation.

P. R. Self-creation, no. Successive reconfigurations, yes.

C. C. But then language is a transformation of the animal cry, which is something you reject.

P. R. I have no access to this first moment of language. Specifically, the problem that you are doomed to ask yourself is that of an institution that begins from nothing.

C. C. I cannot simply remove it.

P. R. I say that we are faced with an institution which comes from institutions. Just as there are always languages that come from languages, similarly there are institutions that come from institutions. We do not know the non-instituted. Put otherwise, as soon as there is the human, there are in fact three things: tools, norms, and language; and perhaps there is fourth, with burial, a specific relationship with the dead.

C. C. Later ...

P. R. And not simply a biological relationship. We do not treat the dead as natural waste, but as ancestors.

C. C. The oldest graves are at least 50,000 years old, and it is certain that the first tools, norms, and even language are much older than that.

P. R. We always arrive after the time when things came to be. I believe that the passage from the biological to the human institution escapes us altogether. That is why we are always in the pre-instituted, in the newly established. And I do not see where you can place the notion of creation unless it has the sense of an event of thought that we will reconfigure exactly as we tell a different story with the same archives. The archives are there, and then we write the history of the French Revolution. But we couldn't have an innovation in thinking without some kind of large reserve of events, a large array configured in a certain way by our predecessors – and that we reconfigure differently. Innovations always go from configurations to configurations and reconfigurations.

C. C. Yet again, this discussion only makes sense if we distinguish levels ... Consider Thales. He is not a mythical character, and he is the confluence of many continuities: his language, his education, the content of his theorem, which he perhaps learned from the Egyptians, or by visiting masons, architects ... But at some point, as the story goes, he was not content with this acquired knowledge or with the use of boards; he wanted to *demonstrate* this property of triangles. There, we are no longer in a simple continuity; all of a sudden, there *emerges* a new figure of history which, like other contemporary figures, has the same meaning, or rather the same magma of meanings: the *logon didonai*, the giving of accounts and reasons. That is the absolute rupture, which marks the singularity of our history: to give an account and to reason when I say that the square of the hypotenuse is equal, etc., but also when I claim that these are the laws that the city should adopt, or that the Persians live according to these customs and the Egyptians by other ones. And to give an account and to reason without ending up with a mythical story, with Tables of the Law, or with the stories of the ancestors.

P. R. Nothing in that contradicts me. I am saying exactly the same thing: With Thales, a previously unexpressed and unheard mode of thought emerges, but at the same time, humans continue to live. I will thus never be faced with a complete discontinuity.

C. C. Let's not continue on about that; it is absolutely certain.

P. R. And that is how there can be a humanity. I begin here but I continue there.

C. C. I completely agree with you. And I myself have written that the most radical political revolution conceivable will leave intact many more things than it will transform – billions of people, forests, fields, buildings ... The question that matters to me here is the emergence of a new figure. So, when you say that this inexhaustibility of things in the past is linked to our ability to innovate for the future ...

P. R. I will focus on a concept that Lacan highlighted in Freud: the notion of the *after-effect* [*après-coup*].[19] It corresponds to a word that is more personal to me that I used earlier, which is the word *retroaction*. I come back to this because this concept is quite important for us: When there is a breakthrough of truth, we are at the same time able to reconnect it, precisely because we are not at an absolute beginning. We are not the absolute beginning of everything. In order to be creative, we must be able to remember what we have abandoned in order to include it in what we have found.

C. C. Absolutely. But I have the impression that we are talking, as they say in English, *at cross purposes*, a little bit past each other.[20] Maybe this is because you are talking mostly about our European history – and everything that you say is magnificently verified. While I, excuse me, try to go beyond it a little bit and talk about other histories as well. But with Greece, what happens? Whenever something new happens in Europe, we turn anxiously to the Greeks either to say 'it was already there', or to say 'it is in line with the Greeks', or to say 'here we have something that the Greeks could not imagine, but yet ...'

. **P. R.** Yes, the Greeks were the first to do so. Remember Plato, who recalled in memory a *palaios logo*s,[21] an 'ancient saying' ...

C. C. In this famous saying, which is probably not authentic, the Egyptians said that the Greeks were 'eternal children', who were always able to forget one part in order to start another game. Perhaps in this respect we have also remained Greek.

P. R. I was thinking about Nietzsche's beautiful text in the *Second Untimely Meditation* on the advantages and disadvantages of history.[22] It is that, in believing that we are newcomers, we are actually 'late comers'. It is very important for us to negotiate in our own experience this double relationship of early–late arrivals. Think about the arrogance of newcomers. There is at the same time a weakness in Nietzsche's words about the latecomers, which is their derivative character. Among them, there is the arrogance of false prophets ...

C. C. Yes, absolutely, but still with the same difference: This return to history, in order to fertilise the past and enrich it, is specific to us. We have created it, and others have occasionally borrowed it from us. In places other than the West, the relationship to the past is more or less mythical. Obviously, myth also changes, drifts little by little, but never to return to its signification, to question it, to give an account of it, and to reason. Without doubt, and there I am completely with you, the two things go together: it is because we change horizons that we constantly need to return to question our origins. People who don't change their horizon do not need to ...

P. R. We hold on to a certain contingent historical fibre.

C. C. That's it; contingent is the word that matters to me.

P. R. We have the experience of continuity through moments of discontinuity and retroactive recoveries. But we cannot think that this contingency does not have a universal significance: We can only conceive all of humanity as a process of communication that would be placed under the rule of the best argument.[23] No human culture would be so

different that it could not enter into a relationship of mutual translatability with our own. In this respect, one can mention the American philosopher Donald Davidson, who criticised the notion of an 'organising
scheme'.[24] It is impossible, he says, to conceive of absolutely different
civilisations as if they belonged to a radically untranslatable organising
scheme. If they were radically other, we would not even know it. We
can only know that they are other, because we have encountered the
limits of translation. And as a result, translation has already been successful, as we have already said. At that moment, we must indeed put
the relation with difference under the sign of an idea of humanity as
a model of successful communication. I admit that it is an idea in the
Kantian sense of the word, that is, a regulative idea. This regulative idea
holds humanity together and gives coexistence the meaning of not being
many humanities but one single humanity. It is true that it is a task, but
at least we know that we are not working for nothing when we strive
to do so ... This is what Jean-Marc Ferry showed in his thesis.[25] Even
if there is no international community of law, at least we can talk about
international problems. For example, the global debt. Consider the way
that global debt is handled; it is already the beginning of international
law. In other words, we cannot begin with an absolute vacuum of communication, even between different cultures. When we read the Koran
or the *Upanishads* and Lao Tzu, we cannot avoid reading them as texts
to be interpreted and also as texts that have been interpreted. Indeed, it
is our own culture that provides hermeneutical models, but we can also
awaken these hermeneutical models in others. The best evidence of this
is the fact that the great scholars of other cultures are in many ways the
students, the disciples of the great masters of Western hermeneutics. In
this sense, we can presume that there is a single human mode of making
continuity, making a tradition, and making innovation in one and the
same gesture of innovation/tradition.

C. C. Before leaving you the last word, let me make one remark: It is not
possible to think of humanity as a unity. No, that is not true, or else it is
true in some ways but not in others. What is true is that *I want* humanity
to be a unity. It is not a theoretical truth.

P. R. This is exactly what I am saying.

C. C. We agree then on this point: Humanity as a unity is not a regulative idea of reason. It is an imaginary political meaning that animates a
political project.

P. R. There is not only a practical imagination; there is also a practical
reason. It is an act of thought according to the categories of practice and

therefore with legal requirements. We are not able to conceive a total legal vacuum.

C. C. No, there is a human action, a reflective action, which arises on the political level and which, as a result, absolutely must incorporate ethics, the ethical moment. To think the unity of humanity? Yes, but the human sacrifices of the Aztecs, the massacre of the Melians by the Athenians, my ancestors, Auschwitz, the Gulag, I do not see the translation which could bring me closer to that humanity? It removes too easily the monstrous. Hannah Arendt, in her book on totalitarianism,[26] said that the phenomenon of totalitarianism brings about the collapse of the traditional categories of understanding history. And she was right.

P. R. We have not talked about evil at all. I am totally on your side.

C. C. You call it evil; I call it the monstrous, but it is there.

P. R. I mean that there is something unrecoverable in the construction of sense [*sens*].

C. C. And that too is still a sense [*sens*], on its own level.

P. R. You are heading in my direction [*sens*], if I dare say: I can only recognise the unacceptable, the unbearable, and the intolerable within the limits of a search for understanding which thus falls under the rule of the best argument. And the limit to argument is the fact of violence. I can only exclude it through a practice of argumentation. The point of blindness is what cannot be admitted into the order of argumentation.

C. C. But this blind spot, this point of blindness, is constitutive of reality. The rule of the better argument is worthless in face of Hitler, the Stalinists, Khomeini, etc. Beautiful argumentation is something that I can always carry with me to the other world …

P. R. The expression 'worthless' is situated precisely in the universe of sense. I refuse nonsense, but I could not be like Adorno,[27] who knew perfectly well what evil was but had no idea of the good. And if I did not have, like Habermas[28] or others, the limit idea of successful communication (and hence certain practices of successful communication, though limited), I could not ethically say 'no' to horrible motives. I can only understand it imaginarily on the following condition; in this work, I continue my task as a translator. I am the universal translator even of that which I refuse and that I absolutely reject from my horizon.

—Translated by Scott Davidson

NOTES

1. *Le Bon Plaisir* de Paul Ricoeur, *France-Culture*, March 1985. *Editor's Note*: All notes to the dialogue were compiled by Johann Michel, editor of the French edition, with the exception of those indicated as *Editor's Note*, which were added for the English publication.

2. *Editor's Note*: The Imaginary Element (*l'Élément imaginaire*) was Castoriadis's great but ultimately unfinished work. He referred to it directly in the preface of *The Imaginary Institution of Society*, where in discussing the limitations of the book, he noted that '[l]ikewise, the properly philosophical aspect of the question of the imaginary and of the imagination has been reserved for another work, *l'Élément imaginaire*, which will be published soon' (1987, 2). There is a large amount of unpublished texts and working notes on *The Imaginary Element* held in the Castoriadis Archives. Some work was published from it, for example, the essay 'The Discovery of the Imagination' (Castoriadis 1997) and the posthumously published fragment, 'The Imaginary as Such' (Castoriadis 2015).

3. Here Ricoeur is referring to Castoriadis (1987).

4. For Fichte, reflection itself is empty; it thus implies production [*produzieren*], which is to say, the reflection about something or on something (images, concepts, etc.).

5. Ricoeur (1977).

6. Ricoeur (1984–1988).

7. Cochin (1979).

8. Furet (1985).

9. André Malraux uses the expression 'coherent deformation' (where Ricoeur speaks of a 'regulated deformation') in Malraux (1978).

10. Foucault (1972).

11. Spinoza, *Ethics* [1677]. 'The infinite continuity of existence' refers to the definition of duration in the *Ethics* (Eth. 2, Def. V).

12. *Editor's Note*: The Spanish conquest of the Aztec Empire was led by Hernan Cortes, not Christopher Columbus.

13. *Editor's Note*: Castoriadis used the term *Eingebung* in the original. In the context of 'the bestowal of meaning', however, *Sinngebung* is a more appropriate conceptual translation, and has been accordingly substituted. Although *Sinngebung* as 'sense bestowal' is a Husserlian term that Heidegger used only occasionally, he did not use the notion of *Eingebung* at all. I thank Johann Michel and Jean-Luc Amalric for drawing this issue to my attention, and Johann Arnason, Ingo Farin, and Jeff Malpas for further clarification.

14. Canguilhem (2008).

15. Reinhart Koselleck (1923–2006), German historian and philosopher, who renewed historical epistemology. Ricoeur refers to his masterpiece (Koselleck 2004).

16. The Bielefeld school is a current of German historiography (affiliated with the University of Bielefeld). This current is distinguished by the desire to reconnect history to the methods of the social science in an approach that is sometimes close to the French Annales school. *Editor's Note*: Although Koselleck spent the most important part of his career in Bielefeld, he was not a member of the Bielefeld school per se, as his whole line of enquiry was different from the School in fundamental respects.

17. Heidegger (1990).

18. Castoriadis is alluding to the theory of 'mimetic desire' by René Girard in Girard (2005).

19. The after-effect is the translation of the Freudian concept drawn from the substantive term *Nachträglichkeit*, which signifies the reworking of past events by the mind. See the reprise of this concept as a conception of mental causality and its structuralist extension in Lacan (2007, 123–60).

20. *Editor's Note*: In the original French version, Castoriadis deployed the phrase 'at cross purposes' in English.

21. This expression can be found in Plato's *Phaedo* (70c). *Palaios logos* can also be translated as 'a certain ancient saying, a certain tradition'.

22. *Untimely Meditations* collects a series of four philosophical works by Friedrich Nietzsche. Ricoeur is referring to the second one of these, called 'On the Uses and Disadvantages of the Study of History for Life' (1997 [1874], 59–123).

23. Habermas (1990).

24. Ricoeur refers to Donald Davidson's notion of a conceptual scheme, which he translates here as 'organizational scheme'. See Davidson (1973–1974, 5–20).

25. Ferry (1987).

26. Arendt (1951).

27. Horkheimer and Adorno (2002 [1944]).

28. See Habermas (1990).

REFERENCES

Arendt, Hannah. 1951. *The Origins of Totalitarianism.* New York: Schocken Books.

Canguilhem, Georges. 2008. *Knowledge of Life.* Translated by Stefanos Geroulanos and Daniela Ginsburg. New York: Fordham University Press.

Castoriadis, Cornelius. 1987. *The Imaginary Institution of Society.* Translated by Kathleen Blamey. Cambridge, MA: MIT Press.

———. 1997 'The Discovery of the Imagination'. In *World in Fragments.* Translated and edited by David Ames Curtis. Stanford, CA: Stanford University Press.

————. 2015. 'The Imaginary as Such'. Translated by Johann Arnason. *Social Imaginaries* 1:1, pp. 59–70.

Cochin, Augustin. 1979. *L'esprit du jacobinisme: Une interprétation sociologique de la Révolution française.* Paris: PUF.

Davidson, Donald. 1973–1974. 'On the Very Idea of a Conceptual Scheme'. *Proceedings and Addresses of the American Philosophical Association* 47: 5–20.

Ferry, Jean-Marc. 1987. *Habermas: L'Éthique de la Communication.* Paris: PUF.

Foucault, Michel. 1972. *The Archaeology of Knowledge.* Translated by Alan Sheridan. New York: Pantheon Books.

Furet, François. 1985. *Penser la Révolution française.* Paris: Gallimard.

Girard, René. 2005. *Violence and the Sacred.* Translated by Patrick Gregory. London: Bloomsbury.

Habermas, Jürgen. 1990. *Moral Consciousness and Communicative Action.* Translated by Christian Lenhardt and Shierry Weber Nicholsen. Cambridge, MA: MIT Press.

Heidegger, Martin. 1990. *Kant and the Problem of Metaphysics.* Translated by Richard Taft. Bloomington: Indiana University Press.

Horkheimer, Max, and Theodore W. Adorno. 2002 [1944]. *The Dialectic of Enlightenment.* Translated by Edmund Jephcott. Stanford, CA: Stanford University Press.

Koselleck, Reinhart. 2004. *Futures Past: On the Semantics of Historical Time.* Translated by Keith Tribe. New York: Columbia University Press.

Lacan, Jacques. 2007. 'Presentation on Psychical Causality'. In *Ecrits: First Complete Edition in English.* Translated by Bruce Fink. New York: Norton.

Malraux, André. 1978. *The Voices of Silence.* Translated by Stuart Gilbert. Princeton, NJ: Princeton University Press.

Nietzsche, Friedrich. 1997 [1874]. 'On the Uses and Disadvantages of the Study of History for Life'. In *Untimely Meditations.* Edited by Daniel Breazeale, 59–123. Cambridge, UK: Cambridge University Press.

Ricoeur, Paul. 1977. *The Rule of Metaphor.* Translated by Robert Czerny. Toronto: University of Toronto Press.

————. 1984–1988. Time and Narrative, 3 vols. Translated by Kathleen Blamey and David Pellauer. Chicago, IL: University of Chicago Press.

Part II

ESSAYS

Chapter Two

On the Cusp

Ricoeur and Castoriadis at the Boundary

George H. Taylor

The 1985 conversation between Castoriadis and Ricoeur offers an enthralling crystallisation of numerous themes that allows for closer examination of their similarities and differences. My title, 'On the Cusp', signifies three themes that this essay will pursue. First, the debate between Castoriadis and Ricoeur itself exists against a basically unstated background that they hold in common. Each grants the primordiality of the social imaginary in social life. This agreement needs our initial attention. They are both 'on the cusp' in being at the forefront boundary of the development of the ineluctability and significance of the social imaginary as a phenomenon. Second, the discussion between them is 'on the cusp' in revealing the boundary between them. I will focus on their differing attention to productive and creative imagination. I grant particular weight to Castoriadis's promotion of a creative imagination and to Ricoeur's insistence that the productive side of imagination must always arise out of a situated context rather than being simply free. Third, I will emphasise that the discussion between Castoriadis and Ricoeur is *only* 'on the cusp', as it provides a momentary snapshot of a boundary between them that needs contextualising against the larger careers of both thinkers. My argument here is that resources exist in each thinker's corpus over time that may offer a greater sense of similarity between them, even if differences persist. In other of his work, Ricoeur offers much greater support for the creative imagination than he does in the present conversation, and similarly, in other reflections, Castoriadis modulates his position such that creative imagination arises *ex nihilo* but not *in nihilo* or *cum nihilo*. I find that Castoriadis constructively elaborates his position over time, yet he does not accept modification, as the social imaginary would seem to entail, of creation as *ex nihilo* itself. And Ricoeur's stance in the present discussion presents both an explicit debate with Castoriadis and an unnoticed debate with earlier stances of his own. I am more sympathetic to these earlier positions and their advocacy of a creative imagination.[1] Nevertheless, the 1985 conversation remains singular, not only in the uniqueness of the recorded discussion, but in its focalisation of themes of interchange, and its publication should be celebrated for being on the cusp in this way.

THE PRIMORDIALITY OF THE SOCIAL IMAGINARY

I begin with the conversation's largely unstated common background: the agreement that Castoriadis and Ricoeur share regarding the primordiality of the social imaginary.[2] This common background is only briefly referenced, in Ricoeur's opening comment in the dialogue: '[T]his issue of the imaginary foyer of social relations and of social production is, I believe, our shared interest' (see chapter 1, p. 3).[3] Given the decisive attention Castoriadis gave to the social imaginary throughout his corpus, the inexorability of the social imaginary in his work seems a commonplace, although I shall briefly return to his and Ricoeur's differentiation from structuralism, Weber, and Marx. In Ricoeur, the attention to the social imaginary may be less familiar. More dedicated Ricoeur readers are aware that the imagination is a significant and continuing subtext in his work, as Jean-Luc Amalric has admirably shown in great detail (Amalric 2013; Kearney 2004). The publication of Ricoeur's *Lectures on Imagination* (Ricoeur 2018), which I am co-editing, should demonstrate in systematic form his larger thesis in support of the productive (and creative) imagination. I return to this volume at greater length in the third part. As for Ricoeur's more specific development of the social imaginary, it is important to appreciate that his volume, *Lectures on Ideology and Utopia*, claims that discussion of ideology and utopia must be framed within the social and cultural imagination (Ricoeur 1986, 1).[4] In these *Lectures*, Ricoeur argues for 'a symbolic structure of action that is absolutely primitive and ineluctable' (Ricoeur 1986, 77). Ricoeur returns to this theme in *Time and Narrative*, where he similarly claims that human action 'is always already symbolically mediated' (Ricoeur 1984, 57). I would contend that his work on metaphor pursues a comparable argument, in maintaining the existence of 'a "metaphoric" at work at the origin of logical thought, at the root of all classification' (Ricoeur 1977, 22). A more detailed analysis would need to demarcate more precisely the interrelations between the symbolic (or metaphoric) and the imaginary, interrelations that Castoriadis calls 'deep and obscure', but for present purposes, it suffices to recognise 'the imaginary component of every symbol and of every symbolism' (Castoriadis 1987, 127).[5]

Because the issue is only one of background importance, the greater significance of Castoriadis's and Ricoeur's emphasis on the ineluctability of the social imaginary can be presented rather succinctly, and by brief contrast to other personages or intellectual trends – to Marx, Weber, and structuralism. Structuralism was the subject of criticism by both Castoriadis and Ricoeur. They both rejected its presentation of a closed system that eliminated the innovative and dynamic event (Castoriadis 1987, 217; Ricoeur 1974; 1975; Dosse 2014, 265). The social imaginary also provides a resource for both thinkers to reject the Weberian assumption of the dominance of instrumental and bureaucratic reason (Castoriadis 1987, 156; 1991, 66–7; Dosse 2014, 253, 272; Ricoeur 1986, 213–14). Of perhaps greatest interest, Castoriadis's and Ricoeur's endorsement of the social imaginary rejects Marx's argument, as customarily understood, for an economic infrastructure from which social and cultural phenomena emanate as superstructure. In the midst of Castoriadis's lengthy critique of Marx in *The Imaginary Institution of Society*, he explicitly rejects a materialist conception of history whose primary motivation is economic and asserts that the reification of human activity is in fact an 'imaginary meaning' (Castoriadis 1987, 29, 140; Dosse 2014; 140; Michel 2015, 126). The economic and the imaginary are intertwined. Similarly, for Ricoeur, the imaginary is infrastructural. 'Take into consideration any culture, and we find that its symbolic framework—its main assumptions, the way in which it considers itself and projects its identity through symbols and myths—is basic. It seems that we can call basic exactly what is usually called the superstructure' (Ricoeur 1986, 153–4). Both Castoriadis and Ricoeur, then, emphasise the pursuit of and inexorability of human meaning rather than grant priority to structural or causal forces. In the present discussion, Castoriadis stresses the vocabulary of the 'domain of meaning' (12), and in Ricoeur's work, citing Clifford Geertz, he gives primacy to analysis that is 'an interpretive one in search of meaning' (Ricoeur 1986, 255, quoting Geertz 1973, 5).[6]

If the present discussion between Castoriadis and Ricoeur concentrates on points of contention and agreement between them, we need to appreciate that the debate is an internecine battle between two figures who agree on the paramount and inextricable character of the social imaginary (Dosse 2014, 265; Michel 2015, 124). If it is obvious that the social imaginary is a fundamental concept for Castoriadis, so also is the imagination a continuing key concept for Ricoeur. While I remarked earlier that the imagination is a continuing subtext of Ricoeur's work, I would insist more forcefully here, along with a number of other readers of Ricoeur, that the imagination and the imaginary are central thematics in his corpus (Revault d'Allonnes 1997, 13; Foessel 2007, 8; Amalric 2013, 13).[7] As I will address in part three of this essay, publication of his *Lectures on Imagination* will make this import even more self-evident. Castoriadis and Ricoeur are 'on the cusp' – in the vanguard – in advancing the thesis that the imaginary is a 'motor of history' (Dosse 2014, 334). Angelos Mouzakitis contends that Castoriadis 'is arguably the only contemporary thinker' who has 'turned creative imagination into *the* central theme of his theoretical construction' (2014, 92). While scholars may debate whether the imagination and the imaginary are 'the' central themes in Ricoeur, it will be my task to show that the creative imagination – and not simply the productive imagination – is indeed central to Ricoeur's writing also. If the present part underscores the priority that Castoriadis and Ricoeur grant to the social imaginary, it remains a separate task to show that in Ricoeur, as in Castoriadis, the social imaginary is creative and not just productive. We cannot assume that the social imaginary is creative by definition. Part two, to which we now turn, explores the discussion and debate in the present text on the differentiation between the productive and the creative imagination.

THE DIFFERENTIATION BETWEEN PRODUCTIVE AND CREATIVE IMAGINATION

This part addresses on its own terms the discussion and debate between Castoriadis and Ricoeur in the present text. It draws on material external to this text simply to amplify the arguments made here. While in their dialogue Castoriadis and Ricoeur show signs of intersection and overlap, the discussion is marked more by different trajectories and ambits of their reflections. At a number of points, although not always, they seem to be arguing past one another. This part then attends principally the cusp of the differences between them that their dialogue reveals. I reserve to part three external material that may suggest the need for modification of theses presently articulated. That part will argue also that the points of intersection between the two thinkers can be amplified, given other parts of their corpora. I begin, in the present part, with Castoriadis and then address Ricoeur's response.

Castoriadis

It is well known that Castoriadis rejects a deterministic view of society. I briefly want to develop this general theme and then will sharpen it to locate more precisely Castoriadis's aim – and then Ricoeur's objection. Castoriadis criticises what he types an 'ensemblist-identitary' social logic, where elements interrelate on a 'well-determined' and conclusive basis (Castoriadis 1987, 177). Instead, as in the present dialogue, Castoriadis advocates for social 'self-institution' and the 'autonomy' that comes from creating new rules (5). New social meanings and forms arise in human history, and they emerge as something other than a 'result of a combination of pre-existing forms' (8). New figures emerge (14), and the enquiry regarding this emergence is the one that most matters to him (14). Human being has 'the potentiality of potentiality' (11). The social imaginary is creative, because determination of what may be is never closed (Castoriadis 1997b, 393).

In his broader work, Castoriadis frequently adverts that he is elucidating the 'radical imaginary'. I understand the meaning of this term to have three overlapping senses. First, whatever the political valences of the 'radical' imaginary, the term means more fundamentally something radical in the sense of going to the root. Castoriadis writes, 'I hold that human history – therefore, also, the various forms of society we have known in history – is in its essence defined by imaginary creation' (Castoriadis 1997b, 84). Humanity at its most basic, at the level of the radical imaginary, is what Castoriadis initially calls a 'productive or creative imagination' (Castoriadis 1987, 146) and then types more precisely as solely 'creative' (199). Given, as we shall see, that

Ricoeur will markedly differentiate between productive imagination –
which in the dialogue he endorses – and creative imagination – which
he does not – it is vital to ascertain that Castoriadis reverses the priority
and defends creative imagination over against productive imagination.
If in the initial citation, he cites productive and creative imagination as
correlative, this is in a lay, non-technical sense. In the second citation,
Castoriadis explicitly rejects the productive imagination, because, as
he notes, the term is limited by Kant to the empirical understanding.
The productive imagination does not bring forward something new. For
Castoriadis, humanity is, at bottom, creative.

The second implication of the radical imaginary is that it creates a
divide or break with existing society. It cannot be encapsulated within
prior norms or determinations. In our present text, Castoriadis goes
so far as to speak of an 'absolute rupture', which marks the singularity within history; continuity is broken (14). This language echoes his
vocabulary elsewhere: '[T]he social-historical element emerges, itself
a rupture of being and an "instance" of the appearance of otherness'
(Castoriadis 1987, 204).[8] In the rupture, 'radical otherness' and the
appearance of the 'absolutely new' occur (172). We find a 'radical
destruction' of society's existing institutions (373). For reasons that
I will return to in part three, I would underscore Castoriadis's terminology that the creative imaginary 'shatters' existing social forms
(Castoriadis 1987, 372; 1997b, 175).

The third implication of the radical imaginary returns us to his claim
in the present dialogue of emergence: New forms emerge in history
(Castoriadis 1987, 40–1). This emergence crystallises the creative
imaginary. The emergence is not simply a deviation or break from
the past but the rise of a new kind of behaviour (14). Castoriadis has
metaphorically characterised this creative emergence as a 'surging
forth' (Castoriadis 1997b, 183). If he characterises as 'magma' (14) the
diverse, interrelated, but non-uniform underpinnings that animate the
social imaginary (Castoriadis 1987, 182; 1997b, 7), the 'surging forth'
evokes the way that magma breaks through the surface of the earth's
crust as lava. Something new, unplanned, and disruptive appears. Part
of the 'potentiality of potentiality' (11) of the human condition is that
the magma lying beneath the human surface may always surge forth.

Likely, the most forceful vocabulary Castoriadis uses for the social
imaginary as creative is that it is 'creation *ex nihilo*', creation out
of nothingness. Although Castoriadis does not use the term in the

dialogue with Ricoeur, the concept seems present in Castoriadis's language, already cited, of 'absolute rupture' (14). I want to address the terminology of 'creation *ex nihilo*' directly, both because it seems to summarise the central thrust of Castoriadis's thematics – evident in the dialogue and in his larger corpus – and because, as we shall see, this concept seems to generate Ricoeur's most critical response in the present conversation. The term 'creation *ex nihilo*' appears but four times in Castoriadis's masterwork, *The Imaginary Institution of Society* (Castoriadis 1987, 2, 3, 153, 361), and as I shall discuss in part three, Castoriadis subsequently modifies the terminology.[9] But throughout his corpus, he retains the term 'creation *ex nihilo*', and in his masterwork, on which I focus here, the concept plays a pervading role, even if the term itself appears infrequently. In his principal volume, Castoriadis discusses how 'the central or primary imaginary significations of a society create objects *ex nihilo*' (Castoriadis 1987, 361). The emphasis, as previously remarked, is on the appearance in history of a 'radical otherness': 'For what is given in and through history is not the determined sequence of the determined but the emergence of radical otherness, immanent creation, non-trivial novelty' (Castoriadis 1987, 184). As radically other, the emergence comes from no determinate source; it is new, unanticipated, unheard of.

In some quite provocative ways, Castoriadis insists on the rise of the creative out of nothingness. The imaginary, like the symbolic, presupposes 'the capacity to see in a thing what it is not'; the imaginary stems from the faculty of 'positing or presenting oneself with things and relations that do not exist' (Castoriadis 1987, 127). The radical imagination makes an initial representation 'arise out of a nothingness of representation, that is to say, *out of nothing*' (283). In later work, Castoriadis even more explicitly links creation *ex nihilo* with the ' "is" not' (Castoriadis 1997a, 305). The 'radical otherness' and the 'absolutely new' previously noted arise from what was not there before. As we now turn to discuss, the concept of creation *ex nihilo* seems quite alien to Ricoeur in the current dialogue and highlights the divergence – the cusp – between them. But the significance of the concept goes further than the seeming divide between the two figures. For in part three, we shall see how Ricoeur, in his independent work on the *creative* imagination, himself predicates the creative as arising out of the 'nowhere'. For now, I want to insist that, in his dialogue with Ricoeur, Castoriadis remains firm in his sense of priority to the creative imagination as a break, a 'cut', something that arises out of nothingness. As he specifically states during the conversation, 'This discontinuity alone is what interests me' (7). Although, as we shall see, at points in the conversation Castoriadis appears to modulate his insistence on the autonomy, the self-predication, of the creative, on its emergence as 'radical otherness', I shall argue that his fundamental stance remains obdurate and unchanged.

Ricoeur

At the outset of our consideration of Ricoeur, it is critical to reinforce that any debate that he has with Castoriadis occurs within the context of a larger framework of similarity. As already noted in part one, they share an emphasis on the primordiality of the social imaginary. Further, while they debate over whether and to what degree a productive imagination can be extended to a creative imagination, they both insist that the productive or creative imagination permits some sense of newness and change. In this, as they recognise in their larger work, their thought argues against the history of Western thought, which in their view almost continuously endorses only a *reproductive* imagination (Castoriadis 1997a, 319; Ricoeur 2018). To be precise, both reject the limitation of the imagination to a weakened version of a perceptual image, the imagination as an 'image of' something else that exists (Castoriadis 1987, 3; Ricoeur 2018, 15.5).[10] The imagination as 'image of' is a reproductive imagination, a replication of existing reality. By contrast, whether as productive or as creative, the imagination for Castoriadis and Ricoeur brings forward something new. In some of his opening lines in the discussion, Ricoeur contrasts an imagination that merely 'reproduces a copy of something that is already there' with one that engages in 'a production of new syntheses and new configurations' (4). He endorses the availability of a productive imagination.

During the debate, Ricoeur grants positive weight to the productive but not to the creative imagination. He finds the notion of creation to relate more to the powers of a 'foundational sacred', while a productive imagination relates to our inextricable existence within an institutional order (4). As we shall discern more in part three, it is odd that Ricoeur here relates the creative imagination to a religious origin, as he does not do so elsewhere. Perhaps, although this is speculative, he is reacting negatively to Castoriadis's emphasis not only on the creative as absolute newness but on it arising *ex nihilo*, which has Christian theological overtones.[11] In any event, Ricoeur's stance in the dialogue is entirely consistent with the remainder of his corpus that the imagination is always situated; it always functions within an existing institutional order – within an existing social and cultural setting. As we shall determine, however, the implications that Ricoeur draws in the dialogue diverge from those he offers elsewhere.

I begin here with Ricoeur's pronouncements on the productive imagination during the dialogue that come closest to Castoriadis's on the creative imagination. I intentionally delay, for a moment, consideration of corresponding Ricoeur statements that modify or seem to pull back on these stronger statements. Ricoeur endorses that humanity proceeds through 'ruptures' and 'discontinuities' (7, 8); he acknowledges the appearance in human history of the 'previously unexpressed and unheard mode of thought' (14) and a 'breakthrough of truth' (14). He accurately indicates: 'I never cease to plead in favour of the concept of an event in thought: there are events in thought, there are innovations' (6). These statements are symptomatic of his larger corpus. As an eminent example of this broader consistency, one of the signal contributions of his book, *The Rule of Metaphor*, is that it demonstrates how metaphor may break the prison of language epitomised in structuralism. Yet, as Ricoeur also makes explicit during the debate, for him, innovation must always be conceived to exist in relation to sedimentation (6). This point, too, is one that Ricoeur maintains across his corpus. In the dialogue, he retains the language of the dialectic between innovation and sedimentation from his work *Time and Narrative* (Ricoeur 1984, 68). He rejects the possibility of 'absolutely novelty' (5), of moving from 'nothing to something' (6). Ricoeur's hermeneutics well reflects this stance (see Michel preface, p. xxxvi): Even as we seek to bridge across distance in our interpretation of the world of another, our interpretation necessarily begins as a situated one arising from our own culture and time. Ricoeur's emphasis on the inextricability of the social imaginary also reflects our situated circumstance. In his larger corpus, Ricoeur describes this setting as one of 'prefiguration' (Ricoeur 1984, 53). During the debate, he speaks similarly of our always being located within the 'pre-instituted' (13), within a 'pre-structure' (5). The non-instituted is not available to us (13). In *Time and Narrative*, Ricoeur develops the notion of 'configuration' of what has already been prefigured (Ricoeur 1984, 64–6), and in the dialogue, Ricoeur

repeatedly returns to the vocabulary of configuration and reconfiguration (4, 6, 8, 9, 13). We can never move from the formless to the form
that we create (5); the configuration does not arise out of nothing (8);
our attempt at innovation occurs only against an environment of existing configurations (6). We are always situated within existing configurations that we try to reconfigure (13). Ricoeur's argument here in the
dialogue is consistent with his larger work, and it is one with which I
happen to agree. I return to Castoriadis's response shortly.

More troubling, however, is Ricoeur's extension of his stance on
configuration in the dialogue to what he calls his 'main argument', on
'retroaction' (11). Admittedly, there is some power in Ricoeur's differentiation between what he calls the continuity at the level of existence
as over against the discontinuities at the level of sense (7). He finds in
this continuity a general condition of humanity as 'living-together' (7).
I hear echoes in this phrasing of comments outside of Ricoeur on how,
genetically and socially, we are all ultimately one humanity in space and
time. In our fractured age, these reminders remain potent. Yet there is a
tonality to Ricoeur's discussion, epitomised in his elaboration of retroaction, that I regret. I disagree with the tone and contend that it skews
what in my mind should be a greater dialectic between continuity and
discontinuity and a greater interrelation between the levels of sense and
existence.

How is Ricoeur's discussion of retroaction his main argument during
the debate? No longer is the matter simply one of configuration, for
the focus is on retrospection, retroaction. The term 'retroaction' is cited
frequently (11, 12, 14). Through a 'retroaction of our new creations on
the old moments, we can deliver possibilities that had been prevented'
(11). We may establish the new by means of a recovery of our legacy
from the past (12). Rupture and innovation is accepted but against the
background of a 'received inheritance' which ensures a 'basso continuo'
(7). Although Ricoeur maintains that through configuration we can now
read the past otherwise (12), his analysis gives primacy to the continuity
of human existence (7). From my perspective, Ricoeur's tonality here
is similar to that in *Time and Narrative*. As I have argued elsewhere
(Taylor 2015a, 130), it is similarly disquieting in that text that Ricoeur's
description of narrative as 'concordant discordance' or as a 'synthesis
of the heterogeneous' (Ricoeur 1984, 66) grants priority to concordance
and synthesis rather than to more of a tension between identity and
difference. I would contend that the framework of figuration and the

social imaginary does not limit us to configuration but remains open to the possibility of *trans*figuration – a recasting or re-envisioning of the old in light of the new, which can include rejection of the parts of the old and moving forward in a new trajectory.[12] As I shall argue in part three, then, the critical differentiation between productive and creative imagination does not rest upon whether we place ourselves within Ricoeur's framework of the symbolic mediation of action and the social imaginary. The dividing line is whether we permit a more robust sense of the transfiguration – the break, the rupture, the newness – that may occur within this framework of figuration. An absolute break with the past is not possible, but a significant break, a significant point of redirection may be. As I shall also pursue in the next part, this contention in favour of the creative imagination may readily draw upon arguments in Ricoeur's corpus that are not attended in the present dialogue or in works such as *Time and Narrative*.

I close the present part with some comments on Castoriadis's response to Ricoeur's arguments in the dialogue. It seems obvious that in the debate, Ricoeur is intent on constant objection to any possibility in Castoriadis of the endorsement of moments of absolute newness in human history. My sense is that Castoriadis's response is twofold: both 'of course' and 'and yet'. These two sides of his response seem congruent with the two levels of Ricoeur's argument I have developed. Castoriadis's response is 'of course' in the sense that he agrees that all human existence is situated historically and culturally. We each function necessarily within existing languages and within existing institutions. Castoriadis acknowledges that 'each sense or each new form that emerges is not the result of a combination of pre-existing forms, even if it does retain a certain reference to the past' (8). To this statement, Ricoeur responds that the two of them are then on the same side (8). As another example, it is a source of continuing fascination to me that throughout his work, as in the dialogue, Castoriadis's orientation to the new continually hearkens back to the lessons and insights of classical Greece (10). Because of the unavoidability of human existence within language and institutions, Castoriadis accepts that in this sense 'there's no absolute rupture' (12).

At first glance, this seems a major concession to Ricoeur. Yet here Castoriadis's additional response of 'and yet' seems to come into play. I noted at this essay's outset that Ricoeur and Castoriadis have important points of overlap, including, as we have seen, the priority they grant to the social imaginary and now the rejection of our inability to extricate ourselves from the social imaginary. Yet as I also forecast, this overlap is part of ambits with quite different directions. Ricoeur moves towards retroaction, and Castoriadis persists in emphasising historical breaks. So, if in a general manner Castoriadis's reaction in the dialogue to Ricoeur's insistence on the inevitability of a situated existence is one of 'of course', his response includes an 'and yet' in the sense that Ricoeur's insistence also misses the point. As previously noted, Castoriadis's emphasis in the conversation is on the availability of historical discontinuity (7); his focus remains on the possibility of the 'emergence of a new figure' (14). After having agreed with Ricoeur that there is 'no absolute rupture' (12) in human language or institutions, a few pages later, he contends that a new figure's emergence breaks with continuity and does present in fact an 'absolute rupture' that 'marks the singularity of our history' (14). While I would not insist on a consistency in vocabulary in the free flow of an intense conversation, there does seem to be a contradiction or at least tension in Castoriadis's conceptual matrix. One question is whether Castoriadis's larger framework can allow no absolute rupture, yet a rupture that is new. The same question can be asked of Ricoeur's larger conceptual model as well. I return to this issue in the context of both thinkers and their larger body of work in part three. To anticipate, despite Castoriadis's agreement with Ricoeur in the dialogue that the appearance of the new in human history is inevitably informed by references from the past (8), the debate does not appear to create a meeting of the minds. This lack of concord seems aptly reflected in a rare statement of Castoriadis on Ricoeur a few years after the conversation occurred. Noting the 1988 publication of the third volume in English of *Time and Narrative*, Castoriadis expresses his admiration for the 'richness and solidity' of Ricoeur's analysis in that work of the philosophical tradition regarding time, yet he also emphasises his own continuing 'obvious and central differences' with Ricoeur (Castoriadis 1997b, 438, n. 1).[13] From the perspective of the dialogue, Ricoeur restricts himself to the availability of productive imagination, because the imagination must always proceed by configuration, whose newness arises from what has gone before, while Castoriadis endorses the creative imagination, because newness not only arises from but also breaks away from the existing social imaginary.

THE CREATIVE IMAGINATION AND
THE IMAGINARY *EX NIHILO*

In this third and concluding part, I move away from the Castoriadis–
Ricoeur dialogue to the wider corpora of these two thinkers. I argue that
the debate in the present text is only on the cusp of the larger potential
interrelation between their thought, as their work as a whole permits
some adjustment to the dialogue's representativeness of the depictions
of their arguments. In particular, I contend that in other of his work,
Ricoeur does endorse a creative, and not just productive, imagination,
and I also reference themes in Castoriadis's broader corpus that situates – but does not eliminate – his endorsement that creation is *ex nihilo*.
I reverse the order of the prior part and begin with Ricoeur and then turn
to Castoriadis.

Ricoeur

My enquiry into the availability in Ricoeur of an endorsement of
creative imagination focuses primarily on his unpublished *Lectures
on Imagination* and also on his books *The Rule of Metaphor* and the
Lectures on Ideology and Utopia. It is relevant that the two volumes
of lectures noted were each the product of sets of course lectures that
Ricoeur delivered in 1975 (at the University of Chicago) and that the
original French version of *The Rule of Metaphor*, *La métaphore vive*
(Ricoeur 1975), appeared during that same year. My thesis in this
section can be baldly stated as follows: Ricoeur's 1985 debate with
Castoriadis would have been significantly different if it had occurred
in 1975. As his work of that year attests, he would have argued in
favour of the existence of the creative imagination, even as he retained
an insistence on the situated character of the emergent or new. My
argument in this section proceeds in three steps. I first examine the
vocabulary in the *Lectures on Imagination* that affirms the availability
of the creative imagination. I then show that this vocabulary reflects
indeed a substantive, not just terminological, variation from Ricoeur's
position in 1985. Finally, I expand the scope to show the substantive
ties between the *Lectures on Imagination*, *The Rule of Metaphor*, the
Lectures on Ideology and Utopia, and other work of that time period.
Part of the task will be to highlight Ricoeur's vocabulary during this

period that endorses, similar to Castoriadis, that the creative imagination may arise from 'nowhere' and that it may 'shatter' existing reality. For whatever reason, Ricoeur himself chose ultimately not to publish the *Lectures on Imagination*; the rationale was not due to a rejection of those lectures' avowal of the creative imagination. Similar themes appear in his published work.

First, then, it is apparent throughout the *Lectures on Imagination* that Ricoeur's object is to carve out a space for the creative imagination in the face of the weight of most of Western thought, which has concentrated solely on the reproductive imagination. The *Lectures* are replete with Ricoeur's references to the positive role of creative imagination. He speaks of 'the creative function of imagination' (3.1, 4.9, 5.3, 5.11), 'the full recognition of creative imagination' (3.9), 'the creative power of imagination' (5.4), the 'creative imagination' as the positive thematic that he wishes to pursue (7.10), and the important implications of 'the notion of creative imagination' (17.15, 18.2). He wants to develop a 'phenomenology of creative imagination' (17.8, 17.9). At many points in these *Lectures*, Ricoeur extends the productive imagination beyond its role in Kant (the subject of lectures 5 and 6) and in fact equates the productive imagination with the creative imagination. He discusses 'the problem of creativity, of productive imagination' (4.7); he claims that imagination is 'the bearer of all productive or creative functions' (5.11); imaginative variation has a 'productive, creative function' (15.12); it is when 'imagination is involved in a creative process of thought and language that imagination itself is productive' (16.1).

My second comment is that Ricoeur's vocabulary of creative imagination does reflect a substantive change from his 1985 discussion and not just a change in vocabulary. In language similar to Castoriadis, Ricoeur talks in the *Lectures* of the 'emergence of something new' (15.16, 16.6). More precisely, the great contribution of the *Lectures* lies in its development of Ricoeur's theory that the productive and creative imagination is best located in a theory of 'creative fiction' (13.19), as fiction allows a distance from existing reality that allows for a refashioning of reality, a shaping of reality in a new way (13.17). In language offering some suggestive parallels to Castoriadis on creation *ex nihilo*, creation out of nothingness, Ricoeur contends that in a theory of fiction, 'we have the full expression of the theory of nothingness', where we seek not to reproduce but to 'produce new entities' (14.12). He argues for an ontological character of fiction. A creative fiction does not seek to reproduce reality, as would a reproductive image. Instead, fiction begins with the nothingness of an image, 'an image without an original', and so permits 'a second ontology that is not the ontology of the original but the ontology displayed by the image itself, because it has no original' (16.1). As I examine in more detail elsewhere (Taylor 2015b), Ricoeur extends the phenomenological concept of intentionality to argue for the fiction as consciousness of the 'absolutely nowhere' (14.15), and this nowhere has ontological implications. Again equating the productive with the creative, Ricoeur contends that 'it's the genius of productive imagination – of the fictional – to open and change reality. Productive imagination may enlarge and even create new world views, new ways of looking at things, and, finally, may change even our way of being in the world' (15.5). The creative imagination can 'reshape' reality (16.4), open new dimensions of reality (19.2, 19.5). The larger ambition of Ricoeur's thesis is to show that the power of the creative imagination extends not only to the poetic imagination but also to the epistemological imagination – for example, in scientific models – and to the social imagination – as in utopias (19.1). He addresses the epistemological imagination in the *Lectures on Imagination* and the utopia in the *Lectures on Ideology and Utopia*. I return shortly to the utopia as exemplary of the social implications of Ricoeur's theory.

Finally, we should respond to any potential critique that Ricoeur may have refrained from publishing the *Lectures on Imagination* because of a decision not to affirm their implications in favour of a creative imagination. It remains the case, though, that he did publish some articles affirming the creative imagination. For example, consider the titles 'The Function of Fiction in Shaping Reality' (Ricoeur 1991) and 'Creativity in Language' (Ricoeur 1978). And, more significantly, he published *The Rule of Metaphor* during this period and subsequently allowed publication of the *Lectures on Ideology and Utopia*. In the *Lectures on Imagination*, Ricoeur devoted one full lecture to demonstrating the positive interrelation between his work on metaphor and his thesis in favour of the creative imagination. Just as the metaphor's disruption of literal meaning allows for a metaphoric reference, so the creative imagination disrupts existing reality and opens a productive reference. There is a connection between the productive aspects of language and the productive conditions of the imagination (16.4). In his article 'Creativity in Language', Ricoeur sharpens the correlation in ways deserving emphasis: '[M]etaphor not only *shatters* the

previous structures of our language, but also the previous structures of
what we call reality' (Ricoeur 1978, 132; emphasis added). We recall
Castoriadis's emphasis also that the emergence of the new arising from
the creative imagination may 'shatter' existing social forms (Castoriadis
1987, 372; 1997b, 175).[14]

In the *Lectures on Ideology and Utopia*, Ricoeur there too insists that
the creative social and cultural imagination may 'shatter' present reality. In contrast to Castoriadis's rejection of the utopia as 'an act of faith'
or 'arbitrary wager' (Castoriadis 1997a, 170),[15] Ricoeur asserts that the
positive power of the utopia lies not in acting as an avenue of escape
from reality but in the 'claim to shatter' reality (Ricoeur 1986, 309).[16]
The utopia has the ability to 'break through the thickness of reality'
(Ricoeur 1986, 309). Ricoeur frequently reiterates in this volume that
the utopia can shatter an existing order (Ricoeur 1986, 173, 179, 273,
285, 289). He returns to this thematic in the *Lectures on Imagination*.
The utopia is literally the 'nowhere' and is another example of a fictional 'nowhere' that can shatter reality. The utopia, Ricoeur says,
offers 'the possibility of the *nowhere* in relation to my social condition'
(14.11). 'The nowhere', he continues, 'is a starting point toward a new
position.... Fictions may produce a new reality, because they don't
reproduce a previous reality' (14.16–17).

The tonality in the *Lectures on Imagination* and other work of
this period is quite different from that of the 1985 discussion with
Castoriadis. The language of the 'nowhere' and of 'shattering' focus not
on continuity with the old but on breaks and the appearance of something new. In the *Lectures*, the language is not one of 'configuration'
but of 'transfiguration' of reality (17.1, 17.7) and of 'restructuration' of
prior categorisation (16.12–13). We must 'reshape' prior concepts in
order to encompass new situations (15.10). The vocabulary of restructuration and reshaping in the *Lectures* does reiterate Ricoeur's emphasis
in the debate with Castoriadis that no absolute rupture occurs. Ricoeur
maintains in the *Lectures* that 'naked creativity' is not available (6.6,
6.14). But we must emphasise both terms in that phrase: Creativity is
never naked, it is always situated; but it is creativity, not productivity,
that is the subject of the discussion. The creative imagination must
arise from the categorical, the structured, in order to be transcategorial (16.11). It is a myth of creativity that it is formless; it 'proceeds
from form to form' (16.14). Ricoeur's work on metaphor renders the

transfiguration and transcategorial activity at work in the creative imagination quite precise:

> Every metaphor, in bringing together two previously distant semantic fields, strikes against a prior categorisation, which it *shatters*. Yet, the idea of semantic impertinence preserves this: an order, logically antecedent, resists, and is not completely abolished by, the new pertinence. In effect, in order that there be a metaphor, it is necessary that I continue to perceive the previous incompatibility through the new compatibility. (Ricoeur 1991, 125; emphasis added)[17]

It may be that the differences in Ricoeur's endorsement of creativity in the 1975 time period and his rejection of it in 1985, as he completes *Time and Narrative*, have to do with the larger subject matter of his works during these years. As he acknowledges in a 1981 conversation with Richard Kearney, analysis of the creative imagination deals with 'creativity in its prospective or futural aspect', while analysis of narrativity assesses it 'in a retrospective fashion' (Ricoeur 2004, 131). The language of retrospectivity resonates with the term 'retroaction' that Ricoeur used in the 1985 dialogue. Whatever the historical factors, in the 1970s, Ricoeur seems consistent in endorsing an imagination that is creative and not just productive. This imagination that can shatter and can arise from the nowhere seems close to Castoriadis, even if it is never a naked form of creativity. It is perhaps fitting to close the discussion of Ricoeur with his rare commentary during this period on Castoriadis, also drawn from his 1981 conversation with Richard Kearney. Ricoeur speaks of how the 'imaginative and *creative* dimension of the social, this *imaginaire social*, has been brilliantly analysed by Castoriadis' (Ricoeur 2004, 133; emphasis added).

Castoriadis

In this section, I address to what degree Castoriadis's writings go beyond his statements in the dialogue with Ricoeur and respond to the critique levied by Ricoeur that creativity is always situated, never an absolute rupture. I examine first Castoriadis's writings subsequent to *The Imaginary Institution of Society* and then return to that major text.[18] In this longer view, I find greater concord between Castoriadis and Ricoeur than the dialogue itself reveals but still not a final commonality.

One of the most significant and commendable changes in Castoriadis's vocabulary is that the language of creation *ex nihilo* that appeared in *The Imaginary Institution of Society* is modified in later writings to that of creation *ex nihilo* but not *in nihilo* or *cum nihilo* (Castoriadis 1991, 64; 1997a, 321, 333, 370, 404; 1997b, 174, 392; Adams 2011, 129).[19] It is essential at the outset to appreciate that Castoriadis does retain his insistence that creation occurs *ex nihilo*, out of nothingness. Although his elaboration of why creation is *ex nihilo* but not *in nihilo* or *cum nihilo* is often brief, Castoriadis clarifies that creation *ex nihilo* remains uncaused or undetermined by external factors but yet under constraints (Castoriadis 1997a, 333, 370; 1997b, 393). Creation does not occur as a matter of a blank slate (Castoriadis 1991, 64; 1997b, 14). 'Neither in the social-historical domain nor anywhere else does creation signify that just anything can happen just anywhere, just any time and just anyhow' (Castoriadis 1997a, 370). The creation is not motivated by external factors but is conditioned by them; something already in existence is utilised. The creation *ex nihilo* of the classical Greek *polis*, for instance, made use of existing Greek mythology (Castoriadis 1997b, 174). In perhaps his most extended development of the meaning of creation *ex nihilo* but not *in nihilo* or *cum nihilo*, Castoriadis identifies four kinds of constraints on creation *ex nihilo* (Castoriadis 1997a, 333–6). First, external constraints include biological and natural factors and instrumental uses of language. These are the products of material life. Second, internal constraints include psychological factors that affect how the psyche becomes socialised. Third, historical constraints relate creation to a past; it exists within a tradition. Finally, creation also faces intrinsic constraints; social imaginary significations must present a general sense of coherence (even if faced with internal tension and contradiction) and must also be complete. These factors do impose important restrictions on what creation *ex nihilo* may produce.

Yet as much as I admire the refinements in Castoriadis's analysis, as I read these factors and the language of constraint, they all seem ultimately external to creation *ex nihilo*. Creation *ex nihilo* is preserved in ways that still seem, in my view, susceptible to Ricoeur's critique that innovation always takes a situated form. Castoriadis discusses creation *ex nihilo* as the 'emergence of a new ontological form – *eidos* – and of a new mode and level of being' (Castoriadis 1991, 64; 1997a, 332). I have an image of creation in Castoriadis as a form like an architectural blueprint, whose achievement may be limited by terrain and the amount and kind of building materials, but the form itself is not affected. To use another metaphor, if magma erupts above the earth's surface as lava, the lava flow will be channelled by conditions on the surface, but the constitution of the lava itself remains unimpinged. The creation as form is not modified. The creation's *meaning* is substantively unaltered; it may be more, it may be less, it may be constructed in wood or in brick, but the creation *ex nihilo* is preserved. Castoriadis's more complex phrasing of creation as *ex nihilo* but not *in nihilo* or *cum nihilo* does not seem to go far enough in redressing the kinds of criticisms Ricoeur launches in the dialogue about the creative imagination – or in his vocabulary there, the productive imagination – always being situated and circumscribed by its conditions. In protecting creation as *ex nihilo*, Castoriadis does not seem to address how the meaning of the creation is itself framed and informed by its circumstances.[20]

To exemplify both the limitations and the potentiality of Castoriadis's argument about creation *ex nihilo*, I return to *The Imaginary Institution of Society* and his discussion there of the role of institutions. My claim is that there seem to be resources in Castoriadis that would allow him to go further than he actually does. As a transition to this argument, I would like to address the challenge whether in his major text, the theme of creation *ex nihilo* but not *in nihilo* or *cum nihilo* is present if not described explicitly in that terminology. My starting point for this enquiry is raised by a suggestive line that appears in Castoriadis's later work. While identifying sources in his recent writings that elaborate on his more complex presentation of creation *ex nihilo*, he also asserts in a parenthetical that 'innumerable passages from *IIS* [*The Imaginary Institution of Society*] show this' as well (Castoriadis 1997a, 404). The implication seems to be that even if this earlier work does not use the same vocabulary regarding creation *ex nihilo* as his later writings, the same substantive stance is present. In consideration of this claim, I find particularly fruitful Castoriadis's early emphasis that the social is both always instituted and always instituting (Castoriadis 1987, 112). Both parts of this statement deserve both acclaim and elaboration. That the social is always instituted has several significant implications. On the one hand, Castoriadis's observation here recognises that institutions are necessary for human societies to operate (Castoriadis 1987, 113–14, 116); social organisation is indispensable. In the dialogue with Ricoeur, he repeats similarly that human communities cannot exist without institutions (12). Second, Castoriadis's observation goes further in rejecting the Marxian claim that institutions are necessarily alienating and that the social goal is to eliminate them, as through the withering of the State (Castoriadis 1987, 114; Dosse 2014, 366). Ricoeur also denies that institutions are necessarily reifying, and it would be intriguing to work out here also the juxtapositions between him and Castoriadis on the human struggle to establish what Ricoeur calls 'just institutions' (Ricoeur 1992, 172).[21] Castoriadis's larger point is that our thought ineluctably belongs to history and to society; every thought 'is but a mode and a form of social-historical doing' (Castoriadis 1987, 3). The social imaginary must manifest itself in and through social-historical institutions (237).

At the same time, the social is always instituting. As we have seen, it is a persistent theme in Castoriadis that we are not limited to deterministic institutions. Creative moments within society and within history are available to us (114). Castoriadis often underscores that the creative arises through social instituting: '[T]he institution is nothing if it is not form, rule and condition of what is not yet' (219). Particularly informative is Castoriadis's example of language as an institution. While language can allow for treating the meaning it provides as determined and circumscribed, it also 'always provide[s] the possibility of new terms emerging' (353). The example of language is generalisable, as language 'shows us how instituting society is constantly at work' (218).

To retrieve the vocabulary of creation *ex nihilo* but not *in nihilo* or *cum nihilo*, we may say that in Castoriadis's earlier framework, the creative can arise – it is new and instituting – but it will do so within institutions – it is not *in nihilo* or *cum nihilo*. This stance is similar to his later argument that 'there can be no radical imaginary except to the extent that it is instituted' (Castoriadis 1997b, 184). In this sense, Castoriadis's conceptual framework regarding creation *ex nihilo* appears similar over time even if the vocabulary of the conception is expanded in his later work.

Yet, I would contend, when Castoriadis frames creativity across his corpus as inextricably arising within institutions, this conceptual structure presses substantively on the viability of the characterisation of creation *ex nihilo*.[22] While, as previously argued, the concept of creativity as break and rupture can importantly be retained, it cannot be as absolute break or rupture. Significantly, this conclusion seems an implication of the very ineluctability of the social imaginary as envisioned by both Castoriadis and Ricoeur. We are never outside or independent of the social imaginary. All of human understanding is mediated and interfused by our social institutions. It is quite pertinent that in the dialogue with Ricoeur, Castoriadis agrees that 'when you say that there's no absolute rupture, that one always remains in the rules of language, that is certainly true' (12). We cannot break absolutely with the framework of language as an institution. We are informed by it all the way down; there is no location separable from the work of language. In the twentieth century, continental philosophy witnessed how the struggle with Western metaphysics of such influential thinkers as Heidegger and Derrida was also a struggle with the language of Western thought; they could not escape how this language instituted even as their own vocabulary pushed it to become instituting in different directions. The same may be said of Castoriadis's own neologisms, such as magma.

I want to retain, then, in both Castoriadis and Ricoeur the availability of the creative imagination and its ability to arise out of 'nowhere' and to shatter current structures of reality. I support Castoriadis's persistent affirmation of the creative imagination and regret the limitations of Ricoeur's apparent retreat in the dialogue and elsewhere to the productive imagination. On the other side, I think that Ricoeur has the better of the argument in maintaining the dialectic of innovation and sedimentation against Castoriadis's defence of the creative as an absolute break. Ricoeur's reflections on the operation of metaphor, the creative imagination as fiction, and the utopia as the shattering of reality also seem to offer more detailed consideration on how the creative may arise, even as he joins Castoriadis in regarding the creative occurrence as ultimately opaque (Ricoeur 2018, 18.20–1; Castoriadis 1997b, 14–15). The endorsement and development of the social imaginary that they both offer remains absolutely vital; in this way, their work remains, years after their death, very much on the cusp of intellectual enquiry.

In *The Rule of Metaphor*, Ricoeur defines metaphor as the depiction of resemblance across difference (Ricoeur 1977, 196). The metaphoric bridging exhibits similarity at the same time that difference is preserved. In their dialogue, as in their writings as a whole, the thought of Castoriadis and Ricoeur offer many moments of metaphoric resemblance, where we experience bridges even as difference remains. Both the synergy of and the divergences between their thought offer rich

resources for further reflection, and we can be grateful that their dialogue has brought these productive (and creative) tensions more keenly
into focus.

NOTES

1. In other writings, I have argued similarly that tensions exist in Ricoeur's
work, such that arguments of which I am critical can be typically challenged by
positions elsewhere in his work that I endorse (Taylor 2012, 2015a).

2. Johann Michel also addresses this point in his preface to the present
volume. I generally will refrain from cross-citation to other commentary in
this book.

3. Hereafter the references to the radio dialogue proper appear as single page
numbers.

4. Greater delineation of the positions of Castoriadis and Ricoeur on the
ineluctable background nature of the social imaginary would need to develop
Ricoeur's reference to this imaginary as both cultural and social. The social,
Ricoeur relates, 'has more to do with the roles ascribed to us within institutions, whereas the cultural involves the production of works of intellectual
life' (Ricoeur 1986, 32, n.1). In this passage, Ricoeur goes on to develop the
differentiation at greater length.

5. For another quick reference to this problem, I have found useful in
Castoriadis the following statement: 'The social imaginary is, primordially,
the creation of significations and the creation of the images and figures that
support these significations. The relation between a signification and its supports (images or figures) is the only precise sense that can be attached to the
term "symbolic" – and this is the sense in which we are using the term here'
(Castoriadis 1987, 238). In the debate with Ricoeur, Castoriadis ascribes the
vocabulary of the symbolic to Ricoeur, while he prefers the language of the
'domain of meaning' (12). For further discussion of this differentiation, see
note 5. As perhaps apparent, in both Castoriadis and Ricoeur, the references to
the 'imaginary' and the 'symbolic' are different from Lacanian vocabulary.

6. In this passage, Ricoeur goes on to interrelate the quest for meaning with
the symbolic mediation of human action (Ricoeur 1986, 255–6). This challenges Castoriadis's differentiation, cited in note 4, between his own focus on
meaning and Ricoeur's on the symbolic.

7. To underscore the argument in the text, it is worth quoting the authors
cited: '[S]'il est un problème philosophique qui cristallise nombre de ses inter-
rogations, c'est bien celui de l'imagination' (Revault d'Allonnes 1997, 13);
'En réalité, la pensée ricoeurienne, depuis l'interprétation de la 'symbolique

du mal' jusqu'aux analyses sur la mémoire, se présente comme une meditation sur les productions de l'imaginaire' (Foessel 2007, 8); '[L]a question de
l'imagination ne correspond pas à un moment déterminé et limité de l'itinéraire
philosophique de Ricoeur mais qu'elle est au coeur de son project philosophique depuis les premières oeuvres jusqu'aux dernières' (Amalric 2013, 13).

8. Suzi Adams comments: 'Creation, in Castoriadis's sense, ruptures
frameworks of being as determinacy – the *eide* as immutable and unalterable –
and, as such, they cannot account for it' (Adams 2011, 52).

9. I thank Suzi Adams for discussion of this topic.

10. In this and subsequent citations to Ricoeur's forthcoming *Lectures on
Imagination*, I refer to the text by lecture number and manuscript page internal
to that lecture. The present citation, then, is to page 5 of lecture 15.

11. I agree with Johann Michel (see Michel Preface, pp. xxxvi–vi) that
Ricoeur's hesitations here have no necessary correlation with his own theological orientation to what may be the powers of a 'foundational sacred'.

12. For development of this argument, see Taylor (2013).

13. In his comment, Castoriadis does not elaborate what these differences are.

14. I find quite suggestive the parallelism in the language of 'shatter' in
both thinkers' work, but emphasise the larger similarity in vocabulary and
conception rather than the identity of the use of 'shatter' in itself. Other terms
used in common, such as 'rupture', also depict this commonality. It is also of
course pertinent that while Ricoeur's invocation of 'shatter' initially occurred
in the *Lectures on Ideology and Utopia*, which were delivered in English,
in Castoriadis, I am referring to a translation of vocabulary originally written in French. In the first citation in the text, the English term is 'shattering'
(Castoriadis 1987, 372), and the French original is 'éclatement' (Castoriadis
1975, 496). In the second citation, the English term is 'shattered' (Castoriadis
1997b, 175), and the French original is 'rompue' (Castoriadis 1997c, 88).

15. For a more extended comparison of the notion of utopia in Castoriadis
and Ricoeur, see Michel (2015, 135–8). For development of Ricoeur's concept
of utopia, see Taylor (2017).

16. Ricoeur originally draws the term from Karl Mannheim (Ricoeur 1986,
173, quoting Mannheim 1936, 192).

17. Greater development of Ricoeur's views across these time periods
would need to assess whether the changes in part result to his latter work
being framed by the concept of *mimesis*. It is of interest that the *Lectures on
Imagination* begin to address that topic, and in that earlier work, Ricoeur differentiates between a reproductive *mimesis*, which he rejects, and 'a productive
mimesis, a creative *mimesis*' (19.6), which he endorses.

18. Because Castoriadis's later writings are often the product of reworking over time across the period, including the dialogue with Ricoeur, I make
no effort to determine whether any might have responded to the challenges

raised by Ricoeur in their conversation. For example, in the endnotes to one of
the articles to which I refer, 'Time and Creation', which appears in *World in
Fragments*, Castoriadis observes that the text was first presented in a 1983 lecture and then modified at points over time until published in 1990 (Castoriadis
1997b, 437).

19. In one of these passages (Castoriadis 1997a, 404), Castoriadis refers
to two other articles in which he had also specified this broader concept:
'PoPA' ('Power, Politics, Autonomy', Castoriadis 1991, 143–74) and 'ISRH'
('Individual, Society, Rationality, History', Castoriadis 1991, 44–80). In the
latter article, the reference to creation *ex nihilo* but not *cum nihilo* is explicit
and cited in my text (Castoriadis 1991, 64); in the former, the vocabulary
of creation *ex nihilo* appears to be absent and the reference seems more
indirect (Castoriadis 1991, 144–45, 170). The diligent reader will note that
in my references here and in the main text, I do not discuss separately when
Castoriadis adds to creation *ex nihilo* that it is not *cum nihilo* or *in nihilo* or
instead simply that it is not *cum nihilo*. Whether this differentiation has much
signification or is more inadvertent is not a subject that I spend time pursuing
here.

20. My argument is then sympathetic to Suzi Adams's claim: 'Castoriadis
does not explicitly acknowledge that the circle of creation is always already
a hermeneutical circle. We are always already inside the web of signification'
(Adams 2011, 118, emphasis deleted).

21. For my pursuit of this topic in Ricoeur, see Taylor (2014). In some
of Castoriadis's later writings, he extends his positive orientation toward the
possibilities of institutions. He writes, for instance, that the object of politics
should be to '[c]reate institutions which, by being internalised by individuals,
most facilitate their accession to their individual autonomy and their effective
participation in all forms of explicit power existing in society' (Castoriadis
1991, 173, emphasis deleted).

22. My argument is supportive of Suzi Adams's criticism that Castoriadis
stumbled when he 'radically separated significatory *meaning* from ensemblistic-
identitarian *organisation*' (Adams 2011, 69).

REFERENCES

Adams, Suzi. 2011. *Castoriadis's Ontology: Being and Creation.* New York:
   Fordham University Press.
Amalric, Jean-Luc. 2013. *Paul Ricoeur, l'imagination vive. Une genèse de la
   philosophie ricoeurienne de l'imagination.* Paris: Hermann.
Castoriadis, Cornelius. 1975. *L'Institution imaginaire de la société.* Paris: Seuil.

————. 1987 [1975]. *The Imaginary Institution of Society.* Translated by Kathleen Blamey. Cambridge, MA: Massachusetts Institute of Technology Press.

————. 1991. *Philosophy, Politics, Autonomy.* Edited by David Ames Curtis. New York: Oxford University Press.

————. 1997a. *The Castoriadis Reader.* Translated and edited by David Ames Curtis. Oxford: Blackwell.

————. 1997b. *World in Fragments: Writings on Politics, Society, Psychoanalysis and the Imagination.* Translated and edited by David Ames Curtis. Stanford, CA: Stanford University Press.

————. 1997c. *Faire et à faire: Les carrefours du labyrinthe V.* Paris: Seuil.

Dosse, François. 2014. *Castoriadis: Une vie.* Paris: La Découverte.

Foessel, Michaël. 2007. 'Introduction: Paul Ricoeur ou les puissances de l'imaginaire'. In *Anthologie de Paul Ricoeur.* Texts chosen and presented by Michaël Foessel and Fabien Lamouche, 7–22. Paris: Points.

Geertz, Clifford. 1973. *The Interpretation of Cultures.* New York: Basic Books.

Kearney, Richard. 2004. 'Between Imagination and Language'. In *On Paul Ricoeur: The Owl of Minerva*, 35–58. Aldershot, England: Ashgate.

Mannheim, Karl. 1936. *Ideology and Utopia.* Translated by Louis Wirth and Edward Shils. New York: Harcourt, Brace and World.

Michel, Johann. 2015. *Ricoeur and the Post-Structuralists.* Translated by Scott Davidson. London: Rowman & Littlefield.

Mouzakitis, Angelos. 2014. 'Social-Historical'. In *Cornelius Castoriadis: Key Concepts.* Edited by Suzi Adams, 89–100. London: Bloomsbury.

Revault d'Allonnes, Myriam. 1997. 'Avant-propos à l'édition française'. In Paul Ricoeur, *L'Idéologie et l'utopie*, 13–16. Paris: Seuil.

Ricoeur, Paul. 1974. 'Structure, Word, Event'. In *The Conflict of Interpretations.* Translated by Robert Sweeney. Evanston, IL: Northwestern University Press.

————. 1975. *La métaphore vive.* Paris: Seuil.

————. 1977. *The Rule of Metaphor.* Translated by Robert Czerny. Toronto: University of Toronto Press.

————. 1978. 'Creativity in Language'. In *The Philosophy of Paul Ricoeur: An Anthology of His Work.* Edited by Charles E. Reagan and David Stewart, 120–33. Boston, MA: Beacon Press.

————. 1984. *Time and Narrative* (Volume 1). Translated by Kathleen McLaughlin and David Pellauer. Chicago, IL: University of Chicago Press.

————. 1986. *Lectures on Ideology and Utopia.* Edited by George H. Taylor. Chicago, IL: University of Chicago Press.

————. 1991. 'The Function of Fiction in Shaping Reality'. In *A Ricoeur Reader: Reflection and Imagination.* Edited by Mario J. Valdés, 117–36. Toronto: University of Toronto Press. [Originally published, in English, in 1979 in *Man and World* 12:2: 123–41.]

————. 1992. *Oneself as Another.* Translated by Kathleen Blamey. Chicago, IL: University of Chicago Press.

————. 2004. 'The Creativity of Language' [1981 dialogue with Richard Kearney] in Richard Kearney, *On Paul Ricoeur: The Owl of Minerva,* 127–43. Aldershot, England: Ashgate.

————. 2018. *Lectures on Imagination.* Edited by George H. Taylor, Patrick Crosby, and Robert D. Sweeney (in press).

Taylor, George H. 2012. 'Ricoeur versus Ricoeur? Between the Universal and the Contextual'. In *From Ricoeur to Action: The Socio-Political Significance of Ricoeur's Thinking.* Edited by Todd S. Mei and David Lewin, 136–54. London: Continuum.

————. 2013. 'Ricoeur, Narrative, and the Just'. *Universitas: Monthly Review of Philosophy and Culture* 470: 145–58.

————. 2014. 'Ricoeur and Just Institutions'. *Philosophy Today* 58:4: 571–89.

————. 2015a. 'Prospective Political Identity'. In *Paul Ricoeur in the Age of Hermeneutical Reason: Poetics, Praxis, and Critique.* Edited by Roger W. H. Savage, 123–37. Lanham, MD: Lexington Books.

————. 2015b. 'The Phenomenological Contribution of Ricoeur's Philosophy of Imagination'. *Social Imaginaries* 1:2: 13–31.

————. 2017. 'Delineating Ricoeur's Concept of Utopia'. *Social Imaginaries* 3:1: 41–60.

Chapter Three

Castoriadis and Ricoeur on Meaning and History

Contrasts and Convergences

Johann P. Arnason

The dialogue between Cornelius Castoriadis and Paul Ricoeur took place in 1985. Both authors later produced important work, some of it posthumously published; a reconsideration of their only direct encounter will obviously have to take note of these subsequent writings. That may help to explain some apparent gaps in the conversation, as well as to identify ways to continue the main lines of the debate that did emerge.

SETTING THE SCENE

A first glance at the text will highlight points where one speaker or the other backs away from confrontations that might have taken interesting turns. When Castoriadis raises the question of the creative imagination, Ricoeur declares that he wants to reserve the idea of creation for 'something infinitely more primordial' (see chapter 1, p. 4),[1] things related to the order of the foundational sacred, and therefore prefers to use the term 'productive' for the human imagination. Castoriadis's failure to challenge this stance seems rooted in his own sweepingly invalidating view of religion and the sacred, discussed in the introduction; he may have thought that the dialogue was reaching the limits of mutual comprehension, and consequently opted for more communicable terms.

But in light of Ricoeur's evolving distinction between philosophy and the hermeneutics of religion, and taking into account the particularly clear-cut statements in later writings, we may suggest a less polarised approach. No claims or assumptions about the sacred or its creative force enter into Ricoeur's philosophical argumentation; he is referring to notions necessary for the hermeneutical work on religion. Moreover, the formulation used in his dialogue with Castoriadis, with its emphasis on the sacred and its foundational role, implies a position closer to Mircea Eliade and (by the same token) more focused on general religious themes than are the later indications mentioned in the introduction. Comparative analyses in the latter vein, with due allowance for the plurality of symbolic patterns, can distinguish between notions of creativity corresponding to different religious traditions and not everywhere of the same importance; and they could in turn be related to historical forms of social creativity, never extensively discussed in Castoriadis's work but easily envisageable in the context of his reflections.

On the other hand, Ricoeur backs off when Castoriadis invokes the Greek *polis* as an example of historical creativity (chapter 1, p. 4). The shift to a philosophy of language and the focus on semantic innovation serve to bring the issue back to more phenomenologically accessible terrain, and to avoid involvement in unending historical controversies. It is not clear how well Ricoeur knew Castoriadis's emerging interpretation of ancient Greece; in any case, it was the posthumous publication of seminars at the École des Hautes Études (Castoriadis 2004–2011) that brought to broader attention many years of work on this exemplary case of human creation. At the same time, the enormous advances of classical scholarship during the past decades have produced results that certainly raise questions about several aspects of Castoriadis's arguments, but can be seen as supportive of his attempts to grasp the *polis* as a total human phenomenon (in a sense reminiscent of Marcel Mauss's anthropological project). Seen from this angle, the Greek experience is obviously relevant to the conversation between Castoriadis and Ricoeur, and the following discussion will return to it in a more specific context.

On both sides, we have thus noted a certain tendency to eliminate the themes least conducive to common ground. What then follows is an effort to find shared horizons and clarify disagreements within their limits. A closer look at these exchanges will reveal some underlying problems and lead to a more sustained confrontation of the two philosophical perspectives. The conclusions thus suggested will, in a fundamental sense, be closer to Castoriadis than to Ricoeur. In particular, the former can be credited with decisive insights concerning the ontology of the social-historical, the role of meaning at that level, and the importance of imaginary significations as the key source of meaning. But as I will try to show, the defence of these ideas calls for conceptual underpinnings going beyond those formulated in Castoriadis's writings, and in some ways prefigured by Ricoeur.

FROM PRODUCTION TO INSTITUTION

As Johann Michel notes in his preface (in this volume), historical innovation is the main thematic point of convergence between the two thinkers (pp. XXXIV–XXXV). But the implications and connotations of this common focus are only in part explored, and logical further questions are not pursued. Ricoeur begins by invoking 'the imaginary production of society' as a shared interest. This is not the only case of assimilating Castoriadis's ideas to the paradigm of production. Alain Touraine (1977; the original French title refers only to production, whereas the English translation uses the more specific term 'self-production') acknowledged his debt to Castoriadis's work on social-historical creativity, but proposed to link that theme more closely to social conflict than Castoriadis had ever done. That is not Ricoeur's agenda, though we should note that Touraine's analysis of rival interpretations rooted in shared cultural models (such as the idea of progress) has certain affinities with the conception of a hermeneutical field of conflicts. But the reference to production raises other questions, and Castoriadis indicates some of them. In response to Ricoeur's coupling of imagination and production, he recalls some landmarks of modern thought; to clarify his own line of argument, a brief look at these earlier variations on the themes of imagination and production may be useful.

Kant's discussion of the productive imagination in the first edition of the *Critique of Pure Reason*, followed by withdrawal from that topic in the second, was part of his unfolding reflection on the constitution of a knowable world. But the imagination, removed from the explicit framework of his project (for a more detailed comment, see Arnason 1993), reappears in the *Critique of Judgment*, albeit in elusive and ambiguous ways. Here, it comes into play through the interpretation of experiential domains that were not given their due in the foundational works on pure and practical reason, namely works of art and the world of living beings (for an extensive discussion of this problematic, see Célis 1977, with a preface by Ricoeur). Heidegger's book on Kant (Heidegger 1997), published soon after *Being and Time* (and much later described by the author as an over-interpretation), returned to the first version of the first Critique and argued against the conventional understanding of Kant's thought as an attempt to dethrone metaphysics. For Heidegger, the underlying and ultimate meaning of Kant's work was a new foundation of metaphysics, and the recognition of the transcendental (by the same token, productive) imagination as a source of theoretical as well as practical reason should be judged in that context: as an empowering extension of a metaphysical principle, the idea of world-making subjectivity. Kant's retreat from the realm of the imagination is then analysed as a failure to confront the final implications of this new approach: that he was working towards an answer to the question of being. As for Marx, the paradigm of production is unquestionably central to his thought, but successive phases of his work bring different aspects of it to the fore. The interpretation most prominent in his later writings, and most influential in the Marxist tradition, stresses the production of material livelihood and its structural constraints. A broader conception, indicated in early texts and arguably still intact as a background presupposition of later ones, refers to an ongoing human production of history and society, and although there is no explicit mention of the imagination, Marx noted in passing that human beings are capable of producing according to the laws of beauty, and was surely sensitive to the Kantian and post-Kantian connotations of that statement.

Before going on to discuss Castoriadis's ambiguous relationship to these traditional sources, Ricoeur's provisional response should be considered. He admits to reactivating pre-Marxist sources but singles out Fichte rather than Kant. Although he – to the best of my knowledge – never wrote an extensive appraisal of Fichte, there are several patent and significant reasons for this choice. The most explicit one has to do with the very idea of the productive imagination. As Ricoeur reads it – without elaborating in detail – Fichte's use of the term 'productive imagination' is a particularly convincing alternative to both reproduction and creation: The focus is on an ongoing production of new syntheses and configurations. Johann Michel's footnote (2017, chapter 1, p. 18, n. 4) signals a second reason. For Ricoeur, Fichte exemplifies the relationship between self-reflection, indispensable as a starting point but incapable of gaining substantive ground, and the production of contents necessary to provide footholds for interpretation. We may add that this reading not only foreshadows Ricoeur's conception of a permanently renewed beginning, but also his more comprehensive vision of philosophy in its unfolding historical shape. In addition to these conceptual affinities, the reference to Fichte suggests certain views on the history of modern thought. To recognise the originality and enduring significance of his philosophy is, by the same token, to cast doubt on the widespread idea of one dominant logic in the trajectory of German idealism, the one that led from Kant to Hegel. Ricoeur can certainly not be accused of underestimating Hegel, but the portrayal of German idealism as a pluralistic configuration of divergent and unexhausted approaches (including, most obviously, Fichte and Schelling) is more in line with his general judgement on thinkers of the past. Finally, if Hegel's work was neither the sole adequate or legitimate summing up of the whole development between 1781 and 1831, nor a pre-refutation of Schelling's final venture in the 1840s, Marx's break with German idealism will appear in a correspondingly different light: neither as a unique and decisive rupture, nor as a reformulation of lasting insights on a higher level. Rather, the Marxian moment is one of several turns, simultaneous as well as successive, and their multiple legacies are still matters of debate (Ricoeur wrote, among other things, an essay on Kierkegaard seen in this context).

Neither the internal plurality nor the diverse posterity of German idealism was an important theme for Castoriadis. He refers to the development from Kant to Hegel as a paradigm case of a pattern known from other phases in the history of philosophy, that is, the necessary transition from critical to dialectical thought (Castoriadis 1987, 54–6). The strong emphasis on Marx's links to Hegel then serves to accuse both thinkers of historical determinism. Given this position, the view of problems raised by the notion of a productive imagination is bound to be very different. Castoriadis's approach draws on crucial sources outside the philosophical tradition, but to grasp his main points, we need another look at the implications of associating production and imagination. The two concepts are, in short, brought together through the problematic of world-making, and with the intention of gaining a more complex picture of the activities and capacities involved on that level. This is, in varying ways, the case with Kant, Marx, and Heidegger, and also with Fichte as read by Ricoeur. For Castoriadis, such perspectives represent an unacceptable shortcut; they bypass or minimise the question of the social-historical. That level tends to shrink to structural determination (as in the most influential versions of Marxism) or to normative expectations (as in Kant and Fichte). In order to anchor the problem of the imagination in social and historical contexts, Castoriadis insists – in his direct response to Ricoeur as well as on numerous other occasions – on its primary link to the institution.

The problematic of institutions had already come to the fore in Castoriadis's critique of Marxism. Three main reasons for this stand out. When the basis-superstructure model is abandoned, on the grounds that the constraints of economic organisation do not account for the historical diversity of human societies, the self-instituting of society becomes a central theme for social theory. When the idea of a revolutionary transformation is reconsidered in light of this shift, it entails not only changes of specific institutions, but also a new relationship of society to its institutions. In this way, the Marxian critique of alienation, invoked at the time by opponents of Soviet-style Marxism, is given a social and historical content that was lacking in the more common humanistic versions, based as they were on general anthropological notions of self-realisation. Castoriadis redefines alienation as a self-inflicted subordination of society to its own institutions. Finally, the idea of autonomy, reformulated as a negation of this condition (and thus clearly akin to Kant's version, but set in a significantly different context), became a criterion for correcting ideological models of emancipation. Castoriadis's arguments in that vein are still geared to a defence of the revolutionary project, albeit understood in a new way, but as Marcel Gauchet's work shows, the social-historical conception of autonomy can be extended beyond this limit, turned against visions of revolution and connected to the problematic of modern democracy.

All these conceptual shifts open up a space where the imagination can come into play. But the institutionalist framework of the whole analysis raises questions about sources, affinities, and differences. The concept of institution was debated in the French human sciences during the 1960s and 1970s, and there is no doubt about the Durkheimian background to this discussion. Closer readings of Durkheim came later, but the legacy of his school was active even when he was not directly invoked. One of the most central tenets of the Durkheimian tradition was the idea of institutions as the sociological theme par excellence. To clarify the content and potential of this claim, it seems best to begin with a classical source: a programmatic essay on the object and the method of sociology, written as an encyclopaedia entry by Paul Fauconnet and Marcel Mauss in 1901 (Mauss 1968, 6–41). Comparison with Mauss's other writings suggests that he was the main author, and this now seems widely recognised. In any case, this text contains the most succinct and suggestive account of the institution as a defining theme of sociological enquiry. It is not being assumed that Castoriadis was directly influenced by Mauss; in fact, the absence of significant contact with Mauss's thought seems equally striking in both Castoriadis's and Ricoeur's work. Castoriadis was well acquainted with the Durkheimian problematic of collective representations, however, and aware of the need to develop his own notion of imaginary significations as an alternative to that approach but also as an upgrading of Durkheim's insights. For Castoriadis as well as Durkheim, the social-historical potential of meaning is realised through institutions, and if the reference to Mauss is to throw further light on this matter, it can only be through comparison with the line taken later, in more explicitly revised conceptual terms, by Castoriadis in his reflections on the imaginary institution. Mauss begins on the sociological and distinctively Durkheimian side, with the opening statement that an institution is a 'set [*ensemble*] of acts or ideas, all established, that the individuals find themselves facing and is more or less imposed on them' (Mauss 1968, 16). This description applies not only to basic social arrangements, but also to more fleeting phenomena, such as 'fashions, prejudices and superstitions' (Mauss 1968, 16). This part of the argument concludes with the claim that the institution is 'in the social order what the function is in the biological order' (Mauss 1968, 17). The implication of this statement, unspoken and unclarifiable without further conceptual innovations, is that closer analysis of the institution will reveal the limits of functional approaches to the social world. That was to become one of the key themes in Castoriadis's main work, *The Imaginary Institution of Society* (1987 [1975]). But Mauss also indicates other roads beyond the strictly Durkheimian view on institutions. They are not simply given or inherited from the past: 'Veritable institutions are alive, that is ever-changing: the rules of action are neither understood nor applied in the same fashion at successive moments, even when the formulas that express them remain literally the same' (Mauss 1968, 17). As will be seen, the question of rules, their conflicting interpretations, and resultant innovations come up in the conversation between Castoriadis and Ricoeur. Finally, Mauss briefly raises the issue

of society beyond institutions. He does not, as Castoriadis did later, distinguish between instituting and instituted society; rather, he considers
social groupings in formation, such as crowds, and describes them as
borderline cases between social life and inferior realms.

If institutions are not only capable of change, but intrinsically and
permanently caught up in it, the medium that makes this possible must
be more clearly identified. Mauss's solution to that problem was the
all-round exploration of the symbolic. According to Tarot, Mauss's
view was that 'every culture, every society is made up of symbolisms,
and social life presupposes them at every turn' (Tarot 2003).[2] Diverse
types and configurations of symbols structure all relationships of
human beings to each other and to their shared world. In general terms,
a symbol is a referring and expressive image, enabling the articulation
of experience, the formation of identities, and the regular flow of communication. Durkheim's mature sociology of religion had already taken
a major step towards a comprehensive grasp of symbolism; the elementary forms of religious life, exemplified by Australian totemism, also
revealed the foundational role of symbolic patterns, rather than explicit
beliefs or verbal teachings. Mauss's move beyond Durkheim, based on
multidisciplinary research (linguistics, comparative mythology, anthropology, Indology, and the history of religions entered into the project),
led to a generalised notion of the symbolic and – as Tarot puts it – a tem-
porary 'eclipse of the sacred' (Tarot 2003, 584). The comparative study
of religions becomes a matter of contextualising their core meanings,
and neither the sacred as such nor its distinction from the profane can
retain the same significance across cultural and historical boundaries.

In Mauss's writings, the broadly understood concept of the symbol,
used as a key to these formative contexts, is not clearly distinguished
from that of the sign. This suggests a proximity to linguistic models,
and there is no doubt that Mauss was aware of advances in that field,
but his attitude to strong claims made on behalf of linguistics was
ambiguous: He acknowledged the omnipresence of language in social
life, but did not regard it as a self-contained and unilaterally determin-
ing component. The inconclusive results of Mauss's ventures into this
field enabled the founder and dominant figure of French structuralism,
Claude Lévi-Strauss, to invoke a model grounded in further developments of linguistics (from Saussure to Jakobson) and propose it as a
solution to the problems inherited from anthropologists and sociologists
working in the Durkheimian tradition. As Tarot argues, the genealogy

of structuralism is thus more complicated than the most influential accounts would have it. There was no unilateral and generalising transfer of a linguistic model to the whole spectrum of the human sciences; rather, the encounter with ongoing reflections and open debates on basic anthropological and sociological issues that gave rise to a new paradigm with transdisciplinary claims.

If Mauss's work explores multiple aspects of the social world and foreshadows a variety of further themes, there is nevertheless a major limitation to be noted. Mauss did not confront the question of the imagination and its role in the constitution of society; his conception of institutions can be seen as an opening to reflection on the imagination, but the next step was not taken. When Castoriadis reconceptualised the link between imagination and institution, he also emphasised the primacy of the imaginary in relation to the symbolic, but did not go on to examine and differentiate the relationship between the two levels. The specific contribution of the imaginary to different constellations of the symbolic has yet to be studied in a comparative view. Provisionally, the signs that generate meaning through their mutual differences and the symbols that evoke latent and disputed meaning may be seen as the extremes of the spectrum.

As we have noted, the initial contrast between production and institution as frameworks of the imagination raises a whole set of questions and perspectives, relating to philosophical traditions, interdisciplinary projects, and reconceptualising turns. But Castoriadis and Ricoeur do not continue along these lines; nor do they try to focus on the imagination as such and different ways of understanding its manifestations in figures, discourses, actions, and sociocultural patterns. The remainder of the conversation deals with the specific themes of innovation, the intertwining of continuity and discontinuity, and of unity and plurality in human history. For both thinkers, these topics seem to constitute the most solid common ground, but also a focus of confrontation, favourable to measured disagreement. The irreducible differences brought to light in the course of the exchange have to do with implicit conceptions of the imagination, but here I will not follow the dialogue step by step. Instead, the main arguments on both sides will be reconstructed in a plausible thematic order. This interpretation will be followed by a sketch of further clarifying points, neither noted in the conversation between Castoriadis and Ricoeur nor covered in their writings, but arguably necessary to spell out the implications of their ideas.

CONFRONTING STRUCTURALISM

Before moving on to these themes, and to the different lines of interpretation proposed by the two thinkers, a shared background should
be noted. Both Castoriadis and Ricoeur insist on demarcating their
approaches from the work of Claude Lévi-Strauss. What Castoriadis
emphatically rejects and Ricoeur dismisses is the idea of innovation as
a rearrangement of fully determined elements, unchanging but available for new combinations. Ricoeur argues, and Castoriadis agrees,
that the emergence of or articulation of a new overall constellation
or project entails new interpretations of the elements that enter into
it. Reinterpretations of history are an exemplary case: They depend
on revised accounts of the events and episodes under consideration.
There is thus no doubt about the common and radical opposition to
structuralism. (Lévi-Strauss was certainly a paradigmatic representative of this current, arguably the only one of that stature.) As other
writings of both authors make abundantly clear, their main concern
was to defend the autonomy and primacy of meaning against a new
and extreme version of reductionism, summed up in Lévi-Strauss's
description of meaning as a derivative effect of elements combined in
a certain fashion. For Castoriadis, this was the second major attempt to
downgrade meaning; the first was the 'materialist' conception of history, centred on the basis-superstructure model, which he had targeted
in the first part of *The Imaginary Institution of Society*. References to
Lévi-Strauss in the second part of that work are at first sight perfunc-
tory, but a posthumously published analysis of the constitutive imaginary (Castoriadis 2015) shows that the structuralist view of language,
meaning, and understanding is one of the challenges that Castoriadis
wanted to counter.

Both Castoriadis and Ricoeur responded to the rise of structuralism in
innovative ways, with lasting consequences for the orientation of their
thought, and growing recognition of their stature must therefore affect
received views on the history of French thought during the period in
question. As Johann Michel (2014) shows in his book on Ricoeur and
his contemporaries, the inclusion of the two thinkers blurs the picture
commonly associated with the notion of poststructuralism. But then it
would seem advisable to go one step further than Michel does and drop
the very idea. Poststructuralism is an Anglo-American term, rarely and
reluctantly adopted by French writers, and suggests a unifying pedigree

and perspective that cannot be substantiated. Strictly speaking, we should only speak of post-structuralist thought when structuralist views are reconceptualised in ways that move beyond the original framework and into a different context. There is probably no better example of that procedure than Derrida's classic essay on sign, structure, and play in the human sciences (Derrida 1978). It is much less obvious that the same applies to Derrida's later work, not to mention other authors initially counted among the structuralists but later reclassified as post-structuralists (Foucault, Lacan, Althusser). And there is no justification for subsuming the fundamentally autonomous philosophical projects of Castoriadis and Ricoeur under this category. They perceived structuralism as a challenge, and they developed defences and alternatives in the spirit of their pre-decided philosophical choices. That is not a reason for calling them post-structuralists. All things considered, it seems best to consign the latter notion – at least in the broad sense taken to define a moment or a turn in intellectual history – to oblivion as an artificial construct, invented by outsiders in search of a new 'postism'.

CREATIVITY IN CONTEXT

It remains to clarify the affinities and differences between the two conceptions of innovation in language, culture, history, and society. The general line of the following argument will tend to support Castoriadis's stronger views on the subject, against Ricoeur's more moderate ones, but to strengthen the case, interpretations and formulations going beyond those used by Castoriadis in the dialogue will have to be brought in. On the other hand, this will not entail a defence of the most extreme statements found elsewhere in Castoriadis's writings. *Creatio ex nihilo* is an unfortunate expression, out of tune with the overall thrust of Castoriadis's thought, and when it is admitted (as he did in response to critics) that human creation can neither occur *in nihilo* nor *cum nihilo*, that is, that means and circumstances always have a role to play, it is not clear what the reference to nothingness can still mean. In fact, the creativity discussed in Castoriadis's work is always contextual, and in multiple senses. On the most general ontological level, we can distinguish between a fundamental cosmic creativity (invoked through the resurrected notion of *physis*), the specific creativity of living beings, and the more transformative creativity

at work in the social-historical world (Adams 2011); what gives the
latter its particular force is the double-edged role of the imagination,
released from functional constraints on the level of the psyche but then
channelled into specific direction on the level of institutions. Further
distinctions will highlight the differences between historical epochs
and constellations. Durkheim had already noted cases and phases of
'collective effervescence', and Castoriadis singles out the creative
flowerings of the Greek *polis* as well as the Western European world
from the twelfth century onwards. Other examples could be added,
not least the period known as the Axial Age (the middle centuries of
the last millennium BCE), although it does not figure prominently
in Castoriadis's vision of the past. In short, uneven development and
varying direction of creativity are basic features of history. Finally, the
patterns of creativity that unfold in different spheres of social life – the
aesthetic, the intellectual, and the political, to mention obvious cases –
will vary in character and impact.

If we discard the notion of *creatio ex nihilo*, contextual creativity may thus be seen as a common theme of the two thinkers, with
Castoriadis unmistakably defending a more emphatic version. It seems
appropriate to start on the more moderate side and with the most cautious approach. That seems to be Ricoeur's statement to the effect
that we can only produce according to rules (chapter 1, p. 5); he goes
on to argue that when faced with established rules, we can innovate
through what he calls (quoting Malraux) 'coherent deformations'. He
had already mentioned metaphor as an example. But a closer look at
that very case raises doubts about 'production according to rules'. If
metaphors are generated by making one semantic field interfere with
another, we are working with different sets of rules, and using one of
them to disrupt the other; the interference is not rule-governed in the
same sense as each of the fields. There are no rules for the production
of metaphors, only a general and indeterminate possibility inherent in
linguistic practice. Moreover, the whole argument presupposes a certain
conception of language, inspired by the work of Emile Benveniste (he
is now generally regarded as the greatest French linguist of the twentieth century, and Ricoeur was one of those who did most to gain him
due recognition). Benveniste's most important innovation was to move
beyond Saussure's distinction between *langue* and *parole*, thus paving
the way for a linguistics of discourse. The latter notion underlines the
openness and creativity of language, neglected by structuralist schools.

To speak of rules is to speak of institutions, in the broad sense indicated above with reference to Mauss. Castoriadis does not make this point, but it will help to understand his response to Ricoeur. Mauss's reminder of the changing and conflicting interpretations to which institutions are exposed is in line with Ricoeur's conception of the hermeneutical field. The other side of that picture is the capacity of institutions to impose limits and controls on the interpretive potential that accompanies their practices; such restrictions are the joint result of functional logic, power structures, and ideological codes, and it is never easy to disentangle these diverse factors. This dual dynamic affects all kinds of institutions, including the rules of language. It is a commonplace that cultural contexts and traditions are differently conducive to experiments and variations on the level of linguistic conventions.

If the interplay of containing and diversifying sources is a general feature of institutions, it seems plausible to interpret Castoriadis's idea of the imaginary institution as a framework for making sense of this field. The main claim is that institutions presuppose horizons of meaning, and that the interpretive surplus thus made available transcends empirical, rational, and functional conditions in such a way that it can only be understood in terms of an imaginary dimension. Both aspects of the institution draw on this interaction of structural form and excess meaning. The efforts to achieve closure and stability turn the resources of meaning to ideological use, adding an imaginary layer to social crystallisation; conversely, imaginary significations open up a space for variation and can translate into visions of radical innovation, culminating in the capacity for reflective self-transformation that – for Castoriadis – defines an autonomous society.

CONTINUITY AND DISCONTINUITY

The next themes to be considered will take us closer to concrete questions. Pursuing his polemic against the notion of a leap 'from nothing to something', a human analogy to the first day of creation, Ricoeur suggests that historical change is best understood as a reconfiguration of pre-existing configurations; this pattern occurs in varying kinds and degrees, but there is always a transition from one configuration from another, and no conceivable exception to that. Castoriadis, apparently anticipating this turn, refers to different levels and regions of being and their emergence in time. Here, too, we should begin with the more limiting view. The notion of configuration can be compared to more extensively discussed concepts in sociological theory, such as those of *figuration* in Norbert Elias's work or *network* as introduced by Michael Mann (the latter case should not be confused with the mainstream use of the term). They are both designed to grasp the patterns of social life in ways that allow for ongoing change, and thus for an elementary unity of history and society. This in turn presupposes a critique of the traditional emphasis on closure, integration, and stability. Elias and Mann reject systemic images of society and stress the openness, fluidity, and intertwining of the formations to be studied. Their objections to functionalism, systems theory, and – more generally – overintegrated models reflect the same underlying stance as Castoriadis's more rigorous critique of identitarian logic and deterministic assumptions. To clarify affinities and differences, it should be added that Elias and Mann link their conceptual innovations to specific interpretations of social-historical processes. The constellations analysed in their works, whether labelled figurations or networks, are primarily power formations, and they combine various types of social power in different ways. Power and its dynamics figure much less prominently in the writings of Castoriadis and Ricoeur, and Ricoeur's statements, quoted above, refer first of all to configurations of meaning. But bridging steps are possible. There is, in principle, no reason why analyses of the kind developed by Elias and Mann should not be enriched and rebalanced through closer examination of the cultural images and interpretations that enter into the formations and transformations of power.[3]

With that in mind, let us briefly look at the analytical potential of the concepts proposed by Ricoeur, and begin with a rough but important distinction. Human societies can reconfigure external models or influences, as well as their internal arrangements and legacies. The Greek experience, already mentioned by Castoriadis, will serve to highlight possibilities on both sides. The first Greeks in recorded history, the Mycenaeans, reconfigured patterns derived from the sacral monarchies and palace economies of regional neighbours, Near Eastern (more specifically the kingdoms and empires of Asia Minor) and Cretan. Given the nature of the archaeological evidence, all aspects of this transfer are disputed, and that applies even more to the question of original features; they were most likely expressed in relations between sacral and political power. And the reconfiguration of an Indo-European legacy, attributable to the conquerors who established the Mycenaean power centres, is the most shadowy part of the picture. This was, in short, a complex but very imperfectly understood set of reconfigurations. But later history has led to it being perceived, first and foremost, as a prelude to another round: the emergence of the Greek *polis* during the archaic period, dated roughly from the eighth to the sixth century BCE.

This historical breakthrough can also be analysed as an interplay of internal and external reconfigurations. The appropriation of skills and themes from the Near Eastern civilisations was so intensive that historians have referred to an orientalising phase of Greek history; they have also distinguished between three main areas and types of intercivilisational encounters. The closest interaction was with the cultures of Asia Minor; the learning of skills and cultural techniques developed elsewhere was most evident in relation to the Phoenicians; the perception of cultural distance was most pronounced with regard to the Egyptians and gave rise to particularly strong interest in alien ways of life and thought (the 'Egyptology' of the Greeks (Hartog 1986) was apparently the first sustained attempt to make sense of another civilisation). These connections to the Near Eastern environment have been invoked (by those who would like to slay the dragon of 'Eurocentrism' at the earliest possible moment) to deny any originality of the Greek achievement. But the other side of the story is a set of interconnected transformations on the Greek side, and only in that context can the borrowings from Near Eastern sources also be described as reconfigurations. After the collapse of the Mycenaean centres, a protracted process of decomposition and recomposition culminated in the formation of the *polis* as a new political order. Familiarity with city-states in the Eastern Mediterranean was probably of some importance for this development, but no convincing case has been made for the *polis* as an overall form of political life being imported from elsewhere. Its early anti-monarchic turn has no parallel in the Near East; not that the monarchic option did not reappear in the practical version of tyranny as well as in imaginary visions of kingship, but this occurred within a new framework and in conjunction with other alternatives. The formation of the *polis* coincided with a major geopolitical and geocultural reconfiguration, somewhat misleadingly known as colonisation but best seen as an enlargement of the Greek world, creating new spaces for the crystallisation of its defining institutions and practices. A further aspect of the process was an imaginary reconfiguration of the Mycenaean past. Traces and memories were reimagined as a heroic age anchored in mythology. The Homeric epics gave a paradigmatic expression to this view of the past and the world, and their version was only to a limited extent dislodged by later advances in philosophical and historical reflection. Their articulation of the religious imaginary was decisive, although the question of their place in the history of Greek religion has not proved easy to settle. In fact, the issue is mostly avoided, but among the few scholars who raise it, we find starkly opposed (yet equally speculative) viewpoints; the Homeric account of the gods has been interpreted not only as the result of an otherwise undocumented but probable religious revolution, but also as a consolidation of religious traditions thus enabled to resist new ventures of the religious imagination (such as Orphism).

It would, in short, be hard to find a historical case where the analysis in terms of configurations and reconfigurations is more rewarding than in the Greek context, and since this is the very example most frequently and forcefully cited by Castoriadis, it becomes all the more important to clarify why he thinks that this view does not go far enough. At the most basic level, his concern is that it overstates the case for continuity. To portray history as no more than a sequence of configurations is to invite the conclusion that innovations realise pre-existing possibilities, and that notions of creative emergence or radical novelty are therefore misguided. To such perspectives, Castoriadis opposes an ontology that stresses the emergence of new modes of being, notably life, the psyche, and the social-historical. These new frameworks generate their own new possibilities; the argument that they must have been potentially contained in earlier stages is an arbitrary simplification, conflating different meanings of possibility and best dismissed as a retrospective illusion. But there is a further twist to Castoriadis's ontological thesis. The pattern of creative emergence is repeated within the social-historical world – or, more precisely, within the human world, demarcated by the interplay between the psyche and the social-historical. The examples cited in the conversation are aesthetic and intellectual innovations of the kind that open up enduring and comprehensive pathways of variation in their respective domains. In this context, the phenomenological concept of world perspectives seems appropriate.

Stronger support for that line of interpretation can be found in Castoriadis's writings, especially in the seminars on ancient Greece. His analyses of Greek civilisation, beginning with the archaic epoch and foregrounding the Homeric epics, centre on a 'Greek grasp of the world', active across cultural genres and successive phases, from mythology to philosophy. Here we need not discuss the specific features of this framework (they include, most prominently, a strong emphasis on the contrast between human mortality and divine immortality, combined with the image of a partial world order superimposed on chaos). The point most relevant to the debate with Ricoeur is the interpretation of archaic Greece as an emerging civilisational formation, marked by new overall patterns encompassing forms of social life as well as articulations of the world. This perspective goes beyond the field of configurations and reconfigurations, with the aim of defining a resultant unity. That is the characteristic approach of comparative civilisational analysis as it has developed in recent historical sociology, and it does not entail any prior assumptions about the unity always being of the same kind. But there is a distinct and shared idea of the general dimension where the unity is constituted: It is the intertwining of social institutions (also understood as rules, more or less disputed, about the definition, distribution, and regulation of social power) and interpretations of the world. For Castoriadis, the core aspects and trends of the Greek world, seen through this civilisational prism, were those that found expression in the joint development of philosophical reflection and democratic rule. It may be suggested (though not further discussed here) that this view underestimates the complexity of the Greek civilisational pattern. The diversity of the *polis* is not given its due, nor is the role of Greek religion (or religions, as some scholars would have it); another perspective, certainly not without affinities to Castoriadis but much less focused on claims to autonomy, is signalled by Blumenberg's remark on the 'antinomy' that the Greeks invented both cosmos and tragedy (Blumenberg 1987, 8).[4]

These modes of creativity are barely adumbrated in the debate between Castoriadis and Ricoeur, and the latter does not confront their implications. Instead, he shifts the case for continuity to another level: towards a 'certain ... continuity of existence ... the perpetuation of a living together as the ground for instituting operations, and that allows us to situate the discontinuities of sense against the continuities of existence' (chapter 1, p. 4). At first sight, this is a conciliatory move. Ruptures on the level of meaning are conceded, but counterbalanced by an enduring substratum. However, the continuity of existence turns out to be a more complex and ramified matter than the first mention would suggest. Its role in Ricoeur's thought can be traced back to

Christian and existentialist beginnings, where it is invoked to stress a lasting effort and commitment. When it is extended to the social-historical level, as Ricoeur does in the formulation quoted above, it acquires stronger connotations. The 'perpetuation of a living-together' involves activities and formations that blur the distinction between existence and meaning; moreover, they lend themselves to intensi-fying processes that result in higher degrees of continuity. Here we must, in the interest of clear exposition, slightly modify the sequence of the dialogue. Ricoeur's most basic claim is that the continuity involves 'properly human life, a life of the mind' (chapter 1, p. 8); such a life presupposes legacies, and hence cultural memory. So far, the argument might seem to turn on the primacy of culture over insti-tutions, but then Ricoeur takes one step further and observes that we have no knowledge of a non-instituted condition (chapter 1, p. 13). The three, and perhaps four, human universals then mentioned – tools, norms, and language, possibly a relationship to the dead – suggest a very broadly defined concept of institution, applicable to regularities of human behaviour and thus converging with the concept of culture. There is no doubt that the reference to burial customs is intended to justify the inclusion of religion among basic institutions. Castoriadis objects that it comes later, but this is hardly conclusive; the presence of religion may be less directly documented than the use of tools and less easily inferred than the necessity of norms and language, but if the appearance of *Homo sapiens sapiens* is regarded as the final phase of the hominising process, there seem to be reasons to assume a religious background. And it may be recalled that archaeologists (especially Cauvin 2008) have made a strong case for religious factors involved in the neolithic revolution.

Whatever view is taken of religion, the two thinkers appear to agree on a point clearly stated by Ricoeur: We cannot aspire to grasp the dynamics or the details of the mutation from the biological to the human and hence instituted level. There is some room for reconstructive ana-lysis of progress in toolmaking, but when it comes to language, it seems implicit in Castoriadis's and Ricoeur's arguments that they agree with their otherwise common adversary, Claude Lévi-Strauss, on an essential point: The emergence of language can only be envisioned as a com-plete and comprehensive transformation. Recent high-profile support from linguists (Chomsky and Berwick 2016) strengthens this thesis; it remains a provocation for those who prefer a seamlessly evolutionary world view, and a borderline area between grounded inference and speculation, but there is no convincing alternative.

The focus of the conversation now shifts to the specific case of 'our' European history, which both thinkers see as a contingent but particularly intensive and revealing interaction between cultural legacies and memories. Greek and Jewish sources, reinterpreted in varying ways at successive junctures, were crucial to this whole trajectory; the result is, in Ricoeur's words, an exemplary manifestation of historicity as the 'power to establish the new in the recovery of the received legacy' (chapter 1, p. 12). The Jewish beginnings are obviously not as important for Castoriadis as they are for Ricoeur, but he does mention the Old Testament alongside Greek traditions, and it is tempting to go further. The core components of Jewish monotheism, the ideas of a sovereign divine legislator and a covenant between him and his chosen people could serve to justify critical views on the performance of rulers as well as on the practices of the community. It is, admittedly, a matter of debate among historians how far this potential was developed by the prophetic movement before the kingdom of Judah was destroyed, or whether it was primarily a result of reflection in exile and a retrospective judgement on the experience of monarchic statehood. Be that as it may, it does not seem far-fetched to interpret this idea complex as a step towards autonomy; but it was inseparably linked to an affirmation of heteronomy through the new and radical version of monotheism, and that implication prevailed in the priestly regime of the Second Temple. This case exemplifies a more ambiguous mixture of autonomy and heteronomy than Castoriadis's vision of history will allow for, and similar claims can probably be made for Indian and Chinese innovations of the Axial Age. If the Greek record during this period can be described as exceptional, that is not because of any dominant or uncontested project of autonomy; rather, the contrast between autonomy and heteronomy was articulated more sharply than elsewhere. But the attitude that corresponds to Castoriadis's emphatic idea of autonomy – radical questioning of beliefs, conventions, and institutions – can hardly be linked to a broader basis than a branch of the sophistic movement of the fifth century BCE.

The agreement on an eminently but not exclusively European interplay of legacy and memory is abruptly terminated. For Ricoeur, the connection between an inexhaustible past and an innovative present reveals 'the great continuity of being behind the discontinuity of productions' (chapter 1, p. 10). Castoriadis objects that we should not speak of continuity, and that the issue involves modes of being – different modes, to be precise. This suggestive but very vaguely contoured dispute is not taken further; we can, however, try to reconstruct the underlying divergences. On Castoriadis's side, the main reasons for highlighting discontinuity are fairly obvious. His ontology assumes not only a succession of emergent realms, from inanimate nature to the social-historical; within the last and most complex one, the pattern of discontinuity reappears in a new guise. Worlds of meaning, structured around different imaginary significations, can enter into contact with each other and/or draw on the ideas, experiences, and achievements of earlier ones, and there is no absolute obstacle to mutual understanding. But it is always partial, dependent on the context of reception, and for Castoriadis, it is the shared resource of the creative imagination – not any basic rules of reason – that ultimately enables cross-cultural understanding. All this adds up to a strong argument for placing the emphasis on discontinuity.

Ricoeur's case for continuity is more elusive, but some connotations may be suggested, even if they might be rejected by many interpreters of his work. His argument hinges on the inexhaustibility of meaning transmitted from the past. He reads the major philosophical works of various epochs as prime examples of this enduring semantic surplus, but his hermeneutic of revelation, discussed in the introduction to his book, leads to even more emphatic conclusions of that kind; and religion, thus understood, remains a key external source for philosophical reflection. It is tempting to single out a certain idea of revelation as the ultimate background to Ricoeur's views on the continuity of meaning. Would this cast doubt on his refusal to be described as a Christian philosopher? That is not obvious. His multi-genre and multi-contextual conception of revelation seems, in principle, compatible with extension into other religious traditions. Ricoeur criticises those who take a shortcut to general theories or universal histories of religion, and insists on starting with hermeneutically anchored reflections; but this does not exclude comparative enquiry with universalistic aims, and some version of the transcendental unity of religions is a conceivable outcome. This reading of Ricoeur is, admittedly, more conjectural than the recapitulation of Castoriadis's ontological premises; but if it makes sense, we are dealing with the confrontation of philosophy and revelation, familiar from other debates in twentieth-century thought and sometimes equated with the contrast between Athens and Jerusalem.

The disagreement, with its far-reaching implications, occurs at a level where the two thinkers share basic terms of reference: They both hold that the historicity of meanings and societies involves continuity as well as discontinuity, but propose very divergent interpretations of their relationship. To round off the picture, it should be noted that they nevertheless agree on some related fundamental issues in the philosophy of history. They admit ruptures of such a radical kind that it is no longer possible to speak of a reappropriated or reconfigured legacy. However, their example – the destruction of Aztec culture by the Spaniards (led by Cortés, not Columbus, as mistakenly stated in the radio dialogue) – suggests that this may be less easy to illustrate than they think. In a ground-breaking work on the genealogy of Mexican nationalism, Jacques Lafaye (1987; the French original was published in 1972) traced connections between Aztec religiosity and colonial Christianity. And if we were to go for the other major Amerindian civilisation destroyed by Spanish conquerors, the Inca Empire was – on the organisational level – more similar to Old World imperial regimes than the Aztec one, and the Spaniards made use of that legacy.

At the other end of the horizon, Castoriadis and Ricoeur share the vision of a unified history enacted by an autonomous human community. One of them calls this vision an imaginary signification, the other a regulative idea, but in both cases, the Kantian affiliation is obvious. Castoriadis sees the project as a political one, but notes that an ethical aspect must be included (thus hinting at a more significant role for ethics than he envisaged on some other occasions); Ricoeur insists on the primacy of ethics, but certainly with political intentions. They join sides in refusing to rationalise the evils and monstrosities of the past.

IMAGINARY SIGNIFICATIONS AND HISTORICAL PROCESSES

For all their cognitive and interpretive dissonances, the two thinkers thus seem to converge on the same answer to a much-quoted Kantian question: What can I hope for?[5] But there is yet another affinity to be noted, this time a common avoidance of questions related to a logical continuation of the dispute. The interest in meaning, reactivation, and creation does not translate into any discussion of historical processes. Since the transformations of meaning and their historical ramifications, however understood, must be envisaged as events unfolding in time, it seems clear that further analyses would have to deal with processual patterns and dynamics. The closest the debate gets to this is Ricoeur's reminder that the Greek *polis* and its culture took shape through 'small developments (*émergences*) that are cumulative' (chapter 1, p. 6), but no clarification follows. If we conclude with some comments on this theme, they should also be read as an attempt to draw on Castoriadis's and Ricoeur's insights in an enlarged context. As will be seen, their conceptions of meaning acquire new content when applied at the level of historical processes, and conversely, processual analysis can benefit from the rethinking of meaning that has been pursued by both thinkers.

It should of course be taken into account that the problematic of historical processes is a highly undertheorised and underdebated field. Classical sociology had dealt extensively with particular processes (capitalist development, bureaucratisation, rationalisation, differentiation), but taken much less interest in the general problem of conceptualising processes, and the subsequently dominant paradigms of social theory tended to obscure the issue. Theories of action focused on means, ends, norms, and values, with more or less extensive allowance for unintentional consequences, but were much less receptive to the idea of processes developing their own logic and imposing it on actors. Systems theories, especially in the Parsonian version, subordinated processes to pattern maintenance and emphasised the programming function of culture (it is a relevant question to what extent this bias was corrected by Luhmann's theory of systems, not least due to a less reductionistic notion of meaning, but this cannot be discussed here). As for the approaches of historians, the most marked reactions against the traditional focus on actors and events were concerned with structural dimensions. This was most pronounced in the Annales school, whose main representatives identified the *longue durée* with enduring structures. Ricoeur tried to integrate that view into his account of time and narrative through a discussion of Braudel's work (Ricoeur 1990: 208–17, 224–5); the book contains no similar discussion of long-term processes.

The author most often cited as a pioneer of reflected processual analysis is Norbert Elias. But it is also a commonplace that his analyses of state formation (and the accompanying 'civilising process') are one-sidedly focused on the transformations of power structures and tend to disregard cultural factors. It may nevertheless be possible to draw on his conception of social processes for the purposes indicated above.

Christian Meier's reflections on historical processes, published in 1978 and taking off from Elias, are still useful, all the more so because Meier's expertise in ancient history brought him into contact with issues that were also crucial for Castoriadis. Meier distinguishes three aspects of Elias's argument about processes. They have a direction, but this should be understood in neither a teleological nor a deterministic sense; this unified meaning of the whole (*Sinnganzes*) emerges from an indeterminate multiplicity of inputs by actors, and the dynamic of the process marginalises their autonomy, but not invariably to the same degree; the complexity and derivative autonomy of the process can increase through interconnections with other processes, and contingent historical events can have significant effects of this kind (Meier 1978).

Let us briefly reflect on the trajectory of the Greek *polis*. From the eighth century BCE onwards, different regimes developed in various city-states, and some of them underwent major changes; political thought played an active role in these transformations. That was, for example, clearly the case with Solon's reforms in Athens. The origins of this political thought, much older than the explicit theorising of alternative regimes, can be traced back to the early archaic period, not least to the Homeric epics (see especially Beck 2013). It is at least a plausible hypothesis that the notion of power as placed in the middle (*meson*), for the *polis* to institute in more specific ways, was at the core of this political imaginary, to use Castoriadis's term. The idea in question was sufficiently innovative, indeterminate, and open to interpretations for the concept of imaginary signification to be obviously applicable. On the other hand, the outcomes of the multiple transformative processes were also determined not only by power struggles within and between city-states but also by broader changing geopolitical constellations, from the Greek colonisation of the Mediterranean and Black Sea areas to the conflict with the new superpower of the Near East, the Persian Empire.

This seems to be a paradigm case of the interaction between imaginary significations and historical processes: A core signification opens up alternative perspectives of change, and at the same time, unfolding processes impose or facilitate specific choices and initiatives. Can we identify a radically different pattern? If we consider a case of imaginary significations containing history, it is tempting to look at debates among historians of late imperial China (with controversial but not altogether implausible extensions into the Communist sequel). The notion of a 'stretched empire' has been proposed in this context (the key source is Chevrier 1996); it refers to the capacity of the imperial order to survive through minimal adaptation to social change, and thus to block the more radical potentialities. This successful containment was surely in part due to the extraordinary resilience of dominant imaginary significations, centred on notions of socio-cosmic order, tradition as a repository of wisdom, and sacral monarchy as a guarantee of harmony.

There are other examples that would merit closer examination. For one thing, the role of imaginary significations in modern revolutions, and in the tradition that has grown up around them, is a complex one. Their transformative impact is beyond doubt, but the mythologising role of the revolutionary imagination is also well known, and this factor has certainly something to do with the obscuring of perspectives and the blocking of possibilities. That is a problematic to be taken up elsewhere. At this point, we should consider a final point of contact and debate between Castoriadis and Ricoeur. One of the most salient and widely noted themes in Ricoeur's philosophy of the imagination is his insistence on a double-edged role: The imagination enables us to gain distance from the world, but it also intervenes in our constitution and transformation of it (the text most frequently quoted is his 'Imagination in Discourse and in Action', Ricoeur 1991). Saulius Geniusas (2015, 2016) credits Ricoeur with being the only author to theorise this as a paradox of the imagination.[6] From Castoriadis's writings, and especially from the text 'The Imaginary as Such' (Castoriadis 2015), it seems clear that he recognised this double-edged character, but he did not call it a paradox; he might have argued that we are dealing with an elementary duality, where each side is constitutive of the other, and that a paradox only arises if the imagination is one-sidedly defined from one or the other point of view. As suggested above, further dualities emerge when we consider imaginary significations in historical contexts; the imagination appears as a source of new meanings and of openness to determination by power structures and processes, a transforming as well as a containing factor. At first sight, we seem to be confronted with two different conceptions of the imagination, one focusing on a central paradox and the other on multiple dualities, and both calling for further development. Ricoeur's work on ideology and utopia shows that he was not averse to closer consideration of social phenomena, but he did not engage with the social-historical realm to the same degree as

Castoriadis did (Ricoeur 1986; but the reference to Husserlian imaginary variation as a source of utopian thought is also a reductionistic
move, confining imagination below the threshold of creation). Further
comparison would, in any case, have to draw on more extensive textual
sources (including, among other things, Ricoeur's still unpublished lectures on the imagination); here we must end on a tentative note.

NOTES

1. Hereafter the references to the radio dialogue proper appear as single page
numbers.
2. This is the most detailed and insightful analysis of Mauss's views on the
symbolic, but see also Karsenti (2011).
3. For an attempt to draw on Castoriadis to revise Elias's theory of state
formation, see Smith (2006).
4. The German word *erfanden* is in my opinion unequivocal: It means
invented, and this is also in line with Blumenberg's whole argument. The translator first uses 'discovered', and then adds 'invented' in brackets.
5. In his discussion of ancient Greek culture, Castoriadis refers to a distinctive and starkly disillusioned view on this issue: 'But to the third question,
"What am I allowed to hope?" there is a definite and clear Greek answer, and
this is a massive and resounding *nothing*' (Castoriadis 1997, 273; emphasis
in original). But despite his unmistakable admiration for this Greek stance, it
cannot be said that he identified with it. If he persisted in defining himself as a
revolutionary (which, needless to say, no ancient Greek ever did), that implies
a certain degree of hope for a better future. And although he and Ricoeur did
not converge on a revolutionary position, they seem to share – in very general
terms – a vision of more autonomous humanity.
6. Geniusas also argues that Ricoeur's attempt to elucidate this paradox
leads to a fragmenting of the imagination into productive and reproductive
capacities, and that a phenomenological correction to Ricoeur's hermeneutical
and overly language-centred approach is needed to solve this problem.

REFERENCES

Adams, Suzi. 2011. *Castoriadis' Ontology: Being and Creation*. New York:
Fordham University Press.
Arnason, Johann P. 1993. 'Reason, Imagination, Interpretation'. In *Rethinking
Imagination: Culture and Creativity*. Edited by Gillian Robinson and John F.
Rundell, 155–70. London: Routledge.

Beck, Hans. 2013. *A Companion to Ancient Greek Government*. Edited by Hans Beck. Malden, MA: Wiley-Blackwell.

Blumenberg, Hans. 1987. *Genesis of the Copernican World*. Cambridge, MA: Massachusetts Institute of Technology Press.

Castoriadis, Cornelius. 1987 [1975]. *The Imaginary Institution of Society*. Translated by Kathleen Blamey. Cambridge, MA: Massachusetts Institute of Technology Press.

———. 1997. 'Done and to Be Done'. In *World in Fragments: Writings on Politics, Society, Psychoanalysis, and the Imagination*. Translated and edited by David Ames Curtis. Oxford and Malden: Blackwell.

———. 2004–2011. *Ce qui fait la Grêce* (Volumes 1–3). Paris: Seuil.

———. 2015. 'The Imaginary as Such'. *Social Imaginaries* 1:1: 59–69.

Cauvin, Jacques. 2008. *The Birth of the Gods and the Origins of Agriculture*. Cambridge, UK: Cambridge University Press.

Célis, Raphaël. 1977. *L'oeuvre et l'imaginaire. Les origins du pouvoir-être créateur*. Bruxelles: Facultés Universitaires Saint-Louis.

Chevrier, Yves. 1996. 'L'empire distendu: esquisse du politique en Chine des Qing à Deng Xiaoping'. In *Les trajectoires du politique, Volume 3: La greffe de l'État*. Edited by Jean-François Bayart, 262–395. Paris: Carthala.

Chomsky, Noam, and Robert C. Berwick. 2016. *Why Only Us? Language and Evolution*. Cambridge, MA: Massachusetts Institute of Technology Press.

Derrida, Jacques. 1978 [1967]. 'Structure, Sign and Play in the Discourse of the Human Sciences'. In *Writing and Difference*. Translated by Alan Bass, 278–95. Chicago, IL: University of Chicago Press.

Geniusas, Saulius. 2015. 'Between Phenomenology and Hermeneutics: Paul Ricoeur's Philosophy of Imagination'. *Human Studies* 38: 223–41.

———. 2016. 'Against the Sartrean Background: Ricoeur's Lectures on Phenomenology'. *Research on Phenomenology* 46:1: 98–116.

Hartog, François. 1986. 'Les Grecs égyptologues'. *Annales. Histoire, Sciences Sociales* 41:5: 953–67.

Heidegger, Martin. 1997. *Kant and the Problem of Metaphysics*. Translated by Richard Taft. Bloomington and Indianapolis: Indiana University Press.

Karsenti, Bruno. 2011. *L'homme total. Sociologie, anthropologie et philosophie chez Marcel Mauss*. Paris: Klimis.

Lafaye, Jacques. 1987. *Quetzalcoatl and Guadalupe: The Formation of Mexican National Consciousness, 1531–1813*. Chicago, IL: University of Chicago Press.

Mauss, Marcel. 1968. *Essais de sociologie*. Paris: Seuil.

Meier, Christian. 1978. 'Fragen und Thesen zu einer Theorie historischer Prozesse'. In *Historische Prozesse*. Edited by Karl-Georg von Faber and Christian Meier, 11–66. München: Deutscher Taschenbuch Verlag.

Michel, Johann. 2014. *Ricoeur and the Post-Structuralists. Bourdieu, Derrida, Deleuze, Foucault, Castoriadis.* London: Rowman & Littlefield International.

———. 1986. *Lectures on Ideology and Utopia.* Edited by George Taylor. Chicago, IL: University of Chicago Press.

———. 1990. *Time and Narrative* (Volume 3). Translated by Kathleen McLaughlin and David Pellauer. Chicago, IL: University of Chicago Press.

———. 1991. 'Imagination in Discourse and in Action'. In *From Text to Action.* Translated by Kathleen Blamey and John B. Thompson, 164–84. New York: Continuum.

Smith, Jeremy. 2006. *Europe and the Americas: State Formation, Capitalism and Civilization in Atlantic Modernity.* Leiden and Boston: Brill.

Tarot, Camille. 2003. *De Durkheim à Mauss, l'invention du symbolique: Sociologie et science des religions.* Paris: La Découverte.

Touraine, Alain. 1977. *The Self-Production of Society.* Chicago, IL: University of Chicago Press.

Chapter Four

Ricoeur and Castoriadis

The Productive Imagination between Mediation and Origin

Jean-Luc Amalric

The interest in publishing the 1985 dialogue between Ricoeur and Castoriadis on history and the social imaginary lies in the fact that this discussion lays the foundations of an unprecedented confrontation between two great contemporary philosophies of the imagination. It thus compensates for the paradoxical absence of written discussion between two thinkers who should have been drawn together by their common field of research.[1]

The two philosophers deal with a wide range of topics: Their dialogue emphasises both the meaning and the status of the concepts of 'institution', 'production', and 'creation' from a social and historical point of view – both thinkers draw their examples from political history, the history of sciences, and the history of arts – and on the alterity of cultures and the possibility of translation. Beyond this diversity of topics, a general reflection on the continuity and discontinuity at stake in the social-historical field, and on the emergence of novelty in the history of human cultures lies in the background. As shown by the wide range of topics we have just evoked, it is both possible and legitimate to · deal with the stakes of this confrontation from different angles.

In this essay, we will focus on the analysis of the conception of *productive imagination* of both philosophers. We will first try to situate the precise general philosophical context of the dialogue, insisting on what we consider as the undeniable convergence of the thought of Castoriadis and Ricoeur: that is, a new reflection on productive imagination related to a common analysis of human action and of the imaginary constitution of social relationships. We will then focus on the terminological discussion running through the entire dialogue so as to assess its scope and meaning. From our point of view, these discussions on the notions of 'institution', 'creation', and 'production' must be relativised because they do not prevent the two philosophers from converging on a common critique of structuralism. In the third part, we will try to assess the gap existing between Castoriadis's ontology of creation and the philosophy of imagination developed by Ricoeur in the renewed frame of a reflexive philosophy of the act.[2] Beyond a mere disagreement over words, whose scope must be balanced, our thesis will consist in showing that these two intellectual projects are laid on different philosophical presuppositions concerning not only the *method* – that is, the ways of access to a philosophical reflection on productive imagination – but also the very *status* of this productive or creative imagination.

THE PHILOSOPHICAL CONTEXT OF THE DIALOGUE: A COMMON DEFENCE OF THE PRACTICAL POWER OF PRODUCTIVE IMAGINATION

Even if, as we will see throughout our commentary, the dialogue between Ricoeur and Castoriadis reveals some clear oppositions as to the status and scope given to productive imagination, it is clear that the two philosophers share a common aim when they deal with the notions of *history* and the *social imaginary*. It is clear to us that the deep meaning of this confrontation would be missed if we did not first point out the undeniable convergence of these two thinkers as illustrated by their shared attempt to think anew the *power of productive imagination* in opposition to the dominant philosophical tradition.

From this perspective, it is essential to stress the fact that, before diverging on their conceptions of imagination and the imaginary, Ricoeur and Castoriadis have both continuously fought for *the general rehabilitation of imagination in its practical dimension, whether individual or social*. In this respect, it does not seem helpful to specify the philosophical context of this shared struggle to promote the rediscovery and the rehabilitation of the productive or creative power of imagination.

The general philosophical context in which Ricoeur and Castoriadis develop their philosophies in the twentieth century consisted in hostility and persisting defiance towards the notion of imagination. In a radical way, which reminds us of the Heideggerian critique of metaphysics as the 'forgetting of Being', Castoriadis's thought developed as a systematic critique of 'inherited thought'.[3] Even if Castoriadis will draw the inspiration for his critique from the new and fundamental elements brought by *anthropology* and *psychoanalysis* and not from a reflection on 'fundamental ontology', he nonetheless sets his thought in a radical opposition to the dominant philosophical tradition, which he considers as responsible for the occultation and the fundamental and persistent oblivion of the imagination and the imaginary.

For him, indeed, 'inherited thought' has always consisted in occulting the properly originary and creative dimension of imagination, failing to think it for itself and systematically reducing it to a second faculty or function. In other words, from Spinoza to Marx, and with a few remarkable exceptions – notably Kant and Fichte – imagination has been criticised and depreciated as a deluding and illusory power, the negative source of human passions radically opposed to reason. As Castoriadis points out in his article 'The Discovery of Imagination' (1997 [1986], 213–45), it is because the history of philosophy has been mainly deployed as an elaboration of Reason homologous to the position of 'being as determinacy', that it has reduced what does not belong to Reason – and first and foremost imagination – to the 'infra-thinkable' or to the 'supra-thinkable'. Thus, it is against the occultation of imagination as a *continued creative source of new determinations* that Castoriadis's philosophy is fighting, both from the point of view of the social-historical dimension of the *instituting imaginary* and from the psychic point of view of the *radical imagination* of the subject.

As for Ricoeur, even if he also wishes to rehabilitate the productive imagination and to fight against a discrediting of the imagination that dates back at least to Plato (and that can be found also in the French moralists, such as Pascal and Malebranche), he appears more cautious concerning the idea of a 'forgetting' or of a general occultation of the imagination extended to the whole of philosophy. This is the reason why, in his key article of 1976, entitled 'Imagination in Discourse and in Action. Toward a General Theory of Imagination' (1991 [1976], 168–87), he prefers to question more specifically the complex reasons for the *discrediting of imagination in contemporary philosophy*. For him, the abusive use of the term 'image' in the empiricist theory of knowledge is, without doubt, the very origin of this depreciation. Whether it is Husserlian phenomenology, Fregean logic, or contemporary semantics – that of the logicians as well as that of the linguists – the fight against 'psychologism' has essentially appeared as a fight against the notion of the *image* in its gnoseological pretentions. Thereafter, any investigation concerning the phenomenon of image and imagination seems bound to fail, as it will inevitably be suspected of 'psychologism'. For Ricoeur, 'the relative eclipse' of the problem of imagination in contemporary philosophy can also be explained by the structural difficulties faced by any philosophical attempt to think the phenomenon of imagination in its unity in a coherent way. What seems actually understandable in the phenomenon of imagination – and which leads philosophers such as Gilbert Ryle (1939) to doubt the fact that imagination refers to a homogenous phenomenon – is that it refers to experiences that have little in common with each other and that can be moreover radically opposed. Indeed, what is there in common between the imagination thought as the nothingness of perception and imagination thought as quasi-perception, between the imaginative experience of the fascinated consciousness that can, at any time, turn into an illusory and delusory consciousness and the imaginative experience of the critical consciousness capable of taking a distance with reality using some form of power of absence? For Ricoeur, such is the challenge faced by any attempt to theorise and rehabilitate the phenomenon of the imagination.

From this perspective, Ricoeur's philosophy – unlike Castoriadis's thought – is not conceptualised to appear as a radical break with the whole philosophical tradition; on the contrary, it repeatedly evokes 'unemployed potentials' of this tradition and the possibility to renew the philosophy of imagination in the light of a *reflexive philosophy of the act* and towards a *renewed ontology of act and power*. Like Castoriadis, Ricoeur continues his dialogue with the human and social sciences – whether that is Freudian psychoanalysis, the cultural anthropology of Clifford Geertz, or the epistemology of history – but he is deeply convinced – as shown in the reflexive anthropology of *Fallible Man* (1986b), in *The Rule of Metaphor* (2003), and in *Time and Narrative* (1984–1988) – that it is possible to renew the thinking of imagination, starting from a creative reinterpretation of the unemployed potentials of *the Kantian theory of schematism and productive imagination.*[4]

Arguably, the common point between Ricoeur and Castoriadis within their shared diagnosis concerning the *occultation–discreditation of imagination* in the philosophical tradition, and the necessity to think imagination anew, is that they are both convinced that a renewal of the theory of imagination must necessarily proceed as a *central function of imagination in human action* and its foregrounding. For the two thinkers, it is the confinement of the theory of imagination within a theory of knowledge and reason that has led to this critical depreciation of the imagination in relation to these two powers of truth: sensation and concept. In that sense, the two philosophers lead us, each in his own way, towards a regathering of the practical and productive power of imagination.

From *Freedom and Nature* (1950) to the *Lectures on Ideology and Utopia* (1986c) via *From Text to Action* (1986), Ricoeur sought a renewal of the theory of imagination through an innovative approach to the practical function of productive imagination. As will be confirmed in 'Imagination in Discourse and in Action' (1991), there is an essential link between *praxis* and the *social imaginary*, which requires a *general theory of imagination* to take as its starting point the *constitutive and originary dimension of the social and cultural imaginary*. To be more specific, it is only within a reflection on the *originary dialectic between ideology and utopia* and within a critical labour on the pathological forms of the social imaginary – that the contradictions which a simple phenomenology of individual imagination and action must leave as an aporia – are likely to be practically mediated. As for Castoriadis, his theory of the *social imaginary significations* and history obviously also starts from an attempt to rethink praxis in its irreducible creativity without reducing it to a – foreseeable and necessary – historical development. As he writes in *The Imaginary Institution of Society* (Castoriadis 1987 [1975], 146): 'History is impossible and inconceivable outside of the *productive* or *creative imagination*, outside of what we have called the *radical imaginary* as this is manifested indissolubly in both historical *doing* and in the constitution, before any explicit rationality, of a universe of *significations.*'

Now that we have sketched the outlines of the general philosophical context of this confrontation between Ricoeur and Castoriadis, it seems useful, in ending this introductory part, to define the more particular context of this 1985 dialogue. Indeed, it is important to keep in mind the works published by these two philosophers at that date, because they are essential to determine not only the meaning but also the limits of their discussion on the question of the imagination.

First to Castoriadis. In 1975 – that is, ten years earlier – he published his masterpiece, entitled *The Imaginary Institution of Society* (1987 [1975]). As indicated in its title, this work can be wholly read as a progressive disclosure of the power of institution and creation of the social imaginary. Considering the fact that the 1985 dialogue between Ricoeur and Castoriadis opens precisely on this topic, we can consider that the major stakes of the Castoriadian thesis on 'instituting imaginary' led the tone and the orientation of the dialogue. Even if Ricoeur is led to develop some of his ideas on imagination in order to specify some of his oppositions to Castoriadis, his theory of imagination is not central in this discussion.

How can we explain this kind of asymmetry concerning the explicit or implicit references made by the two philosophers to their respective thesis on productive imagination? In my view, the explanation for this asymmetry is quite simple, but it has a decisive impact on the arguments and developments of the dialogue. In 1985, we doubt that Castoriadis could have considered the work already published by Ricoeur as actually focused on the phenomenon of imagination. The question of imagination is obviously repeatedly evoked in all of Ricoeur's published works, but, after all, none of his books are explicitly or directly devoted to an elucidation of the productive imagination. It is only in 1995 – that is, ten years later – that, in his 'Intellectual Autobiography' (1995), Ricoeur will explicitly acknowledge having devoted a large part of his work – from *The Symbolism of Evil* to *Time and Narrative* passing through *The Rule of Metaphor* – to the elaboration of a philosophy of imagination.

Today, it is a fact that a great number of Ricoeur scholars – from Richard Kearney (2004) to George Taylor (2006), from Olivier Abel (1996) to Alain Thomasset (1996) and Michael Foessel (Foessel and

Lamouche 2007) – now agree to consider that an essential part of the Ricoeurian work has been devoted to the patient and progressive elaboration of a general theory of imagination. In this perspective, our latest book – *Paul Ricoeur, L'imagination vive* (Amalric 2013) – is entirely devoted to a detailed genesis of the Ricoeurian philosophy of imagination, insisting on the fact that it already originates in the *Philosophy of the Will*. However, in 1985, it is unlikely that Castoriadis considered Ricoeur's work as essentially devoted to the question of the imagination, and, as a consequence, it is as unlikely that he considered it as a *competing theory concerning the productive imagination*.

As Johann Michel usefully reminds us in his preface (in this volume), in 1985, Ricoeur had already published the first two volumes of *Time and Narrative* and was about to publish the third and last volume of this trilogy, *Narrated Time*. What is essential to us is the fact that, in 1975, Ricoeur had also given two absolutely fundamental lectures on imagination at the University of Chicago. The first series of lectures on social imaginary, today known as *Ideology and Utopia*, was edited by George Taylor and published in English in 1986, but was only translated and published in French in 1997. The second series of lectures is not yet published, but it dealt with philosophical aspects of the imagination, especially in its psychic, phenomenological, and individual dimension.[5] In such a context, nothing indicates that Castoriadis, in 1985 – that is, at the time of the dialogue – knew anything about the content of these lectures; and this could explain why most of the questions he asked Ricoeur appeared less as a confrontation of a particular thesis – on social imaginary, ideology, or utopia – than as demands for precisions so as to better identify possible points of agreement on the question of imagination.[6]

In the following discussion, which we will develop in the following two parts, we will therefore try to keep in mind this asymmetry in the reception each philosopher has of the other's work and thought. In a word, as it is obvious that Ricoeur has closely read *The Imaginary Institution of Society*[7] and that his interventions aim essentially at clarifying some questions or removing perplexities concerning the central thesis of the work, it is on the contrary very likely that Castoriadis has had only partial access to the essential thesis of Ricoeur on social imaginary and on the dialectic between ideology and utopia. This is the reason why he never bluntly deals with the decisive concepts on which Ricoeur's theory of imagination lies.

CREATION, PRODUCTION, AND INSTITUTION: A CONVERGING CRITIQUE OF STRUCTURALISM BEYOND THE TERMINOLOGICAL DISPUTE

The starting point for our commentary on the dialogue between Ricoeur and Castoriadis will be the discussion of the terms 'creation', 'institution', and 'production', which seem to create opposition between the two philosophers throughout their exchange on the status of imaginary and history. In this second part, our aim will be to show that this terminological dispute can be relativised and that it does not stand as an obstacle to a *common converging critique of structuralism* by the two thinkers.

From the beginning of the dialogue, a fundamental dispute seems to appear between Ricoeur and Castoriadis with, what would be, on one side, a Castoriadian defence of the notion of 'creation' conceived as an 'institution' and a radical surge of the new, and, on the other side, a Ricoeurian defence of imagination as *production of meaning* in the sense of the Fichtean *Produzieren*. While Castoriadis insists on the *creation of new forms* – in art, politics, and the sciences – as that which absolutely cannot be reduced to the existing order and determinations, Ricoeur conceives the imagination as a *production of new configurations* – whether narrative, metaphorical, political, or institutional – which can never be assimilated to the surge of absolute novelty because such configurations always lie on a 'prefiguration', a 'pre-structuration', or a 'pre-institution' which regulates and energises any imaginative production.

For Ricoeur, this reluctance to use the term 'creation' when applied to the works of the imagination can probably be explained by the fact that, in his philosophical writings, the term 'creation' has been mostly used for the idea of a 'foundational sacred' or, more broadly, for the idea of the 'primordial' or the 'fundamental' as that which exceeds, overwhelms, or precedes any strictly reflexive or speculative approach of the question of anthropos and human freedom. In the 'General Introduction' to *Freedom and Nature* (1966 [1950]), he evokes indeed the idea of creation as a 'gift of being' and as a 'source of the will' and immediately specifies that the approach of such a notion exceeds the resources of phenomenological description and of reflexive philosophy. For him, the notion of creation could only be developed in a 'Poetics of the Will', which, as a 'pneumatology of the will', would reinsert the 'practical cogito' in being while trying to articulate a poetic inspiration of the will. Beyond the irreducible dualism of freedom and nature which stands as a boundary to a phenomenology of the will, Ricoeur's project of a 'Poetics of the Will' aimed at the *poetic unity of freedom and nature* as a 'unity of creation'.

Even though Ricoeur did not write this third volume of the *Philosophy of the Will*, which was to complete the phenomenological approach of *Freedom and Nature* (1966 [1950]) and the hermeneutical approach of *The Symbolism of Evil* (1969) – which was then conceived as a 'mythics of the will' – he never gave up the idea that a discourse on the 'originary unity of man' or on creation as originary inspiring source of the human will can only be mythical or metaphorical. The conclusion of a phenomenology of the will is that 'willing is not creating' because a regeneration of the will as recreation of our freedom, beyond the slavery of passions, would only have been thinkable within the frame of a poetics of the will.

Even if Ricoeur's philosophy has progressively abandoned the initial project of a 'religious philosophy' of originary creation and has later developed a strictly anthropological perspective – opting for the *agnostic suspension* of a 'philosophy without absolute' – it has always remained faithful to the idea – coming from the Kantian critique of metaphysics – according to which a discourse on originary creation, in its cosmological and/or theological dimensions, is out of reach of any philosophical reflection with speculative pretentions.

He shows the same conviction in 1998, in *What Makes Us Think?* when he evokes the possibility of thinking a unity between the discourse on the *lived body* in its phenomenological and subjective dimension and the discourse on the *body-object* known by sciences. As he writes:

> From this ontological identity arises a third discourse that goes beyond both phenomenological philosophy and science. To my mind this would be either the poetic account of creation in the biblical sense or the speculative discourse that was raised to its height by Spinoza, overcoming the division between the attributes of thought and extension in order to assert the unity of substance. (Changeux and Ricoeur 2002, 28)

But he later adds: 'I do not hesitate to say that as a philosopher I profess considerable skepticism with regard to the possibility of constituting an

overarching discourse of this sort, above and beyond the profound unity
of what appears to me sometimes as a neuronal system, sometimes as
mental experience' (Changeux and Ricoeur 2002, 29).

As we have just seen, Ricoeur has always refrained from developing a speculative discourse of a cosmological type, thus showing a
very Kantian cautiousness as to the possibility of a discourse on the
One and the originary. On the other hand, Castoriadis had a different approach, as, in the last phase of his intellectual work, he clearly
developed a *cosmological reflection*[8] inspired by Greek myths and
the ontology of chaos expressed in them. For him indeed, Greek
myths[9] – notably through the works of Homer, Hesiod, and the great
Greek tragedians – reveal a significance of the world that cannot be
reduced to any form of rationality: They convey a 'magma of significations' which keeps referring to an origin of sense which is 'devoid
of meaning' and thus invites us to think an ontology of creation as
'ontology of chaos' – that is, more precisely, as an ontology of the
interplay of chaos and cosmos.[10] In the same way as on the political
plane, Castoriadis turns to the experience of ancient Greek democracy
to read in it the radical surge of the project of autonomy, so, too, on
the cosmological plane, he turns to Greece – that is, to the mythic and
symbolic emergence of Greece – to try to read in it the surge of an
ontology of chaos and creation which stands as the core of his philosophy of radical imagination.

In my view, we should not discuss this terminological dispute on
the concepts of creation-institution and production too hastily. In fact,
in one of his first texts in which he actually deals with the question on
cultural imaginary in its 'nuclear' and originary dimension, Ricoeur
goes so far as to use the term 'creative nucleus' of cultures to qualify
this 'ethico-mythical nucleus' of a culture, from which it interprets and
originary evaluates life (Ricoeur 1965a, 280). In his article from 1961,
entitled 'Universal Civilisation and National Cultures' (Ricoeur 1965b,
271–84), Ricoeur points out that the values which determine a vision
of the world proper to a specific culture correspond to a 'creative phenomenon', which first expresses itself in a superficial way at the level
of 'practical habits' and then in a deeper way in 'traditional institutions'.
But he later adds: 'The institutions are always abstract signs which need
to be deciphered. It seems to me that if one wishes to attain the cultural
nucleus, one has to cut through to that layer of images and symbols
which make up the basic ideals of a nation' (Ricoeur 1965a, 280).

Ricoeur's connection of habits and institutions to an *originary and creative cultural nucleus* presents a strong analogy with the interplay of the *instituted imaginary* to the *instituting imaginary*, which constitutes the central philosophical gesture of Castoriadis's approach to the social imaginary. The idea of an 'ethico-mythical nucleus' of human cultures is indeed very close to the 'social imaginary significations' in the Castoriadian sense. Beyond this strong convergence, we can consider that, in this key article, Ricoeur sketches a regression to a concept of the originary which obviously announces the 'genetic phenomenology' that he will develop later in *Ideology and Utopia* (1986c).

In fact, in the *Lectures on Ideology and Utopia*, Ricoeur's reflexive endeavour consists in starting from the most superficial significations of ideology and utopia (i.e. their 'pathological' significations) – ideology as *distortion of reality* and utopia as *escape from reality* – to finally reach their most originary and constitutive significations – ideology in its *integrative function*, constitutive of the identity of a group, and utopia as *imagination of a nowhere*, which keeps the field of the possible open – passing through their central significations of, on the one hand, the *legitimation of power* and authority, and, on the other hand, of the radical *critique of power*. When, in the conclusion of the book, Ricoeur uses the term 'constitutive imagination' (1986c, 311) to qualify the more radical meaning of these 'imaginative practices' that are ideology and utopia, it clearly appears that he gives to the social imaginary a status close to that of the Castoriadian 'instituting imaginary'.

Indeed, Ricoeur, like Merleau-Ponty, had earlier criticised Husserlian idealism in his book *A l'école de la phénoménologie* (1986a) and had always denounced the reduction of the problem of the constitution of meaning to that of the auto-constitution of the transcendental absolute ego. Thus, when Ricoeur speaks of 'constitutive' or 'constituting' imaginary, it is never in an egological sense. On the contrary, it is to emphasise the originary character of the social imaginary being thus very close to the Merleau-Pontian and Castoriadian signification of the concept of 'institution'. As early as the *Phenomenology of Perception* (2003a), the central philosophical intention of Merleau-Ponty consisted indeed in criticising the idea of a constituting transcendental subjectivity resulting from the Husserlian *époché*. Unlike the Husserlian reduction, the phenomenological reduction, as conceived by Merleau-Ponty, attempts to return to the unreflected ground of reflection. In Merleau-Ponty, the term 'institution' appears precisely when the philosopher develops the consequences of his criticism of the philosophy of consciousness and of reflection. Unlike the idea of 'constitution', the idea of 'institution' – as developed in Merleau-Ponty's seminars on institution (2003b) – corresponds to a philosophical attempt to think the emergence of a sense susceptible to reconciliation with the passivity of the subject that is also to be shared by other subjects.

Considering what has just been analysed, it therefore seems important to relativise the terminological conflict between the two philosophers because we can see that Castoriadis also sometimes uses the term 'constituting' (1997, 173),[11] as he also uses the term 'productive' (1987, 146)[12] imagination without limiting himself to the use of the term 'creative imagination'.

In that respect, it seems to us that the discussion of the term 'production' must also be interpreted with caution. When, at the beginning of the dialogue, Castoriadis insists on the fact that, for him, the concept of production is too closely linked to Marx (see chapter 1, p. 3),[13] he obviously refers to the whole reflexive work he develops in his critique of Marx, especially in the first chapter of *The Imaginary Institution of Society*, entitled 'Marxism: A Provisional Assessment'. In this critique of Marx, which appears as a *radical critique of the causalistic and deterministic theories of society and of history*, Castoriadis never questions the Marxian idea that human existence cannot be thought independently of the material conditions of the production of social life. However, what he denounces is the reduction of social relationships and historical becoming to the mere development of productive forces.

Here again, this critique of Marx, far from opposing Castoriadis to Ricoeur, in actual fact, brings them together, since, as early as 1953, in an important article entitled 'Work and the Word' (Ricoeur 1965c, 197–219), Ricoeur also develops a critique of the Marxian concept of production with similar arguments to the Castoriadian critique.[14] In this article, Ricoeur outlines a 'mutual overlapping of signifying and acting', a primitive and always renewed dialectic between word and praxis which prevents any reduction of praxis to production and jointly asserts the overwhelming productivity of the word and of the creative power of symbolic imagination in relation to the simple material production.[15] In 1973, in his conference entitled 'Le lieu de la dialectique',[16] Ricoeur will reassert his critique of the Marxian concept of production in terms similar to Castoriadis's.[17] Ricoeur tells us (1975, 104):

> The restriction I reproach Marxism with proceeds from a reduction of the concept of praxis to that of production and even to a reduction of the concept of labour to that of work, as Hannah Arendt has convincingly shown in her book *The Human Condition*.... It is not paradoxical to say that this reduction of praxis to productive work is responsible for the permanent temptation among marxists to fall back on what they themselves call an 'economicist deviation'.[18]

In the five lectures in *Ideology and Utopia* devoted to a detailed commentary of Marx, Ricoeur argues that, in Marx's thought, this reduction of praxis to production has never had the status of an initial presupposition, but has progressively imposed itself through a certain evolution of the Marxian use of the concept of 'production' (Ricoeur 1986c, 21–102). As Ricoeur clearly explains, it is in fact the progressive reduction of the semantic scope of the German concept of *Produktion* which explains, in Marx's thought, the progressive *loss of the creative and imaginary root of praxis*. In the *Economic and Philosophical Manuscripts of 1844*, indeed, Marx's use of the concept of *Produktion* is close to Fichte's *Produzieren*, evoked by Ricoeur at the beginning of the radio dialogue with Castoriadis (chapter 1, p. 3), because it has, at that point, the same extension as the concept of objectivation, and because it means the creative activity in general, the activity as realisation as well as the economic activity in particular. However, in *The German Ideology*, the passage from an *ontology of praxis* to an *ontology of production* leads Marx to evolve in his use of the term *Produktion* (Marx, 1970). But, beyond *The German Ideology*, it is Engels's and Lenin's influences combined that will, for Ricoeur, lead Marxist thought to drastically reduce the concept of *Produktion* to the economic concept of production.

The preceding terminological analysis thus demonstrates that the disagreement between Ricoeur and Castoriadis on the choice of the most appropriate terms to define productive imagination is not sufficient to establish an irreducible opposition between their respective thesis on the imagination and the imaginary. From our point of view, this terminological discussion even enables us to reveal an *essential agreement* between the two thinkers on the *originary and constituting status of the social imaginary*, which is clearly expressed in this *shared critique of structuralism* that they both develop throughout the dialogue.

From the beginning of the dialogue, both Ricoeur and Castoriadis criticise an explanation of imaginative productions that draws from *empiricism* and *associationism*, and that would reduce the novelty of a metaphor, of a narrative, or of a social imaginary signification to a simple 'combination of pre-established elements' (chapter 1, p. 4). For them, it is this same logic of a *reduction of productive imagination to reproductive imagination* – a logic prevailing in the philosophical tradition – that can be found in the central thesis of the structural anthropology of Lévi-Strauss, when it pretends to explain the social starting from a *formal symbolic* entirely reducible to a pure *combinatory logic*. In fact, when Lévi-Strauss (2008) aims at explaining the diversity of cultural forms, from one single combinatory logic corresponding to the symbolic structure of human mind, he merely develops a 'logicist' version of the empiricist reduction of productive imagination to reproductive imagination.

In his 1967 article, entitled 'The Question of the Subject: The Challenge of Semiology' (Ricoeur 2004, 232–62),[19] Ricoeur is grateful to Lévi-Strauss for having perceived the dimension of *radical discontinuity* that represents the *institution of language and symbolism*. In his famous 'Introduction to the Work of Marcel Mauss', Lévi-Strauss indeed wrote: 'Whatever may have been the moment and the circumstances of its appearance in the ascent of animal life, language can only have arisen all at once ... So there is a fundamental opposition, in the history of the human mind, between symbolism, which is characteristically discontinuous, and knowledge, characterised by continuity' (Lévi-Strauss 1987, 59–60).

As shown in this quotation, Lévi-Strauss has perceived the discontinuity implied by the birth of any symbolism, and by denying the possibility to establish a sociological theory of symbolism as Mauss does, he jointly asserts the central thesis of a 'symbolic origin' of society. However, for Ricoeur, *structural anthropology* fails to think the real origin of the social as, by reducing the genesis of language and of the symbolic to a gap, a difference or a simple combination of elements; it may indeed think the conditions of 'semiological order', but it completely misses the problem of the conditions of possibility of the 'semantic order'. For him, what he calls Lévi-Strauss's 'transcendentalism without subject' (Ricoeur 1974, 53) definitely accounts for the *negative and non-subjective condition of language* – that is, the game of differences operating in the system of the language – but it fails to tackle the *positive and subjective dimension of language* – that is, the capacity of human discourse to make sense and, by doing so, to refer to the world.

Even if their arguments differ, the Castoriadian critique of structuralism is obviously very similar to the main points of the Ricoeurian critique. Castoriadis indeed never intends to deny the functional and logical dimension of symbolism and of the social imaginary, but above all rejects the Lévi-Straussian reduction of the social imaginary to a mere combinatory logic, as it misses the 'instituting' aspect. By attempting to reduce the social imaginary to its logical and 'ensidic' dimension, Lévi-Strauss is in fact led to a *reduction of the instituting to the instituted*, which is unable to think the creative aspect and the radical novelty of 'social imaginary significations'. Now, what specifically defines those significations, insofar as they differ from the formal symbolism to which the structuralist theory refers, is that they cannot have any meaning independently from historical becoming and from the concrete lived experience of the subjects in which they are incarnated (Castoriadis 2015).[20] As Nicolas Poirier writes (2011, 258–9):

> To assert, as Lévi-Strauss does, that the series of structures correspond to a series of throws of a dice, is to point out an essential dimension of the social-historical which is precisely the concern of ensemblistic-identitarian logic, and which is ruled by a rationality of probabilistic type.... [But] to reduce the succession of the different societies to a random draw comes round ... to obliterate the question of the very *meaning* of this succession which is, 'par excellence' the problem of *historicity*.

For Ricoeur and Castoriadis, we may thus affirm that, in the same way as time cannot be reduced to the logical, history cannot be reduced to structures, for it is, on the contrary, in its essence, production, or *continued creation of structures*. And in our view, this is exactly the same argument that Ricoeur attempts to develop when (on p. 5 of the dialogue in chapter 1) he opposes a 'productive view' to a 'static view' of cultural and social inventions. For him, *historicity* is the proper characteristic of the productivity of productive imagination, and the latter can only be conceived as an *ever-open and ever-moving process* which has a 'happening' dimension irreducible to a logical combinatory. Symbolic productions actually present a logical dimension, but their dynamism also implies an imaginative dialectic through which the meaning continuously historicises itself through structures.

PRODUCTIVE IMAGINATION: BETWEEN ORIGIN AND MEDIATION, CREATION AND RETROACTION

How can we understand the dispute between Ricoeur and Castoriadis then, despite the strong and undeniable convergences in their conceptions of the productive imagination and the social imaginary that we attempted to show in our two previous parts? In our view, the heart of the debate has to be sought in the dispute that opposes the two philosophers regarding the idea, defended by Ricoeur, that the discontinuities produced by the productive imagination in history should mainly be interpreted as 'discontinuities of sense' standing out in the background of the 'continuity of existence'.

If Castoriadis seems to admit – not without a touch of irony (chapter 1, p. 7) – to the Ricoeurian idea, according to which discontinuity would merely be referring to *sense*, it is because in Castoriadis's view, this 'discontinuity of sense' has an immediate ontological scope: it equates to the position of an imaginary signification of reality that conditions our very access to reality. However, it seems to us that it is precisely under this apparent agreement that the profound difference between the two philosophers' approaches to the theorisation of productive imagination truly lies. When Castoriadis states that, in his view, 'ontologically, society as history, is sense' (7), he states in an eloquent way that the very heart of his philosophical reflection on instituting imagination is *ontological*. In this perspective, thinking the social-historical imaginary means, above all, elucidating a 'mode of being' or a specific and irreducible layer of being. Yet, the conquest of this mode of being specific to the radical imagination is, for Castoriadis, inseparable from the critique of 'inherited ontology', whose essential characteristic, as 'ontology of determinacy', is to lead to a complete occultation of the radical novelty of creation, by confining the philosophical reflection within the borders of the ensemblistic-identitarian logic.

Castoriadis can then very well grant Ricoeur that creation does not happen *cum nihilo* nor *in nihilo* – in so far as that there is always some pre-structured and 'pre-regulated' element resulting from the *sedimentation of the instituted* and applying a form of constraint on creation (pp. 5–6) – yet he maintains throughout his works the idea of creation as *ex nihilo* by defining the imaginary as *primary and unmotivated position* of new forms and new significations. As he summarises in his 1991 interview, entitled 'From the Monad to Autonomy',

> Let us consider the constitutive dimension of society and of history, the instituting dimension. We see therein something that, for lack of a better term, must be called a *source*, a capacity of human collectives to give rise in an unmotivated – though conditioned – way to forms, figures, new schemata that, more than merely serving to organise things, are creative of worlds ... All that is neither necessary nor contingent. It is the way of being that human beings in society create, and each time they create it *ex nihilo* as to what truly matters, that is to say, as to its form or *eidos*. But, of course, never *in nihilo* or *cum nihilo*, for something that was already there is utilised. (Castoriadis 1997, 174)

Thus, beyond this concession made to the 'already there', the profound meaning of the Castoriadian ontology of creation is therefore to affirm that imaginary is *a-causal and unmotivated* and that it is the emergence through creation of a *surplus of being* and of an irreducible alterity. In that sense, the imaginary is the *Being itself* as *Chaos, Abyss, and Groundlessness*: It is the Being as *time of creation* and of *radical alteration*. As Castoriadis himself notes, it is difficult to speak of the instituting social imaginary without defining it as a 'source' or a 'radical origin'[21] of new determinations. In this respect, the essentially *negative critical method* he displays throughout *The Imaginary Institution of Society* aims at progressively isolating that which, in our understanding of history, exceeds the principle of sufficient reason and ensemblistic-identitarian explanations. If the Castoriadian critical method appears indeed as a patient and obstinate analysis of the insufficiencies of Marx's theory of history and of 'inherited thought', it has an essentially ontological objective, that is, to unveil a 'surplus of being', which is the one of the imaginary sources of our societies.

As Arnaud Tomès (2008, 181–95) rightly stresses, the path that leads to a renewed ontology of creation is narrow, as there is, in the affirmation and definition of the social imaginary as *origin*, an apparent 'positivity' risking at any time to make us fall back into a *substantialist* and *causal* approach of the phenomenon of imagination. Temptation is strong, indeed, to forget the meaning of the immense critical effort developed by Castoriadis's philosophy and to reduce the specific *mode of being* of the social-historical imaginary to the three types which the 'inherited thought' has continuously pointed at: the *thing*, the *person*, or the *idea*. This being done, it is the specificity in the mode of being of society and history as constituting poles of the *anonymous collective creative capacity* that is at risk once more of being lost and occulted.

We believe that it is this risk or 'temptation' that draws Ricoeur's attention and orients it towards a very different interpretation of the productive imagination. Greatly influenced, as we saw, by the Kantian *critique of metaphysics*, Ricoeur has always considered the philosophical project of elaborating a renewed ontology as highly problematic. In this regard, constant references by Ricoeur to ontology must not mislead us: As shown in the tenth study of *Oneself as Another* (1992), ontology never plays the role of a *primary philosophy* for Ricoeur, but instead remains the 'horizon' or the 'promised land' of his philosophical reflection. In that sense, ontology is always characterised by its *exploratory and unachieved status*: It is the very thing that a philosophy of human action aspires to in its phenomenological, reflexive, and hermeneutical developments, although it always remains secondary and subordinate to the reflexive conquests of the reflection on action. As he stresses in the *Conflict of Interpretations* (1974 [1969]), a 'separate ontology' is beyond our grasp: It is only within the movement of the interpretation of symbols, texts, and actions that we perceive some dimension of the interpreted being.

For these reasons, we do not find any 'ontology of the imaginary' in Ricoeur's work, nor at any point is the philosopher drawn to place the social imaginary in a position of *radical origin* by identifying the instituting imaginary with the *being itself of historical becoming*. If he does not challenge the term of 'source' to define the social imaginary since, as we saw, he, like Castoriadis, defends the idea of an *originary imaginary and symbolic constitution of the social bond*, the fact remains that most of his theorisation of productive imagination falls within the renewed framework of a *philosophy of the act*[22] that consists in thinking the activity of the imagination first and foremost as an *activity of synthesis and mediation*.

From the *Philosophy of the Will* to *Time and Narrative* (1984–1988), Ricoeur continually insisted on the *inscrutable and structurally aporetic nature of the question of origin* – whether it be the origin of evil or the origin of time – and for the same reasons, he never placed the imagination in a position of origin. Therefore, he keeps supporting the thesis according to which our relationship to the origin can only be of a *poetico-practical* nature. As our relationship to the origin is never immediate and can only express itself through the indirect discourse of symbols and myths, it can be first described as *poetic* in the sense that it shows an irreducibly metaphorical dimension. But this reference to the poetic is not sufficient to define our *relationship to the originary*. For Ricoeur, the profound meaning of this relationship is to be a *practical relationship* rather than a theoretical and speculative relationship. Thus, it is only in action and in the *dialectic inherent in the human praxis* that what could be described as a productive 'contact point' with the origin keeps forming itself.

What are then the consequences of this poetico-practical thinking of productive imagination that never places the imagination in a position of radical origin but always provides it with the status of a *productive mediation*?

In our judgement, there is first a *methodological and critical* consequence of this positioning regarding the phenomenon of imagination. All the developments of Ricoeur's philosophy of imagination take as a starting point the *effective experience* that we have of the productivity and creativity of imagination, and maintain the methodological decision never to move away from the field of experience and from its *reflective reappropriation*. In that context, it is not surprising that the main objection made by Ricoeur to Castoriadis throughout the dialogue should precisely be to deny the fact that we could have an 'experience' of creation or of absolute novelty. As highlighted by Ricoeur, 'we do not know the non-instituted' (chapter 1, p. 13), and in that sense, the idea of an *absolute discontinuity* can only result from a form of 'subreption' in our reflection on productive imagination. Indeed, we have no choice but to note that our experience of imagination is first and foremost one of *an imaginary and symbolic medium* 'always already' there and one of an *origin always beyond our grasp*.

At the same time, we are merely describing half of this experience here, for the sole fact of being able to refer reflexively to this 'imaginary medium' which is always already there implies that we are capable of a 'critical distanciation' that creates the complementary and inseparable pole of our 'experience' of productive imagination. For Ricoeur, there is therefore a *tensional nature in our relationship to productive imagination* which – in its *indissolubly active and receptive dimension* – precisely leads to making any immediate or direct experience of the imagination's productivity impossible. It should be stressed that, in this regard, we do not know what is a *pure productive imagination*, no more than we know what is a *pure reproductive imagination*. Our experience is one of the *mixed*, of the 'in-between', and of the 'impure', which is why Ricoeur constantly insists on the fact that the productivity of the imagination to which we have access is always one of a 'regulated imagination' and never of a purely anomic and anarchic imagination.

This is the reason why, from *Fallible Man* (1986b [1960]) – so to speak from the first sketch of his philosophical anthropology – to *The Rule of Metaphor* (1977 [1975]) and *Time and Narrative* (1984–1988 [1983–1985]), Ricoeur favours a Kant-inspired approach to the productive imagination that emphasises its *power of mediation and synthesis*. At the opposite end of the dominant philosophical tradition, the emergence of the entirely new problematic of *synthesis* in the Kantian philosophy entails, according to Ricoeur, a true revolution when dealing with the question of imagination. For the first time in the history of philosophy, the problem of *imagination* as *production* or as 'doing' indeed prevails on the problem of *image* conceived as *reproduction* of the perceived thing. In so doing, both the epistemological primacy of perception over imagination and the phenomenological primacy of representation over act are contested. All through his work, there is thus no doubt that Ricoeur constantly considers the elaboration of his philosophy of imagination as a *renewal and a creative extension of the Kantian theory of schematism and productive imagination*. In this perspective, he will take also his inspiration from the Bachelardian conception of the imagination (2014),[23] the main contribution of which is to reveal the constitutive relationship between productive imagination and language by conceiving imagination as 'emergent signification' and not as 'vanishing perception'.

From *The Rule of Metaphor* (2003) to *Time and Narrative* (1984–1988), therefore, it is a productivity of imagination conceived as *synthesis and mediation* that the Ricoeurian philosophy endeavours to think, focussing essentially on the inventive power of imagination operating in discourse. As underlined by the preface of *Time and Narrative* (1984–1988), neither metaphor nor narrative is likely to produce a *semantic innovation* unless they both apply a 'synthesis of the heterogeneous'. In the case of the metaphor, the synthetic activity of the imagination lies in producing a *new resemblance* by crossing the gap between terms that at first seem 'distant'. As Ricoeur stresses: 'The productive imagination at work in the metaphorical process is thus our competence for producing new logical species by predicative assimilation, in spite of the resistance of our current categorisations of language' (Ricoeur 1984, X).[24] In the case of the narrative, this synthetic work of imagination consists in the *invention of a plot*: By means of the plot, heterogeneous elements such as agents, goals, causes, chance, or circumstances are brought together within the temporal unity of a whole and complete action. In other words, the plot of a narrative invents a human action configuration which 'refigures' our *practical experience* while resting upon its previous symbolic prefiguration.

In our view, this theorisation of the 'regulated imagination', in his attempt to think together the work of *invention* and *mediation* of imagination, reflects Ricoeur's resistance to the interpretation of Kant that Heidegger offers in the *Kantbuch* (1997). Since *Fallible Man* (1986b), Ricoeur indeed critically positions himself regarding the Heideggerian interpretation of productive imagination as *source* or *radical origin*, that is to say, as *common root of understanding and sensibility*. In his view, 'transcendental imagination' can legitimately be thought as *origin of transcendence*, as the very possibility of our *openness to the world*, but it is not sufficient to account for the *objectivity* and the *constitution of an intelligible order*. In that sense, it seems illusory to see in the *schematism* of transcendental imagination an *absolutely originary temporality*, as it does not offer us much more than a vague and formless transcendence, a simple field of apparition, and fails to explain the problems of *validity* and of intellectual determination. For Ricoeur, the real function of productive imagination is therefore not only to make possible our openness to the world, but most fundamentally, to produce *a mediation of appearance and expressibility*, that is to say, a *synthesis of finitude and rationality*. In his dialogue with Ricoeur, Castoriadis in turn seems to distance himself from the *Kantbuch* (1997) as he reproaches the Heideggerian interpretation for not overcoming the Kantian conception of imagination as 'imagination of a subject', and for thus missing the specificity of the *instituting social imaginary* as created by the *anonymous collective* (3). Nonetheless, we may question whether his theory of social imaginary placed *as radical origin of our relationship to the world* – that is, as the very root of being and temporality – is not faced with the same difficulties as the ones encountered by the Heideggerian reduction of rationality to originary temporality. In other words, we may wonder whether the radical ontological orientation that, in *Crossroads in the Labyrinth*, Castoriadis gave to his philosophy of the imaginary first presented in *The Imaginary Institution of Society* – that is, an ontology insisting on Being as 'Chaos' and on an originary 'creative-destructive' time – leads to a satisfactory definition of rationality and of critical reason.[25]

Therefore, if we want to grasp the specificity of Ricoeur's theory of imagination, we must absolutely resituate it in the framework of a *reflexive philosophy of the act* as inspired by Jean Nabert. In this perspective, to assert that productive imagination is, above all, *mediation* means that, in terms of individual existence as well as in social terms of the 'living together',[26] it always mediates our actions by making correlatively possible *a passage from act to sign and a reflexive movement from signs to act or to the originary affirmation that constitutes us.* The imagination constantly *mediates* a passage from act to sign, from *force* to *meaning*, or from *act* to *representation*, but the essence of this mediation is to remain unseen in this intentional process of emerging synthesis. This is the reason why Ricoeur chooses the 'long path' of critical hermeneutics of symbols, texts, actions, and cultural objectivities in order to reappropriate in a reflexive and indirect way the productive power of our act to exist, rather than the 'short path' of ontology.

What can be the specific contribution of this *philosophy of imaginative mediation* which is itself based on a *philosophy of expression* conceived as an expression of the act in the sign? Arguably, it consists, above all, in closer attention paid to phenomena directly linked to our *lived experience of imaginative productivity* – phenomena which tend to be concealed in the Castoriadian theory of imagination. If we had to schematically summarise the common characteristic of these phenomena, we could say that they all refer to *originary experiences of receptivity or belonging*. This implies that human action must always be conceived within the reflexive and hermeneutic frame of a *dialectic of affection and self-affection*.

From *Freedom and Nature* (1966 [1950]) to *The Course of Recognition* (2005 [2004], Ricoeur has kept defending a certain conception of human freedom as 'receptive initiative' or as 'dependence without heteronomy'. In his phenomenology of the will, these expressions first referred to the relationship of a finite *freedom* to the *motives* which orientate and energise it without compelling it; however, it does not appear exaggerated to say that in the following part of his work, they appear to characterise very precisely *our relationship to productive imagination in its poetical and practical dimension.*

As a matter of fact, what qualifies this relationship is that it is constitutively structured as a *tensional and dialectical relationship between activity and receptivity*, innovation and sedimentation, rupture and continuity, invention and discovery, distanciation and belonging, negation and mediation. In that sense, *productive imagination is what continually mediates activity and receptivity in the human experience, both individual and social.* Let us give but two examples. In a living metaphor, the *invention* of an impertinent attribution and the *discovery* of a relationship of similarity between two predicates, which at first seem distant, always coincide. In the *invention of a narrative*, the synthesis of the heterogeneous which operates the plot is only pos-sible because it operates at the same time as 'a creative *mimesis*' of human action. From that point of view, it is very striking to note that it is precisely when he characterises the *mimetic activity* at stake in the narrative that Ricoeur uses the adjective 'creative'. In other words, it is when imagination has a mimetic intention – which implies an irreduc-ible dimension of receptivity – that it reveals its very creative nature. Such is the meaning, in the dialogue, of the notion of 'debt' which Ricoeur evokes when he speaks of artistic creation and, more particu-larly, of the painting of Monet. Any work of creation is preceded by a lived experience of the world which energises and provokes it, and this is why it is at the same time a creation that 'confronts an unpayable debt' (chapter 1, p. 10).

In this perspective, we can consider that the theory of the 'triple *mimesis*' developed in the first volume of *Time and Narrative* represents the most thorough explanation of this *tensional dialectic of activity and receptivity* which characterises the work of productive imagin-ation. It means that there could not be any imaginative *configuration* and poetico-practical *refiguration* of our experience without a *prefig-uration* of this experience in a symbolic imaginary.[27] Even if Ricoeur, in the same way as Castoriadis, contests the *speculative reduction of imagination to memory* operated by Hegelian philosophy, he insists at the same time on the fact that there is *no imagination without reminis-cence*, pointing out the role and the importance of a *cultural memory* which keeps sustaining and energising the inventions of productive imagination. As shown in the Ricoeurian theory of ideology – in an essential dialogue with the cultural anthropology of Clifford Geertz (1973) – the same process occurs concerning the function of imagination in praxis. There is no initiative of the subject and no inventive praxis without a *symbolic mediation of praxis* made possible by ideology in its integrative function.

We can therefore draw two essential conclusions from this analysis of the fundamental element of *receptivity* which is stressed by the Ricoeurian conception of productive imagination. The first is that, for a philosophy of a 'regulated imagination', the idea of an 'unmotivated creation' in the Castoriadian sense must remain a *mere theoretical hypothesis*. The only productivity of imagination that we experience *practically* is that of a 'motivated production' – that is, a production oriented and energised by a certain experience of receptivity and belonging. Contrary to Castoriadis, who tends to stress the 'closure' and the 'inertia' of the *instituted imaginary* as a progressive concealment of the *instituting imaginary*, Ricoeur therefore gives a more positive function to the instituted imaginary, as he considers it as an *inspiring source of our praxis which orientates it without ever compelling it*.[28] However, if we can qualify our relationship to the instituted imaginary (in its symbolic, mythical, and poetic forms) as a *positive mediation of our freedom* – as an *affection* which cannot inevitably be reduced to an *alienation* – it is only under the condition that this mediation be submitted to a *radical critique*. For Ricoeur, the *utopian pole of imagination* is not only what makes this necessary *critique of ideologies* possible, but it is also what schematises the ways of a *practical transformation of society*. This is the reason why – and this will be our second conclusion – while refusing the idea of an 'authority of tradition', Ricoeur nevertheless defends a certain 'tradition of authority' whose deep meaning, for us, is that of a 'critical tradition' of the *authority of the symbolic productions of the productive imagination* operating in society and history.

What are then the properly ontological consequences of this tensional interpretation of the regulated productivity of imagination developed by Ricoeur? What understanding of the relationship between *continuity* and *discontinuity* in human history results from that interpretation?

In our view, the deep meaning of *the ontology of act and power*, especially sketched by Ricoeur in the tenth study of *Oneself as Another* (1992 [1990]) and re-elaborated in his key article of 1994, entitled

'From Metaphysics to Moral Philosophy' (Ricoeur 1996, 443–58), is precisely to enable a *theory of a dynamic and tensional link between the continuous and discontinuous*, capable of giving a full account of the work of productive imagination in history. But, in the same way as the ontology of creation of Castoriadis had to avoid the pitfalls of falling back into 'substantialism' and 'causalist thinking', the ontology of act and power sketched by Ricoeur must, for its part, also avoid the pitfalls related to a certain *dominant interpretation of the concepts of act and power in the philosophical tradition*. In sum, it must both avoid the assertion of a *primacy of power over act* which would reduce the act or the event in its emergence to the simple achievement of a previous logical determination, and – in an Aristotelian lineage – the assertion of a *primacy of act as determinacy over power*, which would lead to a reduction of the productive power of imagination to the infra-determinable – or what comes down to the same thing, to a constitutive lack of being.

Ricoeur strives to demonstrate that it is possible to conceive a dialectic of act and power in which the *act* – in its power of rupture and discontinuity – is indeed what reveals *power as a continuity of existence* operating through history, but in which *power*, far from being reduced to a pre-determination, is, on the contrary, conceived as a *productive power of determinations*. In other words, Ricoeur's philosophy aims at thinking a *concomitance of the power and of the act* (1966 [1950])[29] from a joint reading of the *phenomenon of imagination as power and act* and *as power and event*. That is the reason why, in the dialogue, the whole argumentation of Ricoeur concerning the dialectic of continuity and discontinuity constitutive of productive imagination leads to the idea of *an innovation conceived as a retroaction*.

In this perspective, even if Ricoeur accepts Castoriadis's idea that imagination is not a passage from the potential to the actual but a *continuous creation of potentialities*, he specifies, however, that this productivity of imagination can only be understood if it is thought as an *epigenesis*, through the idea of 'a sort of retroaction of our new creations on the old moments' (chapter 1, p. 11). It is as if the very nature of every creation was to reveal retroactively a 'point of contact' with the originary: By opening a future, by inventing something unprecedented, we release in fact some *unemployed and repressed potentialities* of our past. In that sense, every creation, every *imaginative production* is indissolubly *invention and discovery*, *act and power*, for in the discontinuity of the act, it reveals retroactively the continuity of existence of the *inexhaustible productive power of imagination*.

Whether it is on the individual plan of the *lived duration* or on the collective plan of the perpetuation of *living together* or on the historical plan of intercultural encounters and praxis, we must understand that there exists a *productivity of the instituted imaginary* which continually mediates the different modes of our continuity of existence from which the creative discontinuities of the works of culture and of the founding events of our societies stand out. This is the reason why, throughout the dialogue, Ricoeur rejects both the idea of *absolute novelty* and that of *absolute alterity*, on the level of the social imaginaries proper to each culture. In this respect, what is paradigmatically exemplified in the *practice of translation* is that it is impossible to think of an absolute discontinuity of cultural imaginaries, as there exists an irreducible practical continuity from which the creations of productive imagination stand out.

In the light of the analysis of the differences between these two interpretations of the phenomenon of productive imagination – as ontology of creation in Castoriadis and as a philosophy of act and sign developed in the prospect of an ontology of act and power in Ricoeur – it is obviously two different understandings of *autonomy* that are adumbrated. With Castoriadis, no doubt, the insistence on the notions of novelty, discontinuity, and radical creation is directly linked to an understanding of the *project of autonomy as a revolutionary project* and to the intention to give an *ontological foundation* to this project. With Ricoeur, it is not the question of denying the legitimacy of a project of autonomy conceived as a revolutionary project, but rather of contesting the reduction of the project of autonomy to a revolutionary project. For him, indeed, praxis should rather be conceived as an activity dialectally situated *between a revolutionary pole and a reformatory pole*.[30] In this respect, asserting the existence of an originary and *irreducible dialectic of ideology and utopia*[31] is refusing the possibility of a *pure autonomy* as well as that of a *pure auto-institution*, and seeking the ways of a human freedom conceived as 'dependence without heteronomy'. It is the 'always already' operating productivity of the instituted imaginary that comes to orient and energise our project of autonomy while, at the same time, defining its limits.

NOTES

1. We can here draw the reader's attention towards the excellent biography by François Dosse (2014), in which is evoked in detail (in chapter 13, entitled 'Changer la culture et la politique' – especially pp. 264–8) the relationship between Ricoeur and Castoriadis and is sketched the confrontation between the two thinkers on the key question of imaginary.

2. It is possible to characterise Ricoeur's philosophy merely as a philosophy of action or of human acting, but, in this essay, we will use the expression 'philosophy of the act', for, in our view, this expression defines what makes the singular originality of the Ricoeurian philosophy of action. The *actus* – Latin translation of the Greek *energeia* – refers indeed to a philosophical concept which is to be found throughout the history of philosophy, taking different forms as the Medieval *actus purus*, the Leibnizian *actuositas*, the Fichtean *Tathandlung*, or the Marxian *Selbstbetätigung*. In Ricoeur's philosophy, the idea of a 'philosophy of the act' refers to the French reflexive philosophy and more precisely to the philosophy of Jean Nabert – that is, a philosophy of the expression of the act in the signs, which refers directly to the Fichtean conception of act and of 'thetic judgement'. In that sense, when Ricoeur attempts to conceive human action and sketches an ontology of act and power, it is always within the specific framework of the French reflexive philosophy.

3. In this respect, the fact that Castoriadis sums up most of the philosophical tradition under the term 'inherited thought' reminds us of the singular of the expression 'metaphysics' used by Heidegger in his radical critique of onto-theology. In both cases, thinkers want to radically break with a philosophical tradition summed up in a singular and unique expression.

4. Incidentally, we can note that, through the different relationships that these philosophers have with the philosophical tradition, there already appears their respective position on the status of imaginative productions – conceived as a radical creative break in Castoriadis' thought and as a creative appropriation of the unemployed potentials in Ricoeur's.

5. Concerning these *Lectures on Imagination* to be published in 2018, the reader may refer to the two essential articles of George Taylor (2006; 2015).

6. Let us keep in mind that in 1985, *From Text to Action. Essays in Hermeneutics II* was not yet published and only three articles of Ricoeur specifically concerning the question of imagination and social imaginary had been already published in journals: 'Science and Ideology' (1974), 'Imagination in Discourse and in Action. Toward a General Theory of Imagination' (1976), and 'Ideology and Utopia as Cultural Imagination' (1976).

7. In his biography of Castoriadis, François Dosse quotes a correspondence between Castoriadis and Ricoeur, dating back to 1978, in which Ricoeur

declares that he 'reads with passion' everything Castoriadis writes and where
he even adds that he has made a lecture for third-year students in Nanterre
University about *The Imaginary Institution of Society* (Dosse 2014, 265).

8. On this topic, the reader may refer to Suzi Adams's essay (2008, 387–
400), which is precisely devoted to the cosmological developments of the
thought of the later Castoriadis, which lead to a renewed philosophy of life as
'autopoiesis', within the frame of an ontology of nature.

9. Even this question goes beyond the present essay; we can wonder if the
relationship that Castoriadis has with the myths in his later works could not
be paralleled with the relationship which Ricoeur has with the symbolic and
mythic thought when he asserts that 'the symbol gives rise to thought'. Indeed,
for Ricoeur, myths are likely to make us think in 'a free speculative register' in
which would be deployed the wisdom resources dissimulated under the narra-
tion of a narrative of the origins.

10. Depending on the texts, it seems that Castoriadis's approach to ontology sometimes emphasises the primacy of 'Chaos', sometimes emphasises the
interplay of 'Chaos' and 'Cosmos'. For instance, he insists first and foremost
on a characterisation of being as 'Chaos', 'Abyss', or 'Groundlessness' and on
an analysis of temporality as 'creative-destructive' (Castoriadis 1984; 1993).
In other texts, which generally refer more precisely to the Hesodian conception of 'Chaos' (Castoriadis 1983; 2004), Castoriadis, in his rethinking of
'Physis', emphasises the interplay of 'Chaos' and 'Cosmos'. As Suzi Adams
writes: 'Castoriadis reinvigorates an ancient Greek schema of being as the
entwining of chaos and cosmos that creates itself as heterogeneous strata and
regions' (Adams 2008, 89–390).

11. We can find an example of this in his interview entitled 'From the
Monad to Autonomy' (Castoriadis 1997, 172–95): 'What appeared to me as a
fundamental lacuna, and more than a lacuna, in Marx's conceptual framework
was not only the dimension of the singular individual, it was the 'imaginary
creation of the social-historical sphere', the imaginary as collective, anonymous, radical, instituting, and *constituting* imaginary' (Castoriadis 1997, 173,
italics mine).

12. Cf. the sentence we have already quoted (p. 81) and which, in *The
Imaginary Institution of Society*, introduces the Castoriadian analysis of 'The
Role of Imaginary Significations' (Castoriadis 1987, 146).

13. Hereafter the references to the radio dialogue proper appear as single
page numbers.

14. For a more detailed analysis of the common points and differences
between the Ricoeurian and the Castoriadian interpretations of Marx, the reader
may refer to the enlightening synthesis proposed by Johann Michel in his preface. As for us, we will mainly focus on the common points between the two
thinkers' critiques of the Marxist concept of 'production'.

15. For a detailed analysis of this question, please refer to chapter 6, part III of our book (Amalric 2013, 484–512).

16. A conference recently published online by the Fonds Ricoeur.

17. Incidentally, this critique reminds us of the critique of the Marxist reduction of the Fichtean concept of activity (as a fundamental activity of the human being producing himself) to the concept of production (as mere instrumental activity) developed in 1968 by Habermas (1994).

18. Translation mine.

19. For a more detailed commentary of this article, the reader may refer to the excellent article by Suzi Adams (2015, 130–53).

20. This is a thesis that Castoriadis strongly asserts, as early as the end of the sixties.

21. Incidentally, this reminds us of the first phrase of 'The Imaginary as Such' where Castoriadis sums up his whole conception of the social imaginary: 'We encounter the imaginary in history: as an ongoing origin, an ever-actual foundation; it is a central component, at work in both the maintenance of every society as a unit, an in the generation of historical change' (Castoriadis 2015, 59).

22. For a more in-depth analysis of the renewed framework of this *philosophy of the act*, we refer to our essay (Amalric 2015; 2016a).

23. Cf. Bachelard (2014).

24. Cf. Ricoeur (1984, X).

25. It is obvious that this question partially overlaps the critique addressed to Castoriadis by Habermas (1990), but, in our view, it remains an open question which cannot be reduced to a mere interrogation concerning the relationship between sense and validity. Raising the essential and difficult question of the imaginary sources of reason, Castoriadis invites us, in fact, to question jointly the relationship between imagination and reason and the relationship between freedom and reason. On this topic, please refer to Castoriadis (1984, 1993, 1997, 1991) and Gely (2008).

26. Even if the question of the dynamic articulation between *individual imagination* and *social imaginary* is not directly dealt with in the dialogue and that it exceeds the limits of this essay, there is no doubt that it represents a decisive question in the Ricoeurian theory of imagination as well as in the Castoriadian theory. As early as *Fallible Man* and his analysis of the 'theoretical synthesis', of the 'practical synthesis', and of the 'affective fragility' of man, Ricoeur strongly asserts that all the being of man consists in 'doing mediation'. But this mediation operated by individual imagination remains still abstract so long as it is not reinserted into the frame of the originary and 'always-already' operating mediation of social imaginary. As the *Lectures on Ideology and Utopia* will show, there exists indeed an *integrative function* of ideology, which precisely corresponds to this *function of symbolical mediation*

of human action constitutive of the social bond and of the identity of a social group. In the same way, with Castoriadis, the elaboration of an ontology of creation and of imaginary being necessarily implies the dynamic relationship between the radical imagination of the psyche and the instituting force of the social-historical imaginary. Unlike the functional imagination already operating in the living being, the imagination of the human psyche is 'nonfunctional': It is pure representative spontaneity, 'unlimited and uncontrollable representational flux'. However, in so far as, in its original form, the 'psychical monad' is radically asocial and antisocial, the decisive role of the instituting social imaginary is to institute the social individual by imposing to the psyche an organisation and common imaginary significations which are radically heterogeneous to it.

27. For a detailed analysis of the relationship between 'implicit symbolism' and 'explicit symbolism' in *Time and Narrative*, and for a synthetic reflection on the relationships between symbol and fiction in Ricoeur's work, the reader may refer to our essay (Amalric 2016b, 131–67).

28. We might say, in that sense, and to use Castoriadian terms, that the central methodological decision of Ricoeur's philosophy of imagination is to situate his analysis of productive imagination in the tensional 'in-between' of instituting imaginary and instituted imaginary. On the contrary, Castoriadis's ontology of creation seems, from our point of view, to oscillate between a theory of productive imagination situated in the tension of instituting society and instituted society, and a discourse on radical autonomy and auto-institution centred on the *instituting*.

29. We use here an expression used by Ricoeur in chapter 3, part I of *Freedom and Nature*. It is indeed in this chapter, developing a reflexive analysis of the 'choice', that Ricoeur defines his conception of freedom and sketches, for the first time, a precise analysis of the relationship between power and act. As he then writes: 'This concomitance of the power and of the act is the radical manner of affirming freedom' (Ricoeur 1966 [1950], 186).

30. Whatever the essentially 'reformist' political positions adopted by Ricoeur from the nineties may be, there is no doubt, in our opinion, that it is his article of 1968 entitled 'Réforme et révolution dans l'Université' which most accurately expresses the meaning of his philosophy of social imaginary and of the *originary dialectic of ideology and utopia*. As Ricoeur then writes: 'We have entered a period in which it is necessary to be reformist *while* remaining revolutionary. In the times to come, the whole art of the legislator will be to set up light institutions, revocable, reparable, opened both to an internal process of revision and to an external process of contest' (Ricoeur 1991, 381, translation mine).

31. As regards our personal interpretation of this originary dialectic of ideology and utopia as emerging from the founding event of a constituting social imaginary, the reader may refer to our essay (Amalric 2014, 9–22).

REFERENCES

Abel, Olivier. 1996. *La Promesse et la règle*. Paris: Michalon.

Adams, Suzi. 2008. 'Towards a Post-Phenomenology of Life: Castoriadis' Critical *Naturphilosophie*'. *Cosmos and History: The Journal of Natural and Social Philosophy* 4:1–2: 387–400.

———. 2015. 'On Ricoeur's Shift from a Hermeneutics of Culture to a Cultural Hermeneutics'. *Etudes Ricoeuriennes/Ricoeur Studies* 6:2: 130–53.

Amalric, Jean-Luc. 2013. *Paul Ricoeur, l'imagination vive. Une genèse de la philosophie ricoeurienne de l'imagination*. Paris: Hermann.

———. 2014. 'Evénement, idéologie et utopie'. *Etudes Ricoeuriennes/Ricoeur Studies* 5:2: 9–22.

———. 2015. 'L'articulation de l'éthique et du politique dans l'horizon d'une philosophie de l'acte I'. *Eco-ethica* 4: 241–55.

———. 2016a. 'L'articulation de l'éthique et du politique dans l'horizon d'une philosophie de l'acte II'. *Eco-ethica* 5: 233–50.

———. 2016b. 'Símbolo, metáfora e narrativa: o estatuto do ficcional em Ricoeur'. In *Pensar Ricoeur: Vida et narração*. Edited by Dir. R. Wu and C. Reichert do Nascimento. Porto Alegre: Editora Clarinete.

Arendt, Hannah. 1998. *The Human Condition*. Chicago, IL: The University of Chicago Press.

Bachelard, Gaston. 2014. *The Poetics of Space*. Translated by Mark Z. Danielewski. New York: Penguin Books.

Castoriadis, Cornelius. 1983. 'The Greek Polis and the Creation of Democracy'. *Graduate Faculty Philosophy Journal* 9:2: 79–115.

———. 1984. 'The Imaginary: Creation in the Social-Historical Domain'. In *Disorder and Order*, Proceedings of the Stanford International Symposium. Stanford Literature Studies 1. Edited by Paisley Livingstone. Saratoga, CA: AnmaLibri.

———. 1987. *The Imaginary Institution of Society*. Translated by Kathleen Blamey. Cambridge, UK: Polity Press.

———. 1991. *Philosophy, Politics, Autonomy*. Translated by David Ames Curtis. New York and Oxford: Oxford University Press.

———. 1993. 'Institution of Society and Religion'. *Thesis Eleven* 35:1: 1–17.

———. 1997. *World in Fragments: Writings on Politics, Society, Psychoanalysis and the Imagination*. Translated and edited by David Ames Curtis. Stanford, CA: Stanford University Press.

———. 2004. *Ce qui fait la Grèce 1. D'Homère à Héraclite*. Paris: Editions du Seuil.

———. 2015. 'The Imaginary as Such'. Translated by Johann P. Arnason. *Social Imaginaries* 1:1: 59–69.

Changeux, Jean-Pierre, and Ricoeur Paul. 2002. *What Makes Us Think? A Neuroscientist and a Philosopher Argue about Ethics, Human Nature, and the Brain.* Translated by M. B. DeBevoise. Princeton and Oxford: Princeton University Press.

Dosse, François. 2014. *Castoriadis, une vie.* Paris: Editions de la Découverte.

Foessel, Michaël, and Fabien Lamouche. 2007. *Anthologie de Paul Ricoeur.* Texts chosen and presented by Michaël Foessel and Fabien Lamouche. Paris: Editions du Seuil.

Geertz, Clifford. 1973. *The Interpretation of Cultures.* New York: Basic Books.

Gely, Raphaël. 2008. 'Imaginaire, affectivité et rationalité. Pour une relecture du débat entre Habermas et Castoriadis'. In *Praxis et Institution. Cahiers Castoriadis n°4.* Edited by Sophie Klimis, Philippe Caumières, and Laurent Van Eyde, 139–82. Bruxelles: Publication des Facultés Universitaires Saint Louis.

Habermas, Jürgen. 1990. *The Philosophical Discourse of Modernity.* Translated by Frederic Lawrence. Cambridge, MA: Massachusetts Institute of Technology Press.

———. 1994. *Knowledge and Human Interests.* Translated by Jeremy J. Shapiro. Cambridge, UK: Polity Press.

Heidegger, Martin. 1997. *Kant and the Problem of Metaphysics.* Translated by Richard Taft. Bloomington and Indianapolis: Indiana University Press.

Kearney, Richard. 2004. *On Paul Ricoeur: The Owl of Minerva.* Aldershot, Hampshire: Ashgate.

Lévi-Strauss, Claude. 1987. *Introduction to the Work of Marcel Mauss.* Translated by Felicity Baker. London: Routledge and Keagan Paul.

———. 2008. *Structural Anthropology, Vol. 1.* Translated by Claire Jacobson and Brooke Grundfest Schoepf. New York and London: Penguin.

Marx, Karl. 1970. *The German Ideology.* Translated by Christopher J. Arthur. New York: International Publishers.

———. 2007. *Economic and Philosophical Manuscripts of 1844.* Translated by Martin Milligan, Mineola, NY: Dover.

Merleau-Ponty, Maurice. 2003a. *Phenomenology of Perception.* Translated by Colin Smith. London and New York: Routledge Classics.

———. 2003b. *L'Institution, La Passivité: Notes de cours au Collège de France (1954–1955).* Paris: Editions Belin.

Poirier, Nicolas. 2011. *L'Ontologie politique de Castoriadis. Création et insti-tution.* Paris: Payot.

Ricoeur, Paul. 1965a. *History and Truth.* Translated by Charles A. Kelbley. Evanston, IL: Northwestern University Press.

———. 1965b. 'Universal Civilization and National Cultures'. In *History and Truth,* 271–84. Evanston, IL: Northwestern University Press.

————. 1965c. 'The Work and the Word'. In *History and Truth*, 197–219. Evanston, IL: Northwestern University Press.

————. 1966 [1950]. *Freedom and Nature: The Voluntary and the Involuntary.* Translated by Erazim V. Kohák. Evanston, IL: Northwestern University Press.

————. 1969. *The Symbolism of Evil.* Translated by E. Buchanan. Boston, MA: Beacon Press.

————. 1974. *The Conflict of Interpretations. Essays in Hermeneutic.* Translated by Don Idhe. Evaston, IL: Northwestern University Press.

————. 1975. 'Le 'lieu' de la dialectique', IIA309. In *Dialectics* (Entretiens de Varna, 1973). Edited by Chaïm Perelman, 92–108. Comité éditorial du Fonds Ricoeur. Text edited by Roberta Picardi. Conference proceedings published by Ricoeur Archives, Paris.

————. 1984–1988. *Time and Narrative, 3 vols.* Translated by Kathleen Blamey and David Pellauer. Chicago, IL: The University of Chicago Press.

————. 1986a. *A l'école de la phénoménologie.* Paris: Editions Vrin.

————. 1986b. *Fallible Man.* Translated by C. A. Kelbley. New York: Fordham University Press.

————. 1986c. *Lectures on Ideology and Utopia.* Edited by George Taylor. New York: Columbia University Press.

————. 1991. *From Text to Action.* Translated by Kathleen Blamey and John B. Thompson. Evanston, IL: Northwestern University Press.

————. 1991. 'Réforme et révolution dans l'Université'. In *Lectures I. Autour du politique*, 380–97. Paris: Seuil.

————. 1992. *Oneself as Another.* Translated by Kathleen Blamey. Chicago, IL: The University of Chicago Press.

————. 1995. 'Intellectual Biography'. In *The Philosophy of Paul Ricoeur.* Edited by Lewis Edwin Hahn and translated by Kathleen Blamey, 3–53. Chicago, IL: Open Court.

————. 1996. 'From Metaphysics to Moral Philosophy'. In *Philosophy Today* 40:4: 443–58.

————. 2003. *The Rule of Metaphor. The Creation of Meaning in Language.* Translated by Robert Czerny, Kathleen McLaughlin, and John Costello, SJ. London: Routledge.

————. 2004. *The Conflict of Interpretations. Essays in Hermeneutics.* Edited by Don Ihde and translated by Kathleen McLaughlin. London and New York: Continuum.

————. 2005. *The Course of Recognition.* Translated by David Pellauer. Cambridge, MA: Harvard University Press.

————. 2018. *Lectures on Imagination.* Edited by George H. Taylor, Patrick Crosby, and Robert D. Sweeney (in press).

Ryle, Gilbert. 1939. *The Concept of Mind.* London and New York: Hutchinson's University Library.

Taylor, George H. 2006. 'Ricoeur's philosophy of Imagination'. *Journal of French Philosophy* 16:1.2: 93–104.

———. 2015. 'The Phenomenological Contributions of Ricoeur's Philosophy of Imagination'. *Social Imaginaries* 1:2: 13–31.

Thomasset, Alain. 1996. *Paul Ricoeur, une poétique de la morale*. Louvain: Leuven University Press.

Tomès, Arnaud. 2008. 'Création et causalité dans le social-historique'. In *Cornélius Castoriadis. Réinventer l'autonomie*. Edited by Blaise Bachofen, Sion Elbaz, and Nicolas Poirier. Paris: Editions du Sandre, pp. 181–196.

———. 2015. *Castoriadis. L'Imaginaire, le Rationnel, et le Réel*. Paris: Editions Demopolis.

Chapter Five

Castoriadis and Ricoeur on the Hermeneutic Spiral and the Meaning of History

Creation, Interpretation, Critique

Suzi Adams

The central theme of the 1985 Ricoeur–Castoriadis radio discussion concerns the possibility – and meaning – of human creation in history. This appears in the dialogue as two overlapping debates. They are: first, the problematic of creation *ex nihilo* versus production and, second, the question of the interplay of continuity and discontinuity in historical creation. Despite their ostensible – and seemingly unbridgeable – differences, Castoriadis and Ricoeur share some common ground. This includes, for example, an understanding of history as the realm of meaning and social change, an approach to the social imaginary that combines the sociological question of social creativity with the philosophical problematic of the creative imagination, the recognition of the bifurcation of the social imaginary in its *instituting-utopian* and *instituted-ideological* aspects, and the connection between meaning and the imagination. Where Castoriadis focuses on the social imaginary creation of institutions and whole societies (see chapter 1, p. 3),[1] with particular reference to ancient Greece, Ricoeur prefers instead to emphasise 'production in the order of language' (4). Here, again, however, there remains openings in their broader oeuvres towards the other's perspective, for example, in Ricoeur's understanding of language as 'the institution of institutions' (1988, 221) and Castoriadis's recognition that imaginary significations in language is its 'widest and most familiar

domain' (1987, 345).[2] The present essay offers two meditations that
engage with these key themes of the dialogue. The first seeks to build
a bridge between Castoriadis's understanding of creation 'out of nothing' and Ricoeur's notion of production 'from something to something'
through recourse to the metaphor of 'chaos' in relation to the imagination and the underdetermination of meaning.[3] The second reflection
begins with the question of continuity and discontinuity in history. It
broadens the scope of reference, however, and, in so doing, reconstructs
an implicit dialogue between Castoriadis and Ricoeur that enunciates a
different vantage point from which to understand their radio encounter
as a rethinking of the hermeneutic circle in relation to history. Before
proceeding further, two things are important to note: First, Ricoeur's
understanding of history as 'history as project' that is oriented towards
the future, and 'history as recounted' that is concerned with the past will
frame the following discussion; and, second, the essay takes its cue from
Castoriadis rather than Ricoeur in its focus on the creative activity of
the social-historical via social imaginary significations in and as society,
rather than on production in the order of language.

MUCH ADO ABOUT 'NOTHING': CREATION
OR PRODUCTION?

As is well known, Castoriadis elucidates human creation as *ex nihilo*:
out of nothing. Ricoeur, however, rejects the possibility of 'absolute
novelty' (5). He contends rather that we are 'never in a passage from
nothing to something, but from something to something' (6). Is it possible to retrieve the sense of 'out of nothing' in Castoriadis's formulation
while still doing justice to the 'from something' in Ricoeur's? How is
such a bridge to be built? Castoriadis had insisted on an understanding of history as creation *ex nihilo* since the mid-1960s (1987, 2),
and remained on this course throughout his intellectual trajectory. For
present purposes, the key point to note in relation to his conception of
self-creation is that new creations – as newly created forms as *eide* –
are neither reducible to, nor producible from their antecedents; thus the
creation of new forms emerges 'out of nothing'. For Castoriadis, this is
epitomised by the ancient Greek invention of democracy. The Greeks
brought a new form – democracy – into being. Thus, social-historical
creation has ontological consequences. The Greek breakthrough to

democracy – and the project of autonomy, more broadly, in its interplay of politics, philosophy, and history – constitutes a rupture, a discontinuity in being itself, in history, and in anthropos more broadly. Beginning with Homeric texts, the upsurge of autonomy as an imaginary signification within instituting society found a hold within institutions as a 'long revolution' from 800 to 500 BCE. The 'new form' emerges as the interaction of nuclear imaginary significations (those that are without a world referent and, as such, are absolutely generative; in this case, 'autonomy') and their articulation and incarnation in institutions, as part of the broader interplay of instituting and instituted society. In his 1989 reply to his critics, Castoriadis (1997a) began to enunciate a more qualified position: Although creation was to still to be considered *ex nihilo*, it was neither *in nihilo* nor *cum nihilo*. He did not, however, further elaborate on the implications for his theory of creation. Clearly, his qualification implicitly acknowledges a contextual – and therefore, interpretative – facet to creation, but the interpretative aspect of creation (and, conversely, the creative aspect of interpretation) was one of Castoriadis's enduring blind spots, and he continued to reject the possibility of a hermeneutic dimension to creation out of hand.[4] Nonetheless, the logic of Castoriadis's own formulations reveals an interpretative aspect to creation (and, conversely, a creative aspect to interpretation). This is seen in, for example, the enigmatic connection between the imaginary element and the symbolic webs through which the imaginary is expressed, and in his postulate that modernity utilises a 'recreation' of the ancient Greek imaginary signification of autonomy in a way that is not a mere copy. Thus, Castoriadis's elucidation of imaginary significations and social-historical creation relies on a hermeneutic framework.

But what does the inauguration of democracy as a new ontological form have to do with meaning? For Castoriadis, the ancient Greek invention of democracy incarnates the social imaginary signification of autonomy as the nuclear imaginary signification of its world formation. Imaginary significations themselves are constellations and patterns of meaning that create each society's own world. On Castoriadis's account, social imaginary significations, as constellations of meaning, are the basis of any social-historical creation of form. This points to Castoriadis's distinction – prior to his ontological turn, at least – between the imaginary element of the social-historical and its articulation, not only in institutions, but through symbolic webs (e.g. he uses the example of the 'pay cheque' symbolising the imaginary

signification of 'rational mastery', which is embodied in the institution of capitalism). There is some overlap here with Ricoeur's take on
Levi-Strauss's critique of Mauss. Ricoeur refers to this discussion in
several places, but does not systematically pursue it. At one point, he
argues: 'For how could illusions and fantasies have any historical efficacy if ideology did not have a mediated role incorporated in the most
elementary social bond, as the latter's symbolic constitution in the sense
of Mauss and Lévi-Strauss? Hence we cannot speak of a pre-ideological
or non-ideological activity' (Ricoeur 1998, 230). Here we can see that
he actually reworks and fuses their approaches: The symbolic institutes
the social world, and it does so symbolically.[5]

Ricoeur rejects Castoriadis's elucidation of creation *ex nihilo*. In the
radio discussion, Ricoeur insists on the Kantian concept of 'production' and (the productive imagination) instead of 'creation'.[6] Where,
for Castoriadis, 'production' remains within determinist ontologies and
identitarian thinking of 'the same', for Ricoeur, 'creation' is reserved
for the domain of the 'foundational sacred' (4); creation – the 'first day
of creation' (5) – is not within history but stands at its threshold. As
'the idea of absolute novelty is unthinkable' (5), Ricoeur considers the
notion of 'production' more appropriate. The production of new figures
in history emerges in an open dialectic of innovation and sedimentation.
In this way, Ricoeur's hermeneutic account of creation is more modest
than Castoriadis's: while allowing for social creativity, the new form
always bears traces of antecedent figurations.

Throughout the dialogue, Castoriadis reduces Ricoeur's understanding of 'production' to Lévi-Strauss's position as a 'combination of
pre-existing elements', which occludes the possibility of creation. This
is perhaps partly due to the fact that Ricoeur's work on the imagination and the social imaginary were all but unpublished at the time
of their radio encounter in 1985.[7] Additionally, the second volume
of *Time and Narrative* (Ricoeur 1985) had been published only a
few months prior to the dialogue, and the third volume was not published until several months thereafter.[8] It was thus highly likely that
Castoriadis was unfamiliar with Ricoeur's reflections on these themes.
Nevertheless, Ricoeur rightly defends his understanding of production
from Castoriadis's reductionism, agreeing that historical creation/pro-
duction cannot be a combination of 'elements already there' (4), and
asserting an alternative approach. Should it, indeed, be possible to
think 'creation', it could only be as an 'event of thought that we will

reconfigure exactly as we tell a different story with the same archives' (13). Ricoeur takes the example of the French Revolution to demonstrate that there are no prior elements to a narrative:

> In contrast, in what I call emplotment, a process is set in motion where the 'elements' are reshaped by the lesson learned from an event. An event is determined by its role in the story that one is telling. Something might be an event for one story, but not for the other. In one plot, the storming of the Bastille is not an event; in another plot, it is an origin. Consequently, there are no elements that are somehow fixed in advance. (5)

Ricoeur devotes a more detailed discussion of this thematic in the first volume of *Time and Narrative* (1984). There he characterises the French Revolution as the 'appearance on the stage of history of a practical and ideological mode of social action that *is nowhere inscribed in what preceded it*' (1984, 222; emphasis added). He arguably finds himself very close to Castoriadis's sense of social-historical creation *ex nihilo*: There is a clear sense in which Ricoeur articulates the French Revolution as emerging out of nothing. But he frames its emergence nonetheless more strongly within historical continuity than does Castoriadis. Ricoeur goes onto say: 'No conceptual reconstruction will ever be able to make the continuity with the *ancien régime* pass by way of the rise to power of an imaginary order experienced as a break and as an origin. This rise to power is itself on the order of an event' (1984, 223).

But back to the task of bridge building. Is there a way to do justice to both Castoriadis's understanding of 'creation out of nothing' and Ricoeur's articulation of production as 'from something to something'? The key, I argue, lies in understanding that *meaning is underdetermined*. Social imaginary significations, as constellations of meaning in Castoriadis's sense, are neither determinate 'things' nor completely indeterminate 'nothings'. As such, meaning, as the basis of historical novelty, is neither 'fully something' nor 'absolutely nothing'. It is not brute 'existence' of a form that makes possible its reconfiguration/recreation, but its meaning for us. And the reason that we can 'be-affected' in different ways by the efficacy of history is because the underdetermination of meaning allows for – calls forth, even – a plurality of interpretations. Being condemned to meaning (to lean on Merleau-Ponty) is to accept its underdetermination as the precondition for the surplus of meaning that makes possible a plurality of interpretations and historical novelty.

It is worth recalling, as noted above, that Ricoeur and Castoriadis share common ground in their linking the productive/creative imagination to their respective theories of meaning, and their characterisation of history as the domain of meaning. Full consideration of Castoriadis's and Ricoeur's respective theories of meaning is beyond the scope of this essay.[9] Through a hermeneutic detour, however, the underdetermination of meaning can be illuminated via reconstruction of the figure of 'chaos' in Ricoeur's and Castoriadis's thought. This is warranted, as, for Castoriadis, social imaginary creativity emerges from the chaos, and Ricoeur himself equates Castoriadis's understanding of creativity with chaos as the 'absolutely formless'. As Johann Michel notes in his preface (in this volume): 'Notably it is the always prior existence of language, whose pre-existing rules prevent Ricoeur from subscribing to the idea that a new form could arise from some kind of formless chaos' (p. xxxvi). Ricoeur twice rejects the possibility of creation *ex nihilo* from the formless in the dialogue. He says: 'We are never in a situation that you would call creation, as if form could be derived from the absolutely formless' (5). Slightly later, Ricoeur reiterates this: 'One is never in a passage from nothing to something ... never from the formless to form' (6).

Both Ricoeur and Castoriadis take up the figure of 'chaos' in their work. Ricoeur discussed it in *The Symbolism of Evil* as the myth of primordial chaos (1967, 175–91), but he was more interested in the myth for its articulation of the entry of evil into the world rather than in the figure of chaos for its own sake. To this end, he explores the Babylonian creation myth *Enuma elish* (Ricoeur 1967, 175ff). He highlights that chaos is anterior to order (177), and that 'evil' is 'coextensive with the primordial'. But evil is 'twice designated: as the chaos in front of order, and as the [theogonic] struggle by which chaos is overcome' (179). In this way, the myth of chaos as the drama of creation posits the origin of evil as coextensive with the origin of things. Interestingly, for present purposes, Ricoeur locates a 'surcharge of meaning' in chaos that makes possible 'the power to produce' (177), but also notes that its 'original disorder' was menacing (179). But what if we were to transgress Ricoeur's reading and shift our lens from the myth of chaotic disorder and see in it a root metaphor for being that brings it closer to Castoriadis's approach?[10] Surely the element (in the Merleau-Pontian sense) that has most often been understood down the ages as unruly and disorderly is the imagination. If this is so, then it is possible to read the imagination as being at the root of the world order and co-extensive with its creation.

The chaos myth did not play an important part in the development of Ricoeur's overall philosophical framework. It is otherwise for Castoriadis, for whom, especially from the early 1980s, the interplay of *chaos* and *kosmos* as a metaphor for being became clearly apparent. Before proceeding further, it is worth noting that there is a widespread but misleading understanding of Castoriadis as a theorist of indeterminacy, to which the articulation of the formlessness of chaos corresponds. Castoriadis himself contributes to this confusion; it points to an internal tension in his thought. For example, in a late essay from 1997, he continues to posit chaos as 'indeterminate' (Castoriadis 2007b, 80). This is no doubt in part due to his embrace of Anaximander's *apeiron*, which has typically been understood as a kind of primordial chaos, as the indeterminate as indefinite in the sense that it is preformed and unlimited/undetermined (i.e. before *eidos* or *peras*) (Castoriadis 1987; 2004, 197). In that Ricoeur seemed to equate Castoriadis's 'nothing' with the 'formless' (in the dialogue, at least), he, too, appeared to cast Castoriadis as a thinker of indeterminacy. At other junctures in his thought, however, Castoriadis reminds us that chaos could not be completely indeterminate: 'If this were the case, [chaos] could not lend itself to any organization or it would lend itself to all; in both cases, all coherent discourse and all action would be impossible' (1987, 341). With his emerging metaphor of being as the interplay of *chaos/kosmos* in the early 1980s, however, Castoriadis developed a clearer – and distinctive – ontological image. He now clearly articulates chaos in a twofold sense: first, as the bottomless depths underlying *kosmos*, but also, second, as a 'formative potential' (Castoriadis 2007c, 241). In general, Castoriadis strenuously critiques the concept of 'potential' (especially in its Aristotelian distinction from 'act'), as for him, it remains within a framework of determinacy: A potential is something that is identifiable, even if incipient, as derivable from its antecedents. In the dialogue – and in his later work – he notes the creation of the 'potentiality of potentiality' (36), which, as the human capacity to create new potentials, becomes a hallmark of his later philosophical anthropology, and his way to recognise the creative merits in 'potentiality' but to (attempt to) sidestep its determinist overtones. In conjunction with his understanding of the 'chaos without', he articulates the psyche (the radical imagination) as the 'chaos within', with formative links to the creation of meaning out of nothing (see Castoriadis 1987, 341–2). But if chaos is neither fully indeterminate nor determined – thus, under-determined – how are we to understand it? Here Castoriadis can help us. In the early 1960s, where he argued if reality is not totally rational, 'it also implies that it is not simply chaos [formless], that it contains grooves, lines of force, veins, which mark out the possible, the feas-ible, indicate the probable and permit action to find points of anchorage in the given' (1987, 79). The *Sinnfähigkeit* of the world offers hinges and pivots (to draw on Merleau-Ponty) for its cultural articulation via imaginary significations.

Finally, a brief note that signposts another hermeneutical spiral to be explored: Castoriadis remarks on a further meaning of chaos (especially in the Hesiodian sense) as 'void' or 'empty chasm'. Here, affinities with Ricoeur's notion of utopia as the critique of ideology and future-oriented vision of counterworlds 'from nowhere' finds unexpected synergies with Castoriadis's understanding of creation 'out of nothing'.

HISTORY, TRADITION, AND THE HERMENEUTIC SPIRAL

As we have seen, Ricoeur raises the question of the French Revolution as a way of refuting Castoriadis's reductive understanding of produc-tion to a (re)combination of a fixed set of elements. As part of his counterargument, Ricoeur also introduces the problematic of continuity and discontinuity. He presents this by way of a critique of Foucault's understanding of absolute historical discontinuity to argue that 'when there is a break in one line, there is continuity in another' (7). Ricoeur acknowledges that he gives a 'certain primacy to the continuity of existence, to the perpetuation of a living-together as the ground for instituting operations', as it is that which 'allows us to situate the dis-continuities of sense against the continuities of existence' (7). But the question of continuity and discontinuity in history opens onto broader questions. To this end, we shall follow a short excerpt of the dialogue fairly closely, as it goes to the crux of their dispute.

Ricoeur argues in the dialogue that there are 'discontinuities of sense [*sens*] against the continuities of existence. There is a relation of sense and existence: it is on the level of sense that there can be ruptures, events, and emergences' (7). Castoriadis accepts Ricoeur's distinction between existence and meaning – at least, in the sense that continuity and discontinuity are evident in human history. The social-historical is the region of meaning par excellence in Castoriadis's ontology, and it is at this level that historical discontinuity appears.[11] Castoriadis illustrates the difference between discontinuity and continuity by drawing on the example of the (then) Ayatollah Khomeini and the modern West as discontinuous, '[o]therwise', he says, 'we are all talking bipeds; we live in established societies anchored in a shared Jewish past, that of the ·religions of the Book' (7). Note here that he is not merely talking about our biological continuity as 'talking bipeds' but also the shared history of monotheistic religion emanating from our 'shared Jewish past'. Then he goes on to argue: 'But the discontinuity, the cut, occurs on the level of sense [*sens*] – and is also accompanied with other cuts, the cutting of the hands and of other members for thieves and fornicators. This is something that we cannot accept and that we should condemn...' (7). He then adds: 'This discontinuity alone is what interests me' (7).[12] Thus, Castoriadis is particularly interested in a specific kind of historical discontinuity: the discontinuity of the Greco-European tradition of history – dating back to the Homeric poems – from the continuity of the monotheistic heritage and, more broadly, from other civilisational continuities. At the centre of Ricoeur's reflections, however, lies the dual conviction that humanity indeed proceeds via 'ruptures, discontinuities', but 'always within the order of configuration' (8). And in specific response to Castoriadis's foregrounding of ancient Greece, Ricoeur appends the following: 'If we have a great continuity, it is indeed the one that you have stated in which, through the fire, the root, the Greek trunk, we recognize ourselves within a certain continuity' (8). Castoriadis's response is succinct, 'But that is the case for us' (8), whereupon Ricoeur asserts, 'Yes, it is the case for us, and also for those who we call the other' (8).

To attain a fuller understanding of the above exchange, and the wider debates in which they are situated, it is helpful to go beyond the dialogue itself to key themes and issues that Castoriadis and Ricoeur were thinking about at the time. In broadening the space of reference, a submerged interchange becomes visible, which offers an alternative perspective on the central issues at stake in the dialogue proper. This 'unspoken' dialogue, as it were, centres on their different approaches to history and the human condition, more broadly. The frame of reference with which to understand continuity and discontinuity opens onto the human condition more broadly, on the one hand, and the question of our relation to the historical past becomes a question in its own right, on the other. These aspects become visible when key works contemporaneous to the dialogue, and to whose arguments Castoriadis and Ricoeur implicitly refer at crucial junctures, are taken into account. In Ricoeur's case, excerpts from two volumes of *Time and Narrative* are the most relevant. The first is the final chapter of Volume 3, entitled 'Towards a Hermeneutical Historical Consciousness' (1988), and the second is his discussion of *mimesis* in the first volume (Ricoeur 1984). For Castoriadis, the second seminar of *Ce qui fait la Grèce: D'Homère à Héraclite* (2004) – which he presented in 1982 at the *École des hautes études en sciences sociales* (EHESS) – is the most pertinent, with supplementation from 'The Greek Polis and the Creation of Democracy' (1997b), which he wrote in 1983 and summarises the themes of the lectures, and 'Heritage and Revolution' (2007a), which he first presented at a Hannah Arendt conference a few months after the radio dialogue with Ricoeur. With the exception of *Time and Narrative* (Volume 1; Ricoeur 1984), none of the other texts mentioned above were published at the time of the radio dialogue, and thus the other could not be aware of – let alone engage with – them.

Castoriadis

Let us begin with Castoriadis. What does he mean by his assertion that 'that is the case for us', exactly? Arguably, it signals an internal tension to Castoriadis's articulation of creation in history. Creation in history is social-historical, that is, anthropological. When the radio discussion ventures into the problematic of continuity/discontinuity in the creation of historical novelty, however, Castoriadis focuses on the historical tradition inaugurated by the ancient Greeks, which links directly to his understanding of the project of autonomy (which is girded by his underlying anthropology of the social-historical, but not reducible to it). Castoriadis understood the historical emergence of the project of autonomy as the 'twin birth' of philosophy (*la philosophie*) and politics (*la politique*) in the strong and explicit sense. This contrasts to their weaker – or, rather, anthropological – forms of 'the political' (*le politique*), as a dimension of all societies, and what I have argued elsewhere is appropriately characterised as 'the philosophical' (*le philosophique*), as a broader range of philosophical traditions that appear in a plurality of civilisational contexts (Adams 2011). In this vein, the internal tension between an anthropology of social-historical creation and the particular Greco-Western historical creation of the project of autonomy is such that we could say that Castoriadis introduces a third distinction between 'the historical' (*l'historique*), as a dimension of the social-historical and the human condition, writ large, and 'history', (*l'histoire*) in the strong sense as founded by the Greeks, which highlights the 'singularity' of the Greco-Western history and is tied to the project of autonomy. As Johann Arnason points out:

> [C]ivilizations vary greatly in regard to the potential for change and differentiation. To take a particularly pronounced example, the ancient Greek civilization of the polis was marked by a high level of transformative capacity and a great variety of resulting socio-political formations. These aspects are stressed in Castoriadis's interpretation of Greek history (2017, 29)

Thus, the Greek creation of *l'histoire* represents a rupture with the continuity of the human condition.

The subterranean discussion that can be reconstructed also concerns the question of creation of the historical tradition of autonomy – history in the strong sense – and our relation to such a history. Is it purely interpretative (i.e. concerning *understanding*), or is there a creative transformation that is wrought in us through the engagement with it, and its connection to a more general philosophical-sociological anthropology? When viewed from this perspective, the debate – on continuity and discontinuity – for Castoriadis, at least, concerns the level of social-historical creation *ex nihilo*, in general, and the ancient Greek creation of history (together with politics and philosophy) in the strong sense as the project of autonomy, and its meaning for us.

To expand on the distinction between Greco-Western history, in the strong sense, and the historical dimension of civilisations, more generally, I now turn to the second seminar in *Ce qui fait la Grèce*, Volume 1 (Castoriadis 2004). Castoriadis opens the seminar by posing questions concerning our interconnections with history. He asks, what kinds of relationships – other than passive – can we have with the past (Castoriadis 2004, 47)? Castoriadis explains that his own central preoccupation with history is to restore the significations and institutions (in which imaginary significations are incarnated), by means of which each society constitutes itself and its particular world as that society in its *singularity*, for example, ancient Hebrew society or contemporary French society, but not any other society (2004, 49). He briefly addresses a range of perspectives on history, but of most relevance for our present discussion is his portrayal of hermeneutics. He takes Gadamer's *Truth and Method* (2013 [1960]) as emblematic and focuses on the problematic of the hermeneutic circle (Castoriadis 2004, 51ff). Castoriadis casts the hermeneutic circle quite rightly as involving a pre-understanding (he uses the Heideggerian term) of the *interpretand*. The pre-understanding makes the text 'speak' in a certain way (2004, 51). The text, however, 'resists' and can speak in ways other than that imposed by the initial preconception, such that the initial interpretation can be modified, and so forth. Thus proceeds the hermeneutic circle. Castoriadis accepts the veracity and importance of the hermeneutic circle, and, shifting more broadly to religious hermeneutics in monotheistic contexts, even finds hermeneutic discourse to be 'rich and subtle' (2004, 53). The limitations of the hermeneutic approach, however, lie elsewhere for him. Castoriadis charges hermeneutics with being only concerned with isolated texts internal to a particular tradition. It is not self-evident, for Castoriadis, that such an approach would be as relevant for the study of a society; he regards the proper object of hermeneutics to be works (*les oeuvres*), and, notably, 'discursive works' (2004, 52). Castoriadis's approach to history (and to Greco-Western history, in particular) is irreducible to a 'simple interpretation of works' (2004, 52); rather, it is a 'project of total understanding' (2004, 52). The aim is not, however, only to understand its world (although that is part of it): It 'is not simply an interpretation, that is to say of a simply theoretical work: when we tackle the birth of democracy and philosophy, what is important ... is our own activity and our own transformation. And it is in this sense that the work which we do is perhaps a political work' (Castoriadis 2004, 52).[13]

Ancient Greece created an 'absolutely new project' (Castoriadis 2004, 53): to understand its own history in order to transform oneself (cf. Castoriadis 1997b, 268ff). And in this, Castoriadis sees the project of autonomy, and the discontinuity of history with world history, more broadly. It is a practical project of political transformation, not a theoretical exercise for the sake of understanding alone (with which he charges hermeneutics). Elsewhere, in a paper written a few months after the radio dialogue (thus, surely in part, in response to it), Castoriadis identifies the specific 'heritage' of the Greco-West as the democratic and revolutionary traditions, which is characterised by making, problematising, and changing our institutions (2007a, 106). Central to the 'singularity' of this tradition is thus the activity of critique, of unlimited interrogation, of *logon didonai* (1997b, 268; Castoriadis 2004). Thus, even though Castoriadis is elucidating a version of 'history as recounted', it remains ultimately subordinate to 'history as project', both in the sense of an orientation towards the future and as the transformative project of autonomy.

Let us return to Castoriadis's seminar on ancient Greece. After his brief comments on hermeneutics, he returns to the question of the hermeneutic circle. He agrees that there is, indeed, an element of (pre) understanding involved in the active relation that we have to ancient Greek history, but then the circle 'refracts' and 'multiplies', 'becoming something more and other than a circle' (2004, 52). Although he emphasises the particular case of ancient Greece, the refracting, multiplying hermeneutic circle has implications beyond Greco-Western history (I return to this). But Greece is a special case for Castoriadis, for it is 'our' history, and Greece created the possibility of comprehension in history as an 'absolutely new project' (2004, 53) of understanding history – history in the strong and explicit sense (*l'histoire*) in order to *transform oneself* (as politics in the strong sense of *la politique*). He forcefully differentiates the Greco-Western from the hermeneutic project (now expanded from Gadamer to include hermeneutic traditions within monotheistic religions; Ricoeur 2004, 53). Such traditions find radical limits in sacred texts that they cannot transgress. These limits are bound by the religious inability, on Castoriadis's account, to ask what he casts as a mandatory question concerning the *origin of meaning*. Thus, for him, there is a 'radical limit' which distinguishes a work of interpretation from the project of understanding as simultaneously radical and practical. For hermeneutics, the phenomenon of *meaning* (of the text, of pre-understanding) is to be 'disclosed' (again, he uses the Heideggerian term), not created. But this cannot account for the production of sense; it cannot account for the moment of creation (2004, 53). Elsewhere, Castoriadis refers to this as the 'circle of creation', which he illustrates in the following way:

> Did the Geek *politai* create the polis or the polis the *politai*? This is a meaningless question precisely because the *polis* could only have been

created by the action of human beings who were simultaneously transforming themselves into *politai.* (2007a, 113)

Gadamer did not, indeed, examine the creative moment of hermeneutics, but Castoriadis considered only Gadamer in these seminars. What
happens when Ricoeur is reintroduced into the mix?

Ricoeur

The question of the interplay of historical continuity and discontinuity is
more significant for Ricoeur's intellectual project than for Castoriadis.
As noted above, Ricoeur argues in the dialogue for the discontinuity of
meaning (*sens*) against the continuity of existence. While recognising the
discontinuity of history, his approach 'gives a certain primary to the
continuity of existence, to the perpetuation of a living-together as
the ground for instituting operations, and that allows us to situate the
discontinuities of sense against the continuities of existence. There is a
relation of sense and existence: it is on the level of sense that there can
be ruptures, events, and emergences' (7).

This 'open dialectic' appears at different levels in Ricoeur's
thought. It can be seen in, for example, his distinction between the
human condition writ large and the human condition in modernity.
In this vein, his philosophical anthropology is 'aimed at identifying the most enduring features of [our] temporal condition ... those
which are the least vulnerable to the vicissitudes of the modern age'
(Ricoeur 1983, 60), where institutional and cultural change certainly
occurs but has been 'over-evaluated' in light of historicism (and other
theoretical trends). This stands in contrast to Castoriadis's emphasis
on political change as ongoing, active, and explicit (e.g. Castoriadis
2007a, 105). In *Time and Narrative* (Volume 3), Ricoeur expands on
this point:

> [T]he very reception of the historical past by present consciousness ...
> seems to require the continuity of a common memory, and because, on the
> other hand, the documentary revolution brought about by the new history
> seems to make breaks, ruptures, crises, and the irruption of changes in
> thinking – in short, discontinuity – prevail. (1988, 217)

Where Castoriadis emphasises history in the strong sense as a future-
oriented project of change, creativity, and political transformation,

Ricoeur is more interested in highlighting the enduring features (of the political dimension) of the human condition, such as the family, politics, religion, violence, and sovereignty, although he allows, following Husserl, for their 'imaginative variation'. For Ricoeur, the entanglement of continuity and discontinuity occurs as events within the order of history. In this way, the French Revolution, as we have seen, must be understood both in continuity with the *Ancien régime* and in discontinuity as the emergence of new modes of action and power. But continuity and discontinuity in a particular current of history play out at a different level than that noted above (i.e. between his philosophical anthropology and modern history).

Let us recall (and extend) Castoriadis's questions concerning our relation to history, and then consider Ricoeur's response. The questions are: What is our relation to history (as recounted)? Can it be something other than passive? What kind of insight does the hermeneutic circle provide in this regard? The following reflections are organised around three aspects: first, consideration of 'traditionality' as elucidated in *Time and Narrative* Volume 3 (Ricoeur 1988); second, incorporation of Ricoeur's refiguring of the hermeneutic circle into the hermeneutic spiral of *mimesis* in the first volume of *Time and Narrative* (Ricoeur 1984); and, third, discussion of his notion of 'retroaction'. In the final chapter of *Time and Narrative*, Ricoeur aims to rework and deepen Gadamer's hermeneutic notion of *Wirkungsgeschichte* as historically effected consciousness (Ricoeur 1988, 217), as the interplay of *effective history* and our *being-affected-by this effectiveness* (1988, 224) in order to clarify his understanding of tradition. But 'being-affected' is neither purely receptive nor purely passive. Rather, Ricoeur argues, to the contrary (and in rejection of Foucault's position), that only an understanding of history as living and open has the capacity of 'joining together vigorous political action and the "memory" of snuffed out or repressed possibilities from the past' (1988, 219). Ricoeur's rearticulation of 'tradition' in this third volume is itself a refinement of his earlier intervention in the Gadamer–Habermas debate. In *Time and Narrative*, Ricoeur articulates a threefold understanding of 'traditionality' as a living, underdetermined current of history.

Ricoeur (1988, 211) draws on Koselleck's argument on the 'temporalization of history' in modernity as his starting point. The concept of *Geschichte* brings together the twofold characteristics of history in modernity as a *project to be made* and as the *past to be recounted*

(1988, 209, 212). Following Koselleck, Ricoeur reconfigures these as the 'space of experience' and 'horizon of expectation' as philosophical anthropological transcendentals (Ricoeur 1988, 208, 213–14; see also Koselleck 2004 [1985]). They meet in an 'imperfect meditation' of the present. Three *topoi* characterise the temporalisation of history in modernity: new times, the acceleration of history, and the mastery of history, which alter the interplay of the space of experience and the horizon of expectation (1988, 212–14). When all three *topoi* are taken together, Ricoeur argues that the temporality of modernity irrevocably alters our access to the historical past. They 'contributed to the unfolding of a new horizon of expectation that by a kind of recoil effect transformed the space of experience within which the acquisitions of the past are deposited' (Ricoeur 1988, 210). This transformation is surely, however, an implicit acknowledgement of the fundamental change – the profound rupture – that the modern human condition wrought on an understanding of anthropos that emphasises continuity.

The future-oriented temporalisation of history, with its accent on human action as history-to-be-made – the theme of mastering history, as taken up by Foucault, for example, and by extension, Castoriadis – tends to neglect that we are also *affected by* history: '[I]t is precisely this tie between historical action and a received past, which we did not make, that preserves the dialectical relation between our horizon of expectation and our space of experience' (Ricoeur 1988, 213). An important part of what Ricoeur is trying to do is to rearticulate the past similarly as we understand the future, that is, as more open and contingent – as an *underdetermined* realm of meaning (as discussed above) – instead of 'unequivocally closed' (1988, 216).

Ricoeur makes clear that he wants to avoid reducing human receptivity to the efficacy of history to the notion of tradition that was proposed in the Gadamer–Habermas debate. Instead, he articulates a tripartite notion of tradition: traditionality, traditions, tradition. This speaks to the pre-understandings that we bring to the hermeneutic circle. Traditionality comprises a core feature of the temporality of history, alongside the space of experience and horizon of expectation; it comprises a dialectic internal to experience between 'the efficacity of the past that we undergo and the reception of the past that we bring about' (Ricoeur 1988, 220), as a process of mediation between remoteness and distanciation. The formal condition of traditionality opens onto Ricoeur's central problematic: the tension between the horizon of the past and that of the present. For Ricoeur, it signifies that temporal distance from the past is not a 'dead interval'; instead, it generates meaning. He tells us that, 'before being an inert deposit, tradition is an operation that can only make sense dialectically through the exchange between the interpreted past and the interpreting present' (1988, 221).

Traditionality opens onto the second aspect: *traditions*, in the plural. This middle characteristic resonates with Ricoeur's critique of Castoriadis's stance towards creation/production, and continuity and discontinuity. It means that we can never be 'absolute innovators' but rather are always first 'heirs' to particular historical traditions (Ricoeur 1988, 221). Here, however, his linguistification of the imagination comes to the fore, for traditionality has its roots in the 'language-like structure of communication' (Ricoeur 1988, 221). At this point, Ricoeur links his analysis of traditions to *mimesis1* in its 'reference to the primordial aspect of action as being symbolically mediated' (1988, 221), where action through the structuring activity of emplotment is understood as a text. Ricoeur can be seen to provide a response to Castoriadis's charge that hermeneutics is primarily the study of texts, not societies and their imaginary significations. Ricoeur notes that historiography in great part depends on texts that provide the past with a 'documentary status. It is in this way that the understanding of texts inherited from the past can be set up, with all the necessary reservations, as a kind of exemplary experience as regards every relation to the past' (1988, 222).

With the consideration of the third variety of traditionality – *tradition*, in the singular – Ricoeur reconsiders the problematic that invited his intervention in the Gadamer–Habermas debate (1988, 222ff). Foregrounded here are the question of meaning and its connection to truth – that draws on modes of belief – which confer reasonableness on the threefold *plaidoyer* for prejudice, authority, and tradition. Gadamer introduces his notion of consciousness in its encounter with effective history. The prejudged for Gadamer becomes a structure of the pre-understanding 'outside of which the "thing itself" cannot make itself heard' (Ricoeur 1988, 223). Authority is at play as the claim to truth augments simple 'meaning'. In the reception of a particular tradition, it is a matter of the 'recognition of superiority' rather than of 'blind obedience'; this brings it close to Hegel's *Sittlichkeit*. Gadamer's analysis of 'method' is a reminder that we are immersed in a traditional truth claim before we can subject that to critical inspection. Thus, Gadamer's notion of 'historical research' holds an implicit moment of critique. The second moment of critique – distanciation – allows for the critique of ideologies (understood as rival traditions) (Ricoeur 1988, 224).

Thus, Ricoeur's reconfiguration of tradition articulates a living connection that presupposes the underdetermined, open dimension of history as recounted to be met in the present to make the future as history as project. It allows for the interplay of reflexive critique and the productive aspect of interpretation as undergirding our pre-understanding as we traverse the hermeneutic circle. It also links up to his discussion of the spiral of *mimesis* in the first volume of *Time and Narrative*. Importantly, for present purposes, although for Ricoeur, the hermeneutic circle is focussed on texts, it is also meant to hold good for practical life as well, as the domain of the social imaginary. The social imaginary, especially as the ideological imaginary, continues to haunt Ricoeur's thought on narrative and history, although it is no longer a central focus. But the symbolic mediation of action that is central to *mimesis* is anchored in social imaginary contexts. Ricoeur's account of traditionality and being-affected by history deepens the hermeneutic spiral he articulated via *mimesis*. In brief, *mimesis1* refers to the prefiguration of the field of action, which Ricoeur enunciates in formal terms via three features, structural, temporal, and symbolic (1984, 54ff), which are then brought from the virtual to the actual realm of discourse/action as and via narrative. Of interest here is that the *circle of mimesis* is prefigured in symbolically mediated contexts of action, where symbols 'understood as interpretants, provide the rules of meaning as a function of which this or that behaviour can be interpreted' (Ricoeur 1984, 58). The symbolic webs are themselves anchored in historical traditions, and together they provide the context of our pre-understanding. *Mimesis2* refers to the configuration of the field of action via emplotment (as per the example of the French Revolution, above) as the work of the productive imagination; the mediation of events into a meaningful narrative order and temporal signification; this activity, too, stands in living traditions of pre-understandings and historically effected consciousness, and bears similarity to the interplay of *chaos* and *kosmos* (as a beautiful order and ordering) that was important for Castoriadis's thought. *Mimesis3* provides the 'reader' with the opportunity to integrate the imaginative worlds of *mimesis2* into their own lived experience – this is the transformative aspect, but is more muted, as George Taylor (2015) rightly observes, than the arguments in, for example, the function of fiction in shaping reality or in myths as opening new worlds.

There is a further issue with the act of reading belonging to a 'self' or 'agent' which seems to rule out more collective experiences of refiguration but which would be important to reconstruct for a deeper understanding of the social world. It is pertinent in this context that Ricoeur announced the importance from shifting from the hermeneutic circle to the hermeneutic spiral at the end of the *Lectures on Ideology and Utopia* (1986), thus reminding us of its importance for sociality of life, which the literary emphasis in *mimesis3* tends to obscure. As ideology and utopia are not reducible to the agent/self, the emphasis on the hermeneutic spiral in the practical, social realm of life allows for its development in a way that deepens its collective, social dimension. Ricoeur contends,

> It is too simple response, though, to keep the dialectic [between ideology and utopia] running. My more ultimate answer is that we must let ourselves be drawn into the circle and then must try to make the circle a spiral. (Ricoeur 1986, 312)

Arguably, both Castoriadis and Ricoeur reject the image of the hermeneutic circle and have elucidated different versions of the hermeneutic spiral. Despite the differences, their respective account of the hermeneutic spiral anchor it in a theory of meaning and the practical social world of doing. As a spiral, the hermeneutic circle is no longer just about understanding; it also incorporates critical and productive/creative dimensions, although Castoriadis and Ricoeur articulate – and emphasise – the interplay of these dimensions differently. Where Castoriadis prioritises change, creation, explicit critique/interrogation, and the singularity of the Greek historical tradition of autonomy, ultimately remaining focused on history as project, Ricoeur deepens the hermeneutic elements of history as recounted not only to relativise the focus on the openness of the future, but also to impart an understanding of tradition in the dynamism and creativity while incorporating the element of critique. We saw that Castoriadis argued that the hermeneutic circle 'refracted' and became something other than a circle. The image of the hermeneutic spiral offers a fruitful way forward in reflecting on such refractions. It should be noted however that spirals are not predetermined to travel in an upward direction: A new interpretation is not necessarily a 'higher' interpretation, but its novelty is irreducible to the retracing of the previous 'loop'. The spiral is not even unidirectional; rather, it can refract into multiple directions and mutate into multiple spirals. The idea of the spiral is to open new frontiers, not to be bound to hierarchical modes of thinking.

CONCLUSIONS AND BEGINNINGS: TRAVERSING THE HERMENEUTIC SPIRAL ANEW

This essay has considered Castoriadis and Ricoeur's respective approaches to creation and historical discontinuity as these themes emerged in the dialogue. But it took hermeneutical detours of its own, in order to place these themes in a wider context. Through a consideration of the chaos metaphor, it argued that their respective accounts of history – and the possibility of creation in history – are girt by the underdetermination of meaning, which is fundamentally linked to the mode of being of the creative-productive imagination; this forms the precondition for both the hermeneutic spiral and historical novelty. The focus on the underdetermination of meaning allows Castoriadis to emphasise the 'out of nothing' and Ricoeur to focus on the 'from something'. For both Castoriadis and Ricoeur, history – and our relation to history – is living and active. History is not an inert deposit. For Ricoeur, western history emerges from the intercivilisational encounter of Athens and Jerusalem; for Castoriadis, it appears as the strong version of the Greco-Western inauguration of *l'histoire*. But where Castoriadis wants to argue for the specificity of the Greco-Western trajectory, Ricoeur wants to expand such competencies (such as an active relation to history) to the human condition. Both thinkers demonstrate that we are affected by the efficacy of history; it is not a passive relationship. However, for Castoriadis, it is more explicitly political, more directly transformative, whereas for Ricoeur's richly hermeneutic approach, the transformation is always mediated and indirect, and the extent of the transformation is more measured – or even muted. For Castoriadis, history (*l'histoire*) is primarily understood as history as project, even when he considers its 'recounted' aspects. But for Ricoeur, in *Time and Narrative*, at least, the opposite would appear to be the case. Where Castoriadis emphasises change, creation, and discontinuity, Ricoeur clearly prefers to emphasise overarching lines of continuity internal not only to history but also to the broader interplay of history with the human condition (this is, however, at least in part attributable to what he judges as the overestimation of change in modernity). Castoriadis wants to emphasise the singularity of the Greco-Western tradition of autonomy (as the strong and explicit instauration of history, politics, and philosophy) as a rupture of – and thus discontinuity with – the human condition; he also wishes to emphasise that this 'potentiality of a potentiality' becomes part of the anthropic inheritance more broadly: Potentialities as the 'essence' of the human condition are self-created; this emphasises the anthropic capacity for change. Ricoeur's hermeneutical emphasis on continuity can obscure the significance of world historical ruptures/creation, while Castoriadis's refusal to recognise the interpretative aspect of historical creation and social imaginary significations needlessly closes down, for example, investigations into intercultural versions of autonomy beyond the Greco-Western tradition and the underdetermination of history as recounted to interrogate present and future worlds, and, in so doing, the formation of critical counterworlds.

Thus, overall, their primary disagreement appears to be less about their differing approaches to creation and production, but more to their commitment to and emphasis on the human capacity for change and radical sociopolitical transformation. An alternative approach, such as Blumenberg's recognition that some (philosophical and/or political) questions from a particular historical epoch continue to inform succeeding epochs, could allow for a greater emphasis on social change, but would also require recognition of the hermeneutical basis of the social imaginary. These differences notwithstanding, both Ricoeur and Castoriadis converged on innovative and distinctive approaches to the hermeneutic spiral, as a development of the hermeneutic circle that incorporates not only interpretation and critique, but also creation.

In traversing a single loop of the hermeneutic spiral, new spirals emerge. To deepen the argument presented in this essay, further aspects would need to be taken into account. For example, in what relation does the movement between the 'strange' and the 'familiar', which is the touchstone of hermeneutics and hermeneutic transformations, also rely on its historical discovery with the ancient Greeks, which was Castoriadis's claim? If the 'social' as understood by Ricoeur is primarily intersubjective, or trans-subjective (as the unmotivated movement of the anonymous collective), when viewed through a Castoriadian lens, is there a need to elucidate an intermediate level of sociality to take better account of the collective reflexivity and 'willing' (the activity of willing something) that was inaugurated by the project of autonomy?

Finally, Ricoeur's account of history recounted and history as project also draws on a notion of *retroaction*. In deepening the hermeneutical aspect of 'history recounted', the idea of retroaction points to the under-determination of meaning. In the radio dialogue, Ricoeur raises the question of retroaction repeatedly, but Castoriadis does not pursue it, even though arguably, he recognises the hermeneutic status of retroaction in the reactivation of the project of autonomy in modernity. At one juncture in the dialogue, Ricoeur characterises retroaction as

> [t]he successive forms in which the past, which you yourself character-ized as the inexhaustible, has been revived and reinterpreted themselves contained potential and incompleteness. And through a sort of retroaction of our new creations on the old moments, we can deliver possibilities that had been prevented.... And this unemployed, repressed potential is something that each new creation somehow delivers retroactively. (11)

An earlier articulation of retroaction is found in *The Symbolism of Evil* (Ricoeur 1967, 21–2), where Ricoeur argues that the underdetermined, and openness of the meaning of history – recounted in conjunction with cultural memory and intercivilisational encounters – is central to our understanding of the present. In *Time and Narrative* (Volume 3), Ricoeur expands the discussion on retroaction, strengthened, perhaps, by Koselleck's own usage of the term (1988, 209).[14] In *Time and Narrative*, it is connected to the underdetermined realm of history and tradition, but not to cultural memory, as it was in *The Symbolism of Evil*. Ricoeur's emphasis in *Time and Narrative* is to demonstrate that retroaction presumes the openness, the underdetermination of history that influences our gestalt of the present:

> To do this we must struggle against the tendency to consider the past only from the angle of what is done, unchangeable, and past. We have to reo-pen the past, to revivify its unaccomplished, cut-off – even slaughtered – possibilities. In short, when confronted with the adage that the future is open and contingent in every respect but that the past is unequivocally closed and necessary, we have to make our expectations more determinate and our experience less so. For these are two faces of one and the same task, for only determinate expectations can have the retroactive effect on the past of revealing it as a living tradition. (Ricoeur 1988, 216)

As noted above, in the dialogue, the notion of 'retroaction' was important for Ricoeur as a way to open up contexts of meaning in history as recounted and bring it into play with the present through cultural memory. Although retroaction was not a central theme of Ricoeur's thought, it opens onto interesting debates within tradition, memory, and civilisations. Most recently, Jan Assmann has developed the idea of cultural memory. For Assmann (2015), culture is twofold. It refers, first, to the accumulation and expansion of knowledge across historical generations that enable humanity to transcend its natural limitations. Its second sense is as a 'meaning-producing institution' that relates specifically to memory and recourse, which

> lead to a specifically human form of temporal orientation that tran-
> scends the limits of one's own span of life in both directions ... The
> cultural forms and institutions of social memory keep the dead present
> in the life of a group and maintain the contact between the living and
> the dead. It is this form of memory that provides meaning and orienta-
> tion in a wider, even multi-millennial temporal dimension. (Assmann
> 2015, 327)

Distinctive to Assmann's approach is his rethinking of *tradition* via cultural memory, which allows for greater emphasis on historical experience and its interpretation. The rethinking of tradition via cultural memory is hinted at in Ricoeur's work, but not systematically pursued. Cultural memory is, moreover, instituted in various ways in forms of relative closure or openness. For Castoriadis, critique and critical reflection is 'breaking open the closure' – or, in Ricoeurian terms from an earlier phase in his thought, the 'shattering' effects of utopia (see Taylor 2017). A further delineation of cultural mem-ory, which we might call 'cultural recollection', is required here, to make sense of the critical aspect of the retroaction of history as recounted. Ricoeur does not incorporate a critical aspect to recol-lection, but Dmitri Nikulin's (2017) distinction between collective memory and collective recollection is helpful here.[15] In sum, unlike collective memory, collective recollection is critical and participa-tory (and therefore potentially democratic). This critical aspect – in Castoriadis's terms, in its twofold aspect of the *logon didonai* and unlimited interrogation – sharpens the notion of cultural memory/ tradition in relation not only to retroaction but also to the project of history.

ACKNOWLEDGEMENT

I would like to thank Erin Carlisle for her sterling work in copy-editing this essay. I would also like to thank Johann Arnason for his comments on the chaos section, and George Taylor for his help in locating the 'hermeneutic spiral' in Ricoeur's oeuvre.

NOTES

1. Unless otherwise specified, all page numbers refer to the radio dialogue (from chapter 1).

2. For a discussion of Ricoeur and Castoriadis on their respective approaches to institutions and the social imaginary, see Michel (2014) and Amalric (chapter 4). For a discussion of Castoriadis's approach to institutions, see Arnason (2014b).

3. See Dosse (chapter 6) for a discussion of the importance of the imagination for Castoriadis and Ricoeur's respective theories of history; Amalric (2013) for the most comprehensive account of the imagination in Ricoeur's thought; and Arnason (2014a) for a succinct discussion of the creative imagination in Castoriadis's work.

4. I have discussed this at length elsewhere. See, for example, Adams (2005; 2011).

5. I take this up elsewhere in the context of Ricoeur's general theory of culture. See Adams (2015). See also Helenius (2015) for an alternative approach to Ricoeur's hermeneutics of culture.

6. But also see Taylor's essay in this volume, which argues that, in his imagination lectures, Ricoeur is closer to an understanding of 'creation' not 'production'. See Taylor (chapter 2).

7. See Jean-Luc Amalric's essay in this volume for a more extensive discussion of this issue (chapter 4).

8. *Time and Narrative*, Volume 3, was first published in November 1988.

9. Any comparative discussion of Ricoeur's and Castoriadis's theories of meaning would need to include consideration of the following: the symbolic and the imaginary dimensions of meaning and their interplay; the role of movement, institutions, and action as contexts and bearers of meaning; the phenomenological question of the world and its significance for a theory of meaning; the historicity of meaning (history as project, history as recounted, and retroactive meaning); the question of the 'meaning of meaning', often taken up via Frege's classic account of sense and reference; meaning as interpretative and meaning as generative; the connections between meaning and power; and meaning as

figurative and tropic, to name but the key issues. Such a discussion should not obscure the differences between Ricoeur's and Castoriadis's approaches. These include, for example, Ricoeur's linguistification of the imagination and Castoriadis's focus on meaning in institutions, Ricoeur's positing of a split reference and Castoriadis's account of core social imaginary significations as not having any referent, and Ricoeur's intersubjective understanding of the social, but Castoriadis's trans-subjective elucidation of the social. Any such discussion would further need to reconstruct the shifts and changes – and internal tensions – in each thinker's respective trajectories in relation to their theories of meaning – from Castoriadis's shift away from the symbolic and doing (see, e.g., Adams 2011) in his articulation of social imaginary significations, and Ricoeur's developing account, from the symbols to metaphor to narrative, but also his shift in thinking the productive–creative imagination from the time of the 'Imagination Lectures' and the 'Ideology and Utopia' lectures (both from 1975) to *Time and Narrative* (in the early-mid 1980s) and beyond. For an illuminating discussion of such issues in Ricoeur's thought, see Taylor (2015).

10. See Ricoeur (1976) for a discussion of symbols and metaphors, especially the final section – 'Intermediate degrees between symbol and metaphor' – of chapter 3.

11. For Castoriadis, ontological discontinuity is also evident in the self-creation of new modes of being.

12. Both Castoriadis and Ricoeur reject discontinuity in the Foucaultian sense. See Ricoeur and Castoriadis (chapter 1, p. 6 ff).

13. All translations from *Ce qui fait la Grèce* are my own.

14. Ricoeur does not discuss it however in *Memory, History, and Forgetting* (2004).

15. Nikulin has written extensively on 'recollection', including on the difference between memory and recollection in the ancients. In the present context, his articulation of 'collective recollection' as a response to Halbwachs is of particular interest (Nikulin 2017).

REFERENCES

Adams, Suzi. 2005. 'Interpreting Creation: Castoriadis and the Birth of Autonomy'. *Thesis Eleven* 83:1: 25–41.

———. 2011. *Castoriadis's Ontology: Being and Creation.* New York: Fordham University Press.

———. 2015. 'On Ricoeur's Shift from a Hermeneutics of Culture to a Cultural Hermeneutics'. *Études Ricoeuriennes/Ricoeur Studies* 15:2: 130–53.

Amalric, Jean-Luc. 2013. *Paul Ricoeur, L'imagination Vive: Une Genèse de La Philosophie Ricoeurienne de L'imagination.* Paris: Éditions Hermann.

Arnason, Johann P. 2014a. 'Creative Imagination'. In *Cornelius Castoriadis: Key Concepts*. Edited by Suzi Adams, 43–52. London: Bloomsbury.

———. 2014b. 'Institution'. In *Cornelius Castoriadis: Key Concepts*. Edited by Suzi Adams, 101–6. London: Bloomsbury.

———. 2017. 'Hans Blumenberg: The Philosopher in the Middle of History'. *Social Imaginaries* 3:1: 13–39.

Assmann, Jan. 2015. 'Memory and Culture'. In *Memory: A History*. Edited by Dmitri Nikulin, 325–49. Oxford, UK: Oxford University Press.

Castoriadis, Cornelius. 1987 [1975]. *The Imaginary Institution of Society*. Translated by Katherine Blamey. Cambridge, UK: Polity Press.

———. 1997a. 'Done and to Be Done'. In *The Castoriadis Reader*. Translated and edited by David Ames Curtis, 361–416. Oxford, UK: Blackwell.

———. 1997b. 'The Greek Polis and the Creation of Democracy'. In *The Castoriadis Reader*. Translated and edited by David Ames Curtis, 267–89. Oxford, UK: Blackwell.

———. 2004. *Ce qui fait la Grèce, Volume 1: Séminaires 1982–1983. D'Homère à Héraclite. La création humaine II*. Edited by Pierre Vidal-Naquet. Paris: Seuil.

———. 2007a. 'Heritage and Revolution'. In *Figures of the Thinkable*. Edited by David Ames Curtis, 105–17. Stanford, CA: Stanford University Press.

———. 2007b. 'Imaginary and Imagination at the Crossroads'. In *Figures of the Thinkable*. Edited by David Ames Curtis, 71–90. Stanford, CA: Stanford University Press.

———. 2007c. 'True and False Chaos'. In *Figures of the Thinkable*. Edited by David Ames Curtis, 236–44. Stanford, CA: Stanford University Press.

Gadamer, Hans-Georg. 2013 [1960]. *Truth and Method*. Translated by Joel Weinsheimer and Donald G. Marshall. London: Bloomsbury.

Helenius, Timo. 2015. 'Between Receptivity and Productivity: Paul Ricoeur on Cultural Imagination'. *Social Imaginaries* 1:2: 32–52.

Koselleck, Reinhardt. 2004 [1985]. *Futures Past: On the Semantics of Historical Time*. New York: Columbia University Press.

Michel, Johann. 2014. *Ricoeur and the Post-Structuralists: Bourdieu, Derrida, Deleuze, Foucault, Castoriadis*. Translated by Scott Davidson. London: Rowman & Littlefield International.

Nikulin, Dmitri. 2017. 'Collective Memory: Maurice Halbwachs'. In *Routledge Handbook of Philosophy of Memory*. Edited by Sven Bernecker and Kourken Michaelian, Chapter 44. London: Routledge.

Ricoeur, Paul. 1967. *The Symbolism of Evil*. New York: Harper & Row.

———. 1976. *Interpretation Theory: Discourse and the Surplus of Meaning*. Fort Worth: Texas Christian University Press.

———. 1983. 'Action, Story, and History: On Re-Reading the Human Condition'. *Salmagundi* 60: 60–72.

————. 1984. *Time and Narrative* (Volume 1). Translated by Kathleen McLaughlin and David Pellauer. Chicago, IL: University of Chicago Press.

————. 1985. *Time and Narrative* (Volume 2). Translated by Kathleen McLaughlin and David Pellauer. Chicago, IL: University of Chicago Press.

————. 1986. *Lectures on Ideology and Utopia.* Edited by George H. Taylor. New York: Columbia University Press.

————. 1988. *Time and Narrative* (Volume 3). Translated by Kathleen McLaughlin and David Pellauer. Chicago, IL: University of Chicago Press.

————. 1998. 'Science and Ideology'. In *Hermeneutics and the Human Sciences.* Translated and edited by John B. Thompson, 222–46. Cambridge, UK: Cambridge University Press.

————. 2004. *Memory, History, Forgetting.* Translated by Kathleen Blamey and David Pellauer. Chicago, IL: University of Chicago Press.

Taylor, George H. 2015. 'Prospective Political Identity'. In *Paul Ricoeur in the Age of Hermeneutical Reason: Poetics, Praxis and Critique.* Edited by Roger W. H. Savage, 123–36. New York: Lexington Books.

————. 2017. 'Delineating Ricoeur's Concept of Utopia'. *Social Imaginaries* 3:1: 41–60.

Chapter Six

The Social Imaginary as Engine of History in Ricoeur and Castoriadis

François Dosse

The dimension of the imagination is essential to the work of Ricoeur and Castoriadis, each in their own way.[1] In the first sentences of his introduction to an anthology of the works of Ricoeur, Michael Foessel emphasises the difficulty of defining Ricoeur's philosophy by one central theme due to its abundance of ideas. He identifies, however, a possible thematic unit centred on the question of the imagination. 'It is through the works of the *imagination* that we can reconstruct our sense of the human experience' (Foessel 2007, 8). If Ricoeur did not achieve a poetic of will, as announced in his major thesis, he progresses towards this in his subsequent works, in which he unceasingly stresses the need to rehabilitate in philosophy the dimension of what is imaginary, linking it to other dimensions of human existence and unfolds it on each occasion as a form of action: 'The imagination is the means through which meaning is understood, the world speaks and action is performed. These are the three powers of the imaginary that the philosophy of Ricoeur exhibits masterfully' (Foessel 2007, 10). This idea is in close proximity with that of Castoriadis, who places the radical imagination at the level of the individual and social imagination at the collective level at the heart of the social-historical. Both find themselves breaking away from the Marxian understanding of the imaginary as being relegated to ideological distortions of the superstructure. For Ricoeur and Castoriadis, everything originates in the social imaginary, which constitutes the fundamental background of *praxis*.

DUAL DISCONTENT REGARDING INHERITED THOUGHT ABOUT THE IMAGINARY

Ricoeur's conviction that action is only known and understood indirectly, through mediation, is re-encountered in his treatment of the question of imagination. Images, symbols, and myths play the role of mediators through which access to the ontological dimension of human action can be gained. To underpin this mediating function of the imagination, Ricoeur leans on the decisive contribution of Kant, which he considers a turning point in the history of thought regarding the imagination: 'The essential breakthrough towards a modern philosophy of imagination is to be found in the work of Kant. For him, the problem of imagination as the production of images prevails over imagery as a reproduction of things' (Ricoeur 1974, 9). He thus breaks with a philosophical tradition which, until that point, positioned the imagination on the side of a force whose existence is certainly recognised, but which is considered as being deceptive and misleading to reason, which must dominate it and tame it so as to better abate it. For Kant, the imagination supersedes image and becomes inseparable from the question of doing, from that of productivity. It is striking to note that Kant also represents for Castoriadis a similarly decisive, fundamental break. According to Castoriadis, the dimension of the imaginary could not emerge from purgatory before Kant and his discovery of transcendental imagination in *The Critique of Pure Reason*. However, this release remains incomplete, as Kant neglects his discovery and confines the imagination to the domain of the senses. 'The imagination of which Kant speaks is a secondary imagination' (Castoriadis 2008a, 277). Castoriadis, nonetheless, recognises great merit in the Kantian conception of imagination for having put forward the idea of a schematisation of mediation between categories and sensory data. Furthermore, the imagination is also present in *The Critique of Judgement*, linked to the creation of a work of art.

Ricoeur similarly distanced himself from the narrow conception of objectivity formulated by Kant. The Kantian simplification allows conceptualisation of the mediation that exists between understanding and the sensory, but pure imagination has no 'for itself'. By highlighting a new form of imaginative mediation, Ricoeur suggests a way out of this aporia. 'When Ricoeur underlines the fact that sentiment conjointly operates a *schematisation* of our vital tendencies and a *schematisation* of our aspiration to reason, it is possible to interpret this schematisation of human duality as a work of the imagination' (Amalric 2013, 208). The sentiment that operates this mediation does not pertain to the representation of an object or of a symbol, but rather to the relation between self and others, between self and the world. In situating the act of freedom in the potentialities of the imagination, Ricoeur meets with Sartre's (2004) contemporaneous vision of the imaginary. Sartre's contribution is to link the imagination with the exercise of freedom, given that, in order for the individual consciousness to imagine, it must visualise an absent or unreal object. 'According to Sartre, the consciousness is capable of escaping the world, because unlike things that are "in the middle of the world," the individual consciousness is a "being of the world," capable of extracting itself from the existing present and the given, by denying it' (Amalric 2013, 269–70). In Ricoeur's eyes, the merit of Sartre's philosophy lies in the central place it confers upon the imagination. For Sartre, the imagination holds the capacity to release mankind's freedom, thus concentrating consciousness, in its entirety, on the task of undertaking its own liberation.

At the same time, Sartre does not, however, carry his reasoning on the function of the imagination to its conclusion, as he limits its function to its potential to negate. According to Ricoeur, he fails to acknowledge the overriding purpose of the imagination, its function of mediation. Ricoeur considers that, in limiting his approach to the reproductive function of the imaginary, Sartre is ultimately retreating from the Kantian conception that insists on its productive function. Sartre extends to the imagination a philosophical tradition which confers primacy to perception and for which the imagination plays only a derivative and degraded role next to what is considered as true thought, reason. 'The image carries in itself a spurious persuasive power which comes from the ambiguity of its nature' (Sartre 2004, 120). Sartre considers the act of imagination as an act that has its place in the register of magic, moving it to a secondary place behind the noble act of philosophical understanding. According to Ricoeur, the disparagement Sartre casts on imaginative potentiality stems from his having failed to recognise a capacity for mediation between the visible and the invisible within imagination and he thus remains imprisoned within the sphere of perception.

Ricoeur, on the other hand, insists on the creative capacity of the imagination, including the mediation of the symbol, which 'induces thought' as it manifests a capacity in the productive imagination.[2]

'Unlike the two other modalities of the symbol, hierophanic and oneiric, the poetic symbol shows us expressivity in its nascent stage. In poetry the symbol is caught at the moment when it is a welling up of language' (Ricoeur 1967, 13–14). Dissatisfied by the manner in which Sartre accounts for an imaginary reduced to its function of 'nihalation', Ricoeur turns to Gaston Bachelard, who allows the imagination to be linked not with perception, but with linguistic capacity and semantic innovation. For Bachelard, the poetic image 'places us at the origin of the speaking being' (1994, xix). Bachelard's poetic is situated on the side of symbolism's creative productivity, of its inventive power. Ricoeur thus intends to go beyond the limitations that Kant attributes to the imagination, namely that it is a component of a rationalisation upon which it is conditional. Furthermore, the subjectification of the problem of the imagination in Kant prevents one from attributing any ontological impact to the imagination. These failings encourage Ricoeur to turn to Bachelard: 'The most interesting part of the Bachelardian theory of the imagination is that it leads us instead to see in images a production at once *original* because it is the source of innovation, and *originating*, because it truly corresponds to the creation of a new being' (Amalric 2013, 346). Indeed, according to Bachelard, perceptive reality does not precede imagination, which 'is in the human psyche the very experience of *opening* and *newness*'. What becomes important with Bachelard is what he refers to as 'the realism of irreality' (Bachelard 1988, 5). Ricoeur thus identifies in Bachelard a solid platform from which to show that the symbol not only suggests thought,[3] but is also the bearer of what gives meaning and therefore ontological impact, as demonstrated by Ricoeur in *The Symbolism of Evil* (1967).

The position affirmed by Ricoeur in 1960 in *The Symbolism of Evil* converges with the parallel evolution of Merleau-Ponty concerning the imagination and the critical distance that he expresses towards Sartre's conception in his last works presented in *The Visible and the Invisible* (Merleau-Ponty 1968). Both challenge the radical division which Sartre institutes between perception and imagination, leading him to see the imagination as no more than a 'non-being'. The perceptive experience studied in his *Phenomenology of Perception* becomes 'perceptual faith' in *The Visible and the Invisible*: 'For us, the "perceptual faith" includes everything that is given to the natural man in the original in an experience-source, with the force of what is inaugural and present in person, according to a view that for him is ultimate and could conceivably be more perfect or closer' (Merleau-Ponty 1968, 158). Ricoeur then leaves behind the aporias of solipsism when he opens his theory of the imagination onto the notion of the collective and that of history and identifies an ethical–mythical imaginary that structures the beliefs of a people in the form of a social imaginary. In the philosophy of Ricoeur, which is one of action, the imaginary is not the opposite of the real, but can lead to it in a creative way. The imaginary can be placed upstream from action and empower it by helping it become free of its own constraints. It can also become a driving force of historicity: 'Imaginative mediation is what empowers subjectivity to develop, at the same time that it supports the process of its self-understanding' (Amalric 2013, 454).

The later works of Merleau-Ponty were of interest to Castoriadis just as they were to Ricoeur. In 1971, Castoriadis contributed to the journal *L'Arc*, to the issue that paid homage to Merleau-Ponty and placed an excerpt of the latter's work at the beginning of his article (Castoriadis 1984). Castoriadis welcomes the author's attempt to define a path different to that of traditional ontology and its egology. He follows Merleau-Ponty's lead in distancing himself from the eidetic approach of Husserl in order to depart from the classical discussion of representations, and substitute for it a form of thinking defined by its crossings-over and reversibility. Admittedly, the orientation Merleau-Ponty defines in *The Visible and the Invisible* is not fully satisfactory in the eyes of Castoriadis, but he acknowledges its central merit, that of having tried to escape from the privilege formerly afforded to the object, of having explored the dimension of the imaginary, even if this attempt remains unfinished, interrupted by his untimely death in 1960: 'Thus ... in his last writings, do the term and the idea of "imaginary" return frequently – even if these remain indeterminate due to their equivocality' (Castoriadis 1997, 275). Castoriadis nevertheless perceived in the later works only a partial step away from the overall coherence of Merleau-Ponty's thought, which remained largely dependent on the inherited tradition.

Castoriadis recognises, however, the merit Merleau-Ponty had of having perceived with lucidity and vigour the importance of the imaginary when he claimed that 'perceiving and imagining are now only two modes of *thinking*' (Merleau-Ponty 1968, 29), or that 'the narrow circle of objects of thought that are only half-thought, half-objects or phantoms that have no consistency, no place of their own, disappearing before the sun of thought like the mists of dawn, and that are, between the thought and what it thinks, only a thin layer of the unthought' (Merleau-Ponty 1968, 30). If Castoriadis is not satisfied with the floating sense that Merleau-Ponty accords to the imaginary, he acknowledges its contribution; that of having challenged the common conception of representation as it had been thematised since 1938 by Heidegger, then taken up and considered by his followers as a mask to be removed through philosophy.

According to the later works of Merleau-Ponty, the mind has no representations, but is itself a representative flux, the constant presentation of something that is not here for anyone or anything. 'Perception, dreams, reverie, memory, phantasm, reading, hearing music with eyes closed, thought are first and foremost that, and they rigorously enter under the same heading' (Castoriadis 1997, 281–2). If this is the case, the dimensions of the visible and of the invisible then cannot be separated. Both are caught in a network of inextricable connections through which one cannot speak of the visible without passing through the invisible and thus the imaginary, the subjective, the social: 'When one gauges what speaking means and everything that it conveys, the inherence, in perceiving, of speaking-thinking is nothing other, in a sense, than the shake-up of the distinction posited as absolute, between real and imaginary' (Castoriadis 1997, 302). Over the course of the 1950s, Merleau-Ponty progressively succeeded in performing the beginnings of a fundamental reassessment when he noted that the imaginary completely runs over into the field of perception: 'Our real life, in so far as it is directed at beings; is already imaginary' (Merleau-Ponty 2010, 147).

THE LIVING IMAGINATION IN PAUL RICOEUR

In 1976, Ricoeur expanded on his stance with respect to the role of the imagination, central to his philosophy, by introducing his general theory of the imagination (Ricoeur 1991a). He then drew attention to his planned poetics of the will, which was to shift the concept of the productive imagination beyond the sphere of discourse to that of action, occupying a key position on the border of theory and practice. Ricoeur deplores, as will Castoriadis later, the relegation of the function of the imagination inherited from traditional philosophical thought which suffers 'from the bad reputation of the term *image*, after its misuse in the empiricist theory of knowledge' (Ricoeur 1991a, 169). The imagination allows for the creation of a field of diverse possibilities with respect to the world of perception as well as action. Metaphoric statements seem to break completely from all referential links. Further, a break away from the aporias of theories of perception is allowed through the connection of the imagination to a certain use of language that is more open to semantic innovation. What is truly abolished, however, is the obligatory relationship with ordinary discourse, allowing for an expression of profound belonging to the world of life. Through metaphor, 'the ontological tie of our being to other beings and to being is allowed to be said by poetic discourse. What is thus allowed to be said is what I am calling the second order reference, which in reality is the primordial reference' (Ricoeur 1991a, 175). Being is not envisaged by Ricoeur on a contemplative or purely discursive plane. It opens up onto action, onto the formulation of motivations and projects through which the internal and intimate rapport between action and imagination is established: 'There is no action without imagination' (Ricoeur 1991a, 177). Further, it allows space for ideology and utopia, the inseparable poles of the social imaginary. 'The truth of our condition is in the analogic link which makes fellow man accessible to us across a number of *imaginative practices*, such as *ideology* and *utopia*' (Ricoeur 1991a, 181).

In Ricoeur's thesis dealing with 'The Philosophy of the Will', Jean-Luc Amalric traces the origins of the importance placed on the imagination (Amalric 2013, 109). He demonstrates that Ricoeur attributes the role of mediator, essential to the act of existing, to the imagination despite the break with the *cogito*. He perceives an increase in the power of the imagination, which primarily plays the role of operator of choice at the intersection of need and desire, and which will become central in *Fallible Man* (Ricoeur 1986). The imagination thus finds itself at the heart of Ricoeur's definition of desire. His phenomenological approach reveals a movement from the involuntary to the voluntary. This movement is only made possible by the actions of the imagination, which plays the role of mediator between need and desire, as well as between thought and action. In this first approach, the imagination remains subordinate to perception: 'Imagination cannot charge need's intentionality unless perception appraises it of its object and of the way to obtain it' (Ricoeur 1966, 95). The placement of the imagination as secondary to perception, however, is only a superficial view, as the Ricoeurian understanding of perception and attentive focus amounts to being activities of the imagination. 'For Ricoeur, it becomes apparent that focused imaginings are the very condition of our freedom' (Amalric 2013, 109). Above any consideration of the strictly creative potential of the imagination, Ricoeur assigns a nodal place to the imagination's anticipatory ability, which places representative resources at the service of action. 'Imagination is also, and perhaps primarily, a militant power in the service of a diffuse sense of the future by which we anticipate the actual-to-be, as an absent actual at the basis of the world' (Ricoeur 1966, 97). Jean-Luc Amalric defines the Ricoeurian philosophy of the imagination as an attempt, stemming from the ontology of being as act, to join two domains that traditional philosophy has a habit of separating: poetic discourse and imaginative practice. 'It is this *poetico-practical imagination* which precisely constitutes the *generative tension of human action*, because it represents at the same time a *support* for our acts and a *call* to work on the active transformation of ourselves and the world' (Amalric 2013, 496). This same attempt to articulate with and open towards historicised action is encountered in the work of Castoriadis, Ricoeur's theory being not far removed from his notion of the social-historical.

In the 1960s, Ricoeur faced a challenge to his hermeneutics in the popularity of structuralism. He was to reveal his response in three stages. After grafting hermeneutics onto his work, and prior to making a detour through a discussion of the historical dimension midway between these two tasks, Ricoeur demonstrated how one cannot impose self-closure on a text. With the publication of *La Métaphore vive* in 1975 (see Ricoeur 2003). Ricoeur demonstrates a turnaround from the *upstream* to the *downstream* of the text, reopening it to a field of multiple possibilities in its imaginary poetic dimension. The poetic dimension has always been claimed as essential by Ricoeur. The concept is at the horizon of all of Ricoeur's works following his thesis 'The Philosophy of the Will'. (Already at the time of its completion, he announced his intention to publish a poetic of will.) As well as insisting on the hermeneutic circle, the circular link which binds belief and understanding, Ricoeur establishes a complementarity between the creative behaviour of metaphor and the speculative behaviour of concept. 'Metaphor is living by virtue of the fact that it introduces the spark of the imagination into a "thinking more" at the conceptual level. This struggle to "think more," guided by the "vivifying principle" is the "soul" of interpretation' (Ricoeur 2003, 358). Creation is linked to speculative work and Ricoeur goes so far as to assign to this poetic emergence, to this *autopoiesis*, a truly central place in his theories.

In the days of structuralism, where everything was resolved using stylistic tropes, in particular metaphor and metonymy, which served as an excuse to establish the limits of a text's closure, Ricoeur chose to focus on the study of metaphor. This allowed him to show how in its most intimate essence, metaphor is associated with the connectivity of the verb 'to be' and opens onto a referent, a dimension external to language which confers upon this dimension the same tensional role as the notion of truth. He thus assigns a major role to metaphor while at the same time imposing limitations: 'To *ground* what was called metaphorical truth is also to *limit* poetic discourse' (Ricoeur 2003, 6).

Ricoeur reminds us how the genre to which metaphor belongs, rhetoric, fell into disuse even though Aristotle associated it with a grand ambition, that of governing public discourse. Contrary to the popular idea of considering form as being secondary to message, which relegates metaphor to the status of gratuitous ornament in thought, Ricoeur demonstrates the extent to which Aristotle's metaphor, repositioned in the context of *mimesis*, partakes of a double tension: 'On the one hand the imitation is at once a portrayal of human reality and an original creation; on the other, it is faithful to things as they are and it depicts them as higher and greater than they are' (Ricoeur 2003, 35). From the conclusion of his first study, which explores the rapport between rhetoric and poetic in the theories of Aristotle, Ricoeur opens up the question of action, of the possible awakening of the dormant potential and buried capacities of action, as the very locus of the ontological function of metaphoric discourse.

Metaphors refer back to a meaning, to a referent, and, as such, need to be contextualised. They are subject to the wearing effects of time and then most often fall into the language of common usage. From this moment on, they are but dead metaphors, assimilated, fully absorbed into the language which has forgotten their metaphoric component. So it was, for example, with the common expression 'the leg of the chair'. In the same way ' *"Comprendre"* [comprehend, understand] can have a philosophical sense because we no longer hear *"prendre"* [take, take hold]' (Ricoeur 2003, 346). When the poet asserts that 'time is a beggar' or that old age is like 'a straw of dried hay', new meanings appear; however, a new world seems to reveal itself to the reader through such metaphors, which one can classify as live, based on their capacity to upset the conventions of language and refresh our perspective. The live metaphor does not stand on the side of simple resemblance; its place of predilection is to be found in its distance from common identification. 'Only authentic metaphors, that is living metaphors, are at once meaning and event' (Ricoeur 2003, 115). Metaphor is simultaneously a form of distance and a means of reducing that distance in so far as it carries within itself a conflict – between an old meaning that is resistant to replacement and a new meaning that clears its own path to potential relevance. While metaphor can appear as a fusion of meaning, it is in fact the very subject of a conflict between old and new meaning. Ricoeur thus locates in the trope that is metaphor (the stylistic icon which consists of substituting one signifier with another, both being similar), an internal dynamic of change and of resistance to change. 'Metaphor is the process through which the speaker reduces the deviation by changing the meaning of one of the words' (Ricoeur 2003, 179).

This modification of meaning is conceived by Ricoeur as 'the response of discourse to the threat of destruction represented by semantic impertinence' (2003, 179). It is thus in the surplus of meaning that this creativity resides, carried towards other possible worlds. In this leap towards new possible meanings, the threat which weighs over the destruction of the initial, literal meaning must find a way through, must find a creative opening. Metaphor does not commence from a nothingness of writing, but from sedimental meaning. The new gap takes its force from this existing meaning in order to innovate. Metaphor signals the arbitrary nature of the break between the traditional and the new, and indicates the pertinence of the Gadamerian concept of tradition as live tradition, revisited by the questions of present modernity. Its function is that of expressing singularity, of revealing. It thus connects with an ontological dimension found in the last of Ricoeur's studies, as already outlined at the end of the first section dedicated to Aristotle. Philosophical discourse is thus able to account for the semantic ambition of poetic discourse, thanks to its reflexive capacity. 'Far from locking language up inside itself, this reflective consciousness is the very consciousness of its openness' (Ricoeur 2003, 360). The poetic horizon leads directly to an ontology, a kind of promised land much more than an identity base. At the origin of this process of metaphorisation, the 'ontological vehemence' of the semantic aim only has at its disposal indications of meaning, not determinate meanings (Ricoeur 2003, 354).

This suspending movement reopens onto a referent, within a return to a world which sits within the phenomenological tradition.

Marx plays a definite role in Ricoeur's thinking regarding the necessary task of unveiling meaning, regarding the unfolding of a philosophy of suspicion. In the manner of Freud, Marx brings to the social and political landscape the weapons of critical analysis and suspicion, thus forging a necessary passage away from initial naivety. He also contributes by enriching what Ricoeur, in the middle of the 1970s, came to call the social imaginary; ideology and utopia being considered as its two indispensable expressions. While these two forms of the social imaginary are particularly disparaged – ideology being in fact dismissed as a simple dissimulation of science and utopia as an escape from the real – Ricoeur finds in Marx a means of restoring their double integrative and subversive function. He defines three usages for the notion of ideology (Ricoeur 1991b). The first is envisaged as a means of concealment, like a reversed image of reality which transforms *praxis* into the imaginary, an idea to which the younger Marx resorts in *The Manuscripts of 1844* and *The German Ideology*. The second meaning, however, passes through a process of legitimisation, though a universalisation of particular interests. 'Marx says that the ruling class imposes its ideas as the ruling ideas by representing them as ideal and universal' (Ricoeur 1991b, 317). A third function, that of integration, can be added to these two, manifesting itself notably on occasions of commemorative ceremony. Ideology thus carries positivity, a constructive aim. At the same time, the three levels can fuse; ideology can degenerate by transforming itself from its first manifestation as falsifying into a legitimising dimension. In the context of the 1970s, this re-evaluation of the role of ideology represents an alternative to the contemporary, dominant Althusserian reading of this concept which was purely negative, restricted to its first meaning of illusory living and dissimulation.

In the same way, with regard to utopia, Ricoeur envisages three levels of efficiency in a complementary relationship with ideology. Faced with the integrative function of ideology, utopia is his 'elsewhere', his alternative. It can be a source of inspiration for pathological versions, claiming to announce proven eschatologies. At the same time, utopia can rediscover a liberating function while maintaining the field of possibilities. 'Utopia is what prevents the horizon of expectation from fusion with the field of experience. It is this that maintains the separation between hope and tradition.'[4]

In another piece, Ricoeur examines the coupling of science and ideology, central to the works of Althusser and based on a theme of rupture (Ricoeur 1991c). Here again, he opposes a restrictive definition of ideology, such as that employed by Marxism, which assimilates this dimension with a simple, social instrumentalisation in terms of lies, illusions, and falsification. Behind this strategy which denounces the normative other, Ricoeur reminds whoever adopts this approach of suspicion that he also does so in the name of implicit values, themselves masked by an overhanging stance. It is thus presupposed that 'ideology is the thought of my adversary, the thought of the *other*. *He* does not know it, but *I* do' (Ricoeur 1991c, 248). Aristotle first challenged such a pretentious statement in the name of a science seen as disengaged from all contamination by the Platonists: opposing it with pluralism of methods and degrees of truth. Granted, Ricoeur does not renounce any form of opposition between science and ideology, but it is on the condition that it be reformulated and that it should part with the peremptory character of Althusserianism.

Ideology holds several functions and its interpretation by Marx is only one of the connecting pieces that make up a pluralist phenomenon: its dissimulative, negative side, its distortion of the real. Marx thus marks out a component of ideology that is of clear importance, referring to the symbolic constitution of the social bond (Ricoeur 1977) on which its mystifying function attaches itself and which makes of it 'an unsurpassable phenomenon of social existence, insofar as social reality always has a symbolic constitution' (Ricoeur 1991c, 255). Renouncing all overhanging positions, Ricoeur proposes a more modest discourse of symmetrisation and historicisation of the knowing gaze: 'The elements of a solution seem to me to be contained in a discourse of a *hermeneutical* character on the conditions of all *historical* understanding' (Ricoeur 1991c, 266). The coupling of science and ideology is thus fundamentally transformed on the basis of a number of presuppositions: objectifying knowledge is preceded by a relationship of belonging. A margin of autonomy can thus be seen in this coupling, as the act of detachment is completely necessary. Yet if the critique of ideologies is freed from its engrained constraints, it can only be partially. 'The theory of the ideology is here subsumed to an epistemological constraint of noncompleteness and *nontotalisation*, which has its hermeneutic justification in the very condition of understanding' (Ricoeur 1991c, 268).

Ricoeur also dealt with the philosophy of suspicion in his encounter with the work of Freud between 1960 and 1965, which led him to publish his essay on Freud, *De l'interprétation. Essai sur Freud* (Ricoeur 1965).[5] He follows Freud in his ambition to confer a psychic reality to dreams and fantasy and, beyond this, to the whole imaginary dimension of the drive. The imaginary remains located at the point of origin of desire, in all its manifestations. Freud's work is held yet more closely by Castoriadis, who ended his Freudian journey by becoming a professional psychoanalyst in 1973.

In his masterful trilogy, *Time and Narrative*, published between 1983 and 1985, Ricoeur demonstrated that narrative is the guardian of time, thereby going against structuralist concepts of the eclipse of the narrative in historical discourse and the absence of diachronic logic in synchronic studies. Ricoeur rediscovers the founding character of the reconfigurative power of narrative, starting from an imaginary that reconfigures time, whether it be that of fictional or of historical narrative. On this occasion, Ricoeur delves into fictional narrative in order to examine in what way the latter will achieve a configuration of time. At the crossroads between the prefiguration and refiguration of time, he situates himself within a sole configuration of time, a configuration of a time liberated from the need for documentary archive. This fictional experience of time, detached from all *lieu-tenance* (standing-in)[6] of the text, continues to be placed under the mimetic sign and corresponds to the stage which Aristotle defines as *Mimesis II*. In this respect, the narrative of fiction is related to the historical narrative in a common formulation of plot: 'In this sense, we have simply returned to literature what history had borrowed from it' (Ricoeur 1985, 157). The fables of time explored by Ricoeur in three works, *Mrs Dalloway* by Virginia Woolf, *The Magic Mountain* by Thomas Mann, and *In Search of Lost Time* by Marcel Proust, function due to a kind of Ariadne's thread which brings into being a temporal synthesis of the heterogeneous and manages to bring discordance and concordance together, within a narrative configuration. The comparison of these three works presents the innumerable possibilities that reside in the imaginative variations on time.

With *Mrs Dalloway*, Virginia Woolf insists on the plurality of the experiences of time, caught between the time that is monumental and the time that is mortal. Time is therefore what renders possible the networking of forms of consciousness that remain fundamentally solitary. 'This experience of time is neither that of Clarissa, nor that of Septimus, it is neither that of Peter, nor that of any other character. Instead, it is suggested to the reader *by the reverberation of one solitary experience in another solitary experience*' (Ricoeur 1985a, 112; emphasis added). In *Magic Mountain*, by Thomas Mann, a novel about time marked by a progressive abolition of chronology, the hero, Hans Castorp, gets sucked into the universe of a sanatorium. The whole structure of the novel amounts to this temporal deconstruction, comprising a suite of seven chapters covering a seven-year period. The split between the motionless time of those above and the world of those down below grows bigger, as seen in the hustle and bustle of everyday life. 'Now that the law of those up above has won out, all that is left is to bury oneself deeper in the thickness of time. There are no more witnesses from down below. The time of feeling has eliminated clock time' (Ricoeur 1985a, 121). *In Search of Lost Time*, by Proust, is caught in the tension between the foci of an ellipsis. On the one hand, there is the lost time, perceived as a suspension of time that has been recovered, as eternity and as an extra-temporal form of being. On the other hand, there is the act of regaining the time that has been lost. The final decision to write abolishes this duality and brings about a second meaning in the time that has been regained, that of a lost time resuscitated, a fugitive moment anchored in a sustained piece of writing. The novel succeeds in locating this lost impression through the usage of metaphor, which renders it possible to cross the temporal distance sep-arating vision from recognition. The last word of *In Search of Lost Time* reminds the reader that the ambition of this entire quest was a returning of men to their place 'in Time' (Proust 2003, 532).

From this study of fictional narratives, there appears a major differ-ence in the treatment of time as compared with the manner in which it is employed in a historical narrative. 'Fictional narrative loosens time, enlarging the arch of imaginative variations, historical narrative con-tributes to loosening time by unifying and homogenising it' (Mongin 1998, 156). On another level, that of refiguration (*Mimesis III*), is found the time recounted by the historian. Situated between cosmic and intimate time, it reconfigures time through specific connectors. Ricoeur thus places the historical discourse within a tension specific to it, the tension between narrative identity and the ambition of truth. The poetic of narrative appears as a means of transcending the aporias of a philo-sophical apprehension of time.

Whereas there was a tendency in the 1990s, and with increasing preva-lence ever since, for the past to be memorialised and institutionalised as heritage, once more Ricoeur reacted to preserve the imaginary dimen-sion of a possible future, one that would not be the simple conservation of the past, to retain a future turned towards creativity, towards the void of the new. This is one of the principle motivations behind his writing and publication in 2000 of *Memory, History, Forgetting*. In this work, the concept of *représentance* amounts to something which has occurred, to a factual reality, but not in the fashion of a simple representation or reflection. Between the latter and historical writings, there is, once more, a major role for the imagination, that of the historian as well as of the reader. 'The idea of a deep structure of the imagination owes its indisputable fruitfulness to the tie it establishes between creativity and codification' (Ricoeur 2000, 253). In this reconfiguration of the past in its aftermath, the imaginary finds itself mobilised to allow the his-torian to successfully perform a presentation of the past. Ricoeur thus places emphasis on delinearisation within the relationship with the past which no longer necessarily follows the classic, logical line of consecu-tion for 'one can speak of a rebound-effect of the future onto the past even within the retrospective viewpoint of history. The historian has the opportunity to carry herself in imagination back to back to a given moment of the past as having been present' (Ricoeur 2000, 381). The effort necessary to immerse oneself again in the present of past societies has important epistemological effects. It allows for the reopening of all fields of possible outcomes, whether eventuated or otherwise, which constitute the present of past societies. This amounts to a movement away from fate and a downplaying of strict forms of historical deter-minism, which reintroduces contingency but without denying the field of constraints; of explored expectations, hope, fears, and predictions which have left their mark on the men of the past. This approach, which effectively renders our space of experience more indeterminate, seeks to make the horizons of expectation more closely determined by new imaginative variations, reinvigorating hope in the future.

THE IMAGINARY BETWEEN CHAOS AND INSTITUTION IN CASTORIADIS'S WORKS

The recourse to the imaginary is equally fundamental in Castoriadis's works and allowed him to distance himself from Marxism. Its impor-tance was realised by Castoriadis between 1963 and 1964, when he attended Lacan's seminar and shifted his interest from Marx to Freud, while critiquing Marxism with increasing openness. This shift through which Castoriadis left this worthless surround is a moment of major emancipation which led him to conduct an extensive project about human creation. Through the concept of the imaginary, Castoriadis leaves the theory of reflection which links infrastructure and superstructure in a more or less complex manner. Admittedly, Althusser allowed superstructures to be seen as autonomous through the 'Ideological State Apparatuses', which he conceived as dominant authorities in some modes of production. Ultimately, however, the economic field remains decisive. While Marxist determinism has the effect of relegating all cultural expressions of societies to a secondary position, Castoriadis claims their primal importance for an understanding of the historical process: 'History is impossible and inconceivable outside of the *productive* or *creative imagination*, outside of what we have called the *radical imaginary* as this is manifested indissolubly in both historical *doing* and in the constitution, before any explicit rationality, of a universe of *significations*' (Castoriadis 1987, 146).

During the 1960s and 1970s, a tendency developed, notably among historians under the sway of the third-generation paradigm of the *Annales*, to consider ideological phenomena, mentalities, and culture as authorities that have their own endogenous coherence. Despite this, however, they remained only secondary entities when compared with the socio-economic substrate. Castoriadis, for his part, made the imaginary a crucible of his ontology and gave it a prevalent position in his conception of the social-historical, as attested by the title of his great work, *The Imaginary Institution of Society*, published in 1975. He thus precedes and announces the evolution of the French historical school of the *Annales* that had, under Braudel, favoured social and economic history and then adopted the notion of mentalities, which experienced its peak of influence in the 1970s. This notion continued to be utilised as an extension of categories in use in economic and social history, thus giving rise to a social history that transposes socio-professional divisions on to the level of culture. Only a few years later did the imaginary dimension come to be actually explored, when restoring the world as a representation became a concern, at the time of the 'critical turning point' of the *Annales* in the years 1988–1989 (see Delacroix, Dosse, and Garcia 2007).

Over the course of this evolution, George Duby assumed the role of precursor, as he had in other fields. He expressed his debt to Castoriadis, even when the latter was far removed from the sphere of historians, if not for some Hellenists such as Pierre Vidal-Naquet. From 1973, Duby devoted his seminar to the exploration of a topic in a way that resulted, in 1978, in a publication entitled *The Three Orders: Feudal Society Imagined* (Duby 1980). When interviewed, he attested to the role that Castoriadis's publication had in the choice of the title: 'As for the word "imaginary," I believe I was indebted to Castoriadis, whose book *The Imaginary Institution of Society*, published three years before mine, developed the idea of a society that institutes itself through the image it has of itself' (Duby 1996, 174–92). The connection between Castoriadis and historians could have been fulfilled in 1978, when he was called upon to contribute a text (*L'Arc*, 1978):

> The next issue of *L'Arc* will be dedicated to Georges Duby, and it is strongly hoped that you will participate. It was decided with Georges Duby that this instalment would deal with a question of interest to him rather than with himself … It will be about 'the link that exists between the mental plane and the functioning of society' and 'how the imaginary and the concrete go together in the life of societies'. (Cordier 1997)

Castoriadis, overwhelmed by his activities, did not follow up and this connection has remained imperceptible.

For some young historians among the new generation coming after the 'critical turning point', this relatedness became particularly inspiring. Such was the case of the current managing director of the *Annales*, Etienne Anheim. As a medievalist, dissatisfied at the time by the usages of the notions of ideology or mentalities, he considered the notion of the imaginary, as it was defined by Castoriadis, as an operational heuristic instrument for historical research. Etienne Anheim discovered the work of Castoriadis through his friend Vincent Azoulay in 1992, when he was in the preparatory classes for admission to the *Grandes Écoles*.[7] In 1993, Anheim entered the *École normale supérieure*, a teacher training college in Paris. He was principally interested in attempting to formulate a social history of cultural forms and in reflecting on cultural objects in a transitional phase. As he positioned his work within the perspective of a social history of high culture, Castoriadis became a major reference for Etienne Anheim when, in 1998, he began his thesis devoted to patronage and the court culture of the Popes in Avignon during the mid-fifteenth century. The relationship established in the works of Castoriadis between the institution and the imaginary thus became fundamental for Etienne Anheim.

The centrality of the theme of the imaginary in Castoriadis's works stems especially from his conversion to psychoanalysis, from the influence of Lacan, as well as from the critique of Lacan's views. Although he attended Lacan's seminar, he refuted the Lacanian schema of the symbolic–real–imaginary triad, which strongly favours the symbolic dimension at the expense of the dimension of the imaginary:

> That which, since 1964, I have termed the social imaginary – a term which has since been used and misused in a number of different ways – and, more generally, that which I call the imaginary has nothing to do with representations currently circulating under this heading. In particular, it has nothing to with that which is presented as 'imaginary' by certain currents in psychoanalysis: namely, the 'specular' which is obviously only an image *of* and a reflected image, in other words a *reflection*, and in yet other words a byproduct of Platonic ontology (*eidolon*). (Castoriadis 1987, 3)

Castoriadis did not endorse Lacan's conception of a master-signifier pertaining to the symbolic. For him, as he shared the approach of Piera Aulagnier, who became his wife in 1968, the imaginary dimension is fundamental. This approach is based on the pictogram, the foundation for the construction of the subject. It is here that Castoriadis locates what he later calls the radical imaginary, in a moment where it owes nothing to the *socius*, invalidating any undertaking that reduces the unconscious to its social substrate. This radical imaginary that defines the psyche remains therefore irreducible to its social destiny.

Castoriadis considers Freud's contribution to the question of the imaginary as being fundamentally ambivalent in as much as he seldom uses the noble term that designates the imagination in German. Instead, he repeatedly uses the terms *Phantasy* and *Phantasieren*. However, 'there is nothing in Phantasy, or in phantasm, that the subject has not already perceived; phantasm is reproduction' (Castoriadis 2008a, 292). These phantasms then, in Freudian theory, are not of an original and creative character. Rather, they have a secondary role of combining pre-existing elements. Here, Castoriadis sees a paradox: Freud has only ever addressed elements taken from the imagination; however, he makes this activity secondary and places it in the position of matrix. As Castoriadis points out, for a long time, Freud remained attached to his theory of original trauma based on a supposed primitive scene of real seduction revealed through therapy. However, he came to the recognition that there was no difference in the unconscious between effective perception and representation: 'There are no "indications of reality" in the unconscious. In and for the unconscious the "real" is purely imaginary' (Castoriadis 2008a, 306). While trying to correlate these two dimensions, Freud, however, remained caught in a dualistic perspective opposing the soul to the body, the psyche to the soma.

Beyond Lacan, an entire intellectual context gave precedence to the structuralist paradigm, the formalism of binary relations around structural linguistics and, at its core, the Saussurean algorithm defined by its break with reality. The main scholar of reference for this group is Claude Lévi-Strauss, who, in his anthropological approach, favours the symbolic dimension at the expense of the content of expressed meaning. Castoriadis thus found himself confronted by the challenge that the fruitfulness of this research approach presented in the field of social sciences, at a semiological, ethnological, and psychoanalytical level. Like his friend Edgar Morin, he understood very early on its limits and aporias. The imaginary dimension not only allows him to emphasise the importance of any other stratum than that of the symbolic, but it also shows that structures remain captive to history, change, and diverse projections of meaning, all carried out by collectives that underpin the instituting dimension. Castoriadis does not abandon the dimension of the symbolic, but places it on the side of the instituted society: 'Everything that is presented to us in the social-historical world is inextricably tied to the symbolic ... Institutions cannot be reduced to the symbolic but they can exist only in the symbolic; they are impossible outside of a second-order symbolism' (Castoriadis 1987, 117).

Contrary to what has been attempted by a number of researchers, such as Wilhelm Reich, doubly influenced by Marx and Freud and far from asserting a double determinism, Castoriadis insists rather on the irreducibility of the psyche to conditioning by the social-historical. While Lacan supports the theory of absolute domination of the symbolic over the imaginary, 'What we call the symbolic dominates the imaginary' (Lacan 2006, 686), Castoriadis supports the opposite theory, erasing, over the years, the symbolic in favour of the imaginary. His quest for meaning has the imaginary as its mainstay, especially as 'meaning overflows all rational or functional symbolism, and the term "imaginary" beckons towards the dimension in that which it is rooted, or that comprises it' (Fressard 2006, 132).

For all this, the mediation of the symbolic is not denied, but rather is considered as indispensable to the expression of the imaginary: 'The imaginary has to use the symbolic not only to "express" itself (this is self-evident), but to "exist," to pass from the virtual to anything more than this' (Castoriadis 1987, 127). To grasp the meaning of a society, it is necessary to articulate different levels that are indispensable to each other. Even if there is a dimension that is rational, conscious of the law-makers who establish the institutionalised rules of society, beyond this mastery, '[i]nstitutions have drawn their source from the *social imaginary*. This imaginary must be interwoven with the symbolic, otherwise society could not have "come together"; and have linked up with the economic-functional component, otherwise it could not have survived' (Castoriadis 1987, 131). Society, according to Castoriadis, must necessarily find its limitations and be able to break its own closure. This break is actually that through which a society appears in its singularity. Its historicity unfolds across this original chasm, that from which it comes and what it has instituted, which serves to cover the abyss without ever really successfully eradicating it.

As against the structuralist closure, Castoriadis reminds us of the double dimension of the symbolic, which pertains to a logic both 'ensidic' and imaginary. Ricoeur considers two planes of meaning to be complimentary: the semiological level of rationality, which operates through its combination of signs, and the hermeneutic level, which refers to interpretative plurality through its multiple variations. In the same vein, Castoriadis also brings into consideration the necessary complementarity between the ensidic and the imaginary. While Ricoeur emphasises this function of the imaginary, it also operates in Castoriadis's writings, between Chaos and institution: 'The world as a magma of significations is characterised by a radical "indeterminacy" thanks to which new determinations can emerge' (Legros 2008, 139). Castoriadis opened a new perspective into which, from 1975 onwards, he never ceased to delve. This perspective rejected simplistic alternatives and hyperbolic conceptions, whether they consider that the function of institutions wholly explains society or whether they see in the symbolic the explanatory crucible of the society that is studied. Neither of these levels can be neglected, and he does not question the relevance of functionality any more than the efficiency of the symbolic, provided that they are not understood as covering over the totality of meaning that spills over from all directions:

> Not freely chosen, not imposed upon a given society, neither a neutral instrument nor a transparent medium, neither an impenetrable opacity nor an irreducible adversity, neither the master of society nor the flexible slave of functionality, not a direct and complete means of partaking of a rational order – symbolism determines the aspects of social life (and not merely those it was supposed to determine) while simultaneously being full of interstices and of degrees of freedom. (Castoriadis 1987, 125)

Castoriadis acknowledges the fact that Marx had a strong grasp of the role that the imaginary dimension plays in society when he spoke of 'commodity fetishism'. Marx refers to something that is not within the realm of tangible reality, but does not follow his analysis through to the end: He limits the imaginary to its simple function as expression of alienation, failing to see its opposite pole, which is situated on the side of creation. In the 1970s, faced with the structuralist trend and the success of the theories of Claude Lévi-Strauss, Castoriadis, distanced himself from the conception dominating anthropology which aimed at conceptualising a rationality endogenous to symbolic systems cut off from their institutional and functional substrate: 'Nor can institutions be understood simply as symbolic networks' (Castoriadis 1987, 136). The question unresolved by structuralism is that of knowing why such a system of symbols has prevailed here and not there, as well as the nature of the meanings these symbols carry: 'It is only relative to these significations that we can understand the "choice" of symbolism made by every society, and in particular the choice of its institutional symbolism' (Castoriadis 1987, 146).

From the perspective of Castoriadis, the imaginary dimension allows history and the emergence of the new to be given again a genuine role, whereas synchronic studies of structuralism marginalise the temporal logics specific to the course of history: 'History is impossible and inconceivable outside of the *productive* or *creative imagination*' (Castoriadis 1987, 146). This role of the imaginary is not limited to archaic societies, but also accompanies the progressive rationalisation of social relationships, and thus modernity. Additionally, it is advanced by the increase in the needs created and maintained by contrivances further and further distanced from the natural necessities required for the survival of the species: 'More than any other society, too, modern society permits us to see the historical manufacturing of needs that are produced today before our own eyes' (Castoriadis 1987, 156–7).

As with the synchronic studies of structuralism, the phenomenological tradition is also not satisfactory for Castoriadis, as it rests upon a realist illusion according to which consciousness is consciousness of something. It thus finds itself paradoxically condemned to being a solipsistic consciousness in so far as it is impossible to know what goes on within what is other than the self: 'From a strict phenomenological view, I have no access to the experience of "other people"; they and their "experiences" exist only as "phenomena" to me' (Castoriadis 2008a, 235). As such, the phenomenological approach remains captive to an egological point of view. The evolution of Husserl towards the world of life, as noted in Heidegger's work *Being and Time* (1967), is no more satisfactory, as it swaps the egological view for a self-centred view, on a larger scale. It is true that in contemporary times, Sartre and Bachelard both gave the imaginary a place in their philosophy; however, for Castoriadis, this place is absolutely essential. It is the very matrix of his ontology and occupies a crossroad position in his thought (Castoriadis 2007). For him, Being does not pertain to any system, but to Chaos, to the Abysmal. It is not within time because it is itself time, and it is the source of the creation and the destruction of created forms. According to Castoriadis, being first emerges from its origins in the psyche, and then, second, 'as a socialised individual' (Tomès and Caumières 2011, 157). It is from this that the major role played by the institutions enables the socialisation of a psyche that was formerly unsuited to survival.

Castoriadis clearly intended to deepen his own notion of the imaginary, starting with the Freudian input. He saw in Freud someone who had escaped inherited thought and, with his discovery of the unconscious, managed to break the established division between the real and its representation. Freud embodied a new approach when he claimed that nothing allows one to distinguish, within the psyche, a reality and a representation vested with affect, and when he stated that the unconscious has no experience of time. Herein lies the contradiction: Manifestations of the unconscious lie in interconnections that are neither within nor outside of the subject.

In the course he delivered at the *Collège de France*, Merleau-Ponty expressed his point of view regarding the institution and advocated for a necessary link with a historical dynamic, constantly reusing the past to justify a renewed meaning. Castoriadis's conception is not far different: 'Therefore, by institution, we were intending here those events in an experience which endow the experience with durable dimensions, in relation to which a whole series of other experiences will make sense, will form a thinkable sequel or a history' (Merleau-Ponty 2010, 77). This anchoring in a *praxis* that is historically contextualised cannot help but invoke the constant work of the instituting over the instituted in Castoriadis. One also finds, in the work of Merleau-Ponty, the encroachment of the imaginary on perception, 'namely the fact that our perceptive relation to the world is steeped in unconscious meanings constituting our past, and which the institution has crystalised in the density of our physical being' (Réa 2006, 80).

To illustrate the magmatic pole included in an abundance of possibilities within creation, Castoriadis takes as a concrete example that of the medieval city, referencing the works of Yves Barel (Castoriadis 2008b), with whom he had formed an amiable relationship in 1981 during the decade of Cerisy, dedicated to 'self-organisation'. For Castoriadis, the complexity of objects is due to their initial nature, which is related to magma: 'We will say that an object is magmatic when it is not exhaustively and systematically *ensidisable* – in other words, reducible to elements and relationships pertaining exclusively and in homogenous fashion to ensidic logic' (Castoriadis 2008b, 256).[8] With temporality located next to the emergence of new principles, Castoriadis sees in the historical process, and notably in its periods of change, a terrain that is ideal for identifying these objects of magmatic origin. Around the tenth century, the Western world developed new principles that came to govern the medieval world, in which the city would play a central role. Castoriadis sees in this period a major rupture in the closure, which recalls what Greece realised in Antiquity: One witnesses a decisive step towards social and individual autonomy. Unlike the Athenians of the fifth century, who saw the establishment of a democratic regime, these medieval cities yearned to conquer their autonomy, developing oligarchic systems in what Yves Barel has termed an 'order of urban patricians' (Barel 1978). Castoriadis stands close to Yves Barel, as the major question posed by his study of the medieval city is to know what holds together a society and why the new emerges in history: 'The answers that Yves Barel offers in his case study are essentially true. The appearance of the medieval city is recognised as a "major discontinuity"

(Barel 1978, 74, 165ff.), where one can see the "emergence of new elements" (Barel 1978, 169). The discontinuity is interwoven with a "continuity"' (Castoriadis 2008b, 266). This self-creation cannot be related back to determinations that would explain its upstream meaning. According to Yves Barel, if one nevertheless seeks what can make this more intelligible, it is necessary to examine the 'urban imaginary' (Barel 1978, 182).

The meanings of the social imaginary do not, according to Castoriadis, correspond to the 'ideal types' defined by Max Weber; they are not the result of a 'subjectively targeted' meaning, but are, in contrast, the condition of possibility for concrete, subjective goals: '[S]ocial imaginary significations are "immanent" to the society considered in each case' (Castoriadis 1987, 367). These meanings acquire presence in the institutions that are the gateway into the social imaginary that they support. Castoriadis thus breaks with the theory of reflection. 'The difficulty lies in understanding . . . that the social imaginary is not a substance, not a quality, not an action or a passion; that social imaginary significations are not representations, not figures or forms, not concepts' (Castoriadis 1987, 369). Every society gives itself a global meaning that founds the singularity of its being-together. The common world that society constructs is the result of the constant interplay between the instituting and the instituted that defines its temporal being. The social-historical imaginary both resists the ensemblistic-identarian logic and, at the same time, needs it to exist, to be present and embodied in the instituted, without the instituted escaping the injunctions of innovation conveyed by the instituting.

The social-historical constitutes a dual restriction to the creative powers that echoes the constraints of the present, as much as those of the traditions anchored in the past. This is all the more so, since, according to Castoriadis, certain creations embedded in time constitute 'historical quasi-transcendentals'. Castoriadis does not share Sartre's idea of a philosophy of absolute creation in history. On this level, he is more closely aligned to Merleau-Ponty and Ricoeur, and their concept of 'concrete freedom', which is to say, the exercise of a freedom that finds 'a support in things', with man being 'a product-producer, the locus where necessity can turn into concrete freedom' (Merleau-Ponty 1964, 134).

As Laurent Van Eynde stresses, Castoriadis's thinking around the notion of imaginary must be linked back to a philosophical anthropology whose intention is to consider how singularity can modify the essence while continuing to constitute the essence. In other words, how to understand the constitution of universality through singularity: 'The thought of the possible always leads to reducing singularity to the *a priori* of the universal. At the very least, it is then up to singularity to surprise us and lead us to discover, in its own emergence, the power of the universal' (Van Eynde 2006, 65). According to Laurent Van Eynde, Castoriadis's thinking reaches beyond this insistence on the meaning that disruptive revelations can have over the course of time. He strives to overcome the traditional division between the transcendent and the empirical, which explains his global critique of all that he qualifies as inherited thought. Even if he breaks with transcendentalism, Castoriadis does not mean to adopt relativist stances and to give up on the question of the universal. It is from this perspective, which considers singularity at the same time as universality, that he focuses on the required components of effectiveness and on the concreteness of effectiveness, hence his interest in studies of concrete historical situations: 'All of which means that Castoriadis's thought is an anthropology of effectiveness or, if preferred, an ontology of human creation' (Van Eynde 2006, 67). Thus, it is human creation in history that links the dialectical relationship between the instituting and the instituted, as found at the heart of the historical dynamic:

> The anthropology of the imagination in Castoriadis then truly becomes the centre of all philosophical undertaking because it recognises in the imaginary the impulse for philosophy – the desire to know – and, in my view, allows at the same time a synthesis between the Greek ideal of a philosophy, whose advent is linked to that of democracy, and the *Aufklärer* ideal of individual and social emancipation, synthesis which to my mind is all the more relevant today. (Van Eynde 2006, 74)

Castoriadis explained most clearly this essential position of the imaginary, found at the heart of philosophical reason, in a talk he gave in 1991, published in the journal *Diogène* in 1992: 'At the two extremes of knowledge, but also constantly in its centre, we can find the creative power of the human being, which is to say the radical imagination' (Castoriadis 2008c, 147). Significantly, this point of paradoxical linkage between the two notions most often opposed to each other, those of passion and knowledge, is supported by a connection to the characteristics of the psyche, which Castoriadis can invoke to contradict Aristotle with the claim, 'What the psyche, as well as society, desires, and what both need, is not knowledge, but belief' (Castoriadis 2008c, 164).

A REAL PROXIMITY BETWEEN RICOEUR AND CASTORIADIS

This juxtaposition of Ricoeur and Castoriadis with regard to the notion of the imaginary can appear surprising, given their differences. There is a real proximity, however, between the two. In fact, Castoriadis visited the University of Nanterre in 1967 in order to request from Ricoeur that he supervise his thesis dedicated to *L'élément imaginaire dans l'histoire* ['The Imaginary Element in History'], which never reached completion. When, in 1970, Ricoeur, holding the position of Dean of the University of Nanterre at the time, had rubbish bins emptied over his head, Castoriadis reacted immediately, expressing his support and indignation:

> Regarding the odious incident that took place this week in Nanterre, allow me to express to you all my friendship and at the same time, it must be said, the esteem in which I hold your response. Alas, imbeciles and bastards can be found everywhere. In refusing to respond directly, in revealing in your actions that you do not confuse some maniacs – probably ill, by the way – with their generation nor with a current of ideas, you have not only shown your intelligence in this situation, you have, I believe, also adopted an attitude which will prove to be most profoundly effective in the long term.

The Archives of Paul Ricoeur (*Le Fonds Ricoeur*) hold a dossier written by Castoriadis containing a manuscript in part drafted under the title 'The Foundations of the Social-Historical in the Imaginary'. Undated, this manuscript was sent from Castoriadis's home at the time, *Quai Anatole France*, prior to 1977. It was read closely by Ricoeur, who has underlined the passages that appeared to him to be the most important.

These epistolary exchanges between Ricoeur and Castoriadis attest to a profound and reciprocated esteem. In 1978, Castoriadis wrote to his supervisor, who spent a good part of each year in the United

States, to convey his dissatisfaction at not obtaining a greater response from him:

> We are now friends enough for me to allow myself to tell you of my disappointment before the silence that has met my regular correspondence, for six years at least, and everything I have published during this period? ... You are one of those rare people to whose opinions and reactions I attribute importance. Be sure, in any case, that I will welcome with joy any sign coming from you. (Castoriadis 1978)

Several days later, Ricoeur replied to him:

> I happily accept your friendly protests, for I feel guilty of having neglected to write, but not of neglecting to read. I read with passion all that you write. I have delivered a course at Nanterre on your *Institution Imaginaire de la société* and I have on my desk your last contribution to *Esprit* (Thibaud and Mongin know how much I rejoice that this journal supports your work). (Ricoeur 1978)

Only on one occasion did Castoriadis and Ricoeur have the opportunity of speaking together in public, at the radio program *Bon Plaisir* on *France Culture* broadcast on 9 March 1985 (see chapter 1). This exchange discussed the question of the discontinuity of meaning as against the continuity of existence. They agreed on the need to distance themselves from the notion of the radical break inherent in Michel Foucault's *episteme*, as well as to state that there exists discontinuities in history: 'If you accept discontinuity on the level of sense but not on the level of existence, that suits me perfectly. If I were polemical, I would say that you are granting me what I need' (see chapter 1, p. 7).[9] Ricoeur confirms not having perceived a genuine difference in appreciation with Castoriadis. He admits that each configuration is as such new in comparison with all others, that it hasn't simply arisen from nowhere, and that it links with antecedents. 'And through a sort of retroaction of our new creations on the old moments, we can deliver possibilities that had been prevented' (11).

But the real debate between Ricoeur and Castoriadis was in fact never to take place. This debate should have centred on the question of the imaginary, for each has, in their own way, thoroughly explored this dimension, completely essential to both. Moreover, the reasons that explain their common distance from structuralism pertain precisely to the exclusion of the creative dimension of the imaginary from the repetitive and binary logics of closed systems.

—Translated by Natalie J. Doyle

NOTES

1. *Translator's Note*: My thanks to Elodie Génin, Léa Giry, Shana Heslin, and especially Fleur Heaney, graduate students of the program in Translation studies at Monash University, for all the valuable support they gave me in the preparation of this translation. Additional thanks must be extended to George Sarantoulias and Erin Carlisle for their valued assistance in the finalisation of the manuscript. Already published English translations of French texts have been used and referenced. Where no English translations were already available, the quotes have been translated especially for this chapter, with the references to the original French texts being provided.

2. *Translator's Note*: The author uses the French expression *donner à penser*, normally translated as 'to suggest'. The French expression, however, conveys a meaning which is not encapsulated in the verb 'suggest'.

3. *Translator's Note*: Here again, Dosse uses the French expression *donner à penser*, discussed in note 2.

4. *Translator's Note*: This line does not appear in the English translation of *Ideology and Utopia*.

5. *Translator's Note*: Dosse is referring to the original French-language publication of *De l'interprétation. Essai sur Freud* (Ricoeur 1965). This work was later translated into English as *Freud and Philosophy: An Essay on Interpretation* (Ricoeur 1970). It is important to note here that *Freud and Philosophy* contains additional essays that were not included in the French original.

6. *Translator's Note*: Here Dosse is playing on the etymology of the word *lieutenance* (lieutenancy, authority) from the verb *tenir* (to hold) and the word '*lieu*' (place), which Ricoeur used in the third volume of *Time and Narrative*, along with the word *représentance* (representing), to translate the German word *Vertretung* and to refer to the reconstruction of the past performed by historical narratives.

7. *Translator's Note*: *Grandes écoles* are selective higher education institutions specific to France. Established in the eighteenth and nineteenth centuries, they have written and oral entrance examinations (*concours*), and limited positions available. Candidates normally sit for these examinations after two years of study in dedicated preparatory classes. Among the most prestigious are the *Écoles normales supérieures*, whose original mission was to train university teachers.

8. *Translator's Note*: The term *ensidique* was coined by Castoriadis to refer in shorthand to what he called *logique ensembliste-identitaire*, translated as 'ensemblistic–identitary logic' (or 'ensidic logic'), the logic exemplified in set theory which presumes fully determinable identities for both the sets and their components.

9. Hereafter, the references to the dialogue proper appear as single page numbers.

REFERENCES

Amalric, Jean-Luc. 2013. Paul Ricoeur, *l'imagination vive. Une genèse de la philosophie ricoeurienne de l'imagination*. Paris: Editions Hermann.

Bachelard, Gaston. 1994. *The Poetics of Space*. Translated by Marie Jolas. Boston, MA: Boston University Press.

———. 1988. *Air and Dreams*. Translated by Edith R. Farrell and Frederick C. Farrell. Dallas, TX: Dallas Institute Publications.

Barel, Yves. 1978. *La Ville médiévale: système social, système urbain*. Grenoble: Presses niversitaires de Grenoble.

Castoriadis, Cornelius. 1978. Letter to Paul Ricoeur, '28 juillet 1978'. Paris: Castoriadis Archives.

———. 1984. 'The Sayable and Unsayable'. In Crossroads in the Labyrinth. Translated by Kate Soper and Martin H. Ryle, 119–44. Brighton: The Harvester Press.

———. 1987. *The Imaginary Institution of Society*. Translated by Kathleen Blamey. Cambridge, MA: Massachusetts Institute of Technology Press.

———. 1997. 'Merleau-Ponty and the Weight of the Ontological Tradition'. In World in Fragments: Writings on Politics, Society, Psychoanalysis and the Imagination. Translated and edited by David Ames Curtis, 273–310. Stanford, CA: Stanford University Press.

———. 2007. 'Imaginary and Imagination at the Crossroads'. In *Figures of the Thinkable*. Translated by Helen Arnold, 71–90. Stanford, CA: Stanford University Press.

———. 2008a. 'Imagination, imaginaire, réflexion (1988)'. In *Fait et à faire, Les carrefours du labyrinthe V*, 227–81. Paris: Points.

———. 2008b. 'Complexité, magmas, histoire (1993)'. In *Fait et à faire, Les carrefours du labyrinthe V*, 250–69. Paris: Points.

———. 2008c. 'Passion et connaissance (1992)'. In *Fait et à faire, Les carrefours du labyrinthe V*, 147–68. Paris: Points.

Cordier, Stéphane. 10 October 1997. Letter to Castoriadis. Paris: Castoriadis Archives.

Delacroix, Christian, François Dosse, and Patrick Garcia. 2007. *Les courants historiques en France XIXe-XXe siècle.* Paris: Gallimard.

Duby, Georges. 1980. *The Three Orders: Feudal Society Imagined.* Translated by Arthur Goldhammer. Revised edition. Chicago, IL: University of Chicago Press.

———. 1996. 'L'art, l'écriture et l'histoire'. *Le Débat* 1996/5 92: 174–92.

Foessel, Michaël. 2007. *Anthologie de Paul Ricoeur.* Paris: Points.

Fressard, Olivier. 2006. 'Castoriadis, le symbolique et l'imaginaire'. In *L'imaginaire selon Castoriadis. Thèmes et enjeux, Cahiers Castoriadis no. 1.* Edited by Sophie Klimis and Laurent Van Eynde, 119–50. Bruxelles: Facultés Universitaires Saint-Louis.

Heidegger, Martin. 1967. *Being and Time.* Translated by John Macquarrie and Edward Robinson. Oxford: Blackwell.

Lacan, Jacques. 2006. *Écrits: The First Complete Edition in English.* Translated by Bruce Fink, Héloïse Fink, and Russelle Grigg. New York: W. W. Norton and Company.

L'Arc. 1978. *Numéro spécial de 'Georges Duby',* 72.

Legros, Robert. 2008. 'Castoriadis et la question l'autonomie'. In *Cornelius Castoriadis. Réinventer l'autonomie.* Edited by Blaise Bachofen, Sion Elbaz, and Nicolas Poirier, 131–50. Paris: Éditions du Sandre.

Merleau-Ponty, Maurice. 1964. *Sense and Non-Sense.* Translated by Hubert L. Dreyfus and Patricia Allen Dreyfus. Evanston, IL: Northwestern University Press.

———. 1968. *The Visible and the Invisible, Followed by Working Notes.* Edited by Claude Lefort and translated by Alphonso Lingis. Evanston, IL: Northwestern University Press.

———. 2010. *Institution and Passivity: Course Notes from the Collége De France (1954–1955).* Translated by Leonard Lawlor and Heath Massey. Evanston, IL: Northwestern University Press.

Mongin, Olivier. 1998. *Paul Ricoeur.* Paris: Seuil.

Proust, Marcel. 2003. *Time Regained.* Volume 6, *In Search of Lost Time,* revised edition. Edited by D. J. Enright and translated by Andreas Mayor and Terence Kilmartin. New York: Modern Library Press.

Réa, Caterina. 2006. 'Perception et imaginaire: l'institution humaine entre créativité et sédimentation. Une lecture à partir de Merleau-Ponty et Castoriadis'. In *L'imaginaire selon Castoriadis. Thèmes et enjeux, Cahiers Castoriadis no. 1.* Edited by Sophie Klimis and Laurent Van Eynde, 75–100. Bruxelles: Facultés Universitaires Saint-Louis.

Ricoeur, Paul. 1965. *De l'interprétation. Essai sur Freud.* Paris: Editions du Seuil.

———. 1966. *Freedom and Nature: The Voluntary and the Involuntary.* Translated by Erazim V. Kohak. Evanston, IL: Northwestern University Press.

————. 1967. *The Symbolism of Evil.* Translated by Emerson Buchanan. New York: Harper and Row.

————. 1970. *Freud and Philosophy: An Essay on Interpretation.* Translated by David Savage. New Haven: Yale University Press.

————. 1974. 'Imagination productive et imaginative reproductive selon Kant'. *Recherches phénoménologiques sur l'imaginaire. I*, 9–13. Paris: Centre de Recherches Phénoménologiques.

————. 1977. 'La structure symbolique de l'action'. *Actes de la 14e conference internationale de sociologie des religions* (Symbolisme religieux, séculier et classes sociales? Strasbourg, 1977). 29–50. Lille: Secrétariat C.I.S.R.

————. 1978. Letter to Castoriadis, '7 août 1978'. Paris: Castoriadis Archives.

————. 1985. *Time and Narrative* (Volume 2). Translated by Kathleen McLaughlin and David Pellauer. Chicago, IL: University of Chicago Press.

————. 1986. *Fallible Man.* Translated by Charles A. Kelbley. New York: Fordham University Press.

————. 1991a. 'Imagination in Discourse and in Action'. In *From Text to Action.* Translated by Kathleen Blamey and John B. Thompson, 168–87. Evanston, IL: Northwestern University Press.

————. 1991b. 'Ideology and Utopia'. In *From Text to Action.* Translated by Kathleen Blamey and John B. Thompson, 308–24. Evanston, IL: Northwestern University Press.

————. 1991c. 'Science and Ideology'. In *From Text to Action.* Translated by Kathleen Blamey and John B. Thompson, 246–69. Evanston, IL: Northwestern University Press.

————. 2000. *Memory, History, Forgetting.* Translated by Kathleen Blamey and David Pellauer. Chicago, IL: University of Chicago Press.

————. 2003. *The Rule of Metaphor: The Creation of Meaning in Language.* Translated by Robert Czerny, Kathleen McLaughlin, and John Costello. London: Routledge Classics.

Sartre, Jean-Paul. 2004. *The Imaginary: A Phenomenological Psychology of the Imagination.* Translated by Jonathon Webber. London: Routledge.

Tomès, Arnaud, and Philippe Caumières. 2011. *Cornelius Castoriadis. Réinventer la politique après Marx.* Paris: Presses Universitaires de France.

Van Eynde, Laurent. 2006. 'La Pensée de l'imaginaire de Castoriadis du point de vue de l'anthropologie philosophique'. In *L'imaginaire selon Castoriadis. Thèmes et enjeux, Cahiers Castoriadis no. 1.* Edited by Sophie Klimis and Laurent Van Eynde, 63–74. Bruxelles: Facultés universitaires Saint-Louis.

Biographical Notes on Paul Ricoeur and Cornelius Castoriadis

PAUL RICOEUR (1913–2005)

Paul Ricoeur was a contemporary French philosopher of worldwide renown whose work has been translated into more than thirty languages. Born in a Protestant family, just before the Great War, Ricoeur was marked over the course of his childhood by a series of sorrows (death of his mother shortly after his birth, death of his father at the Battle of Marne, and death of his older sister from tuberculosis). Raised by his grandparents in Rennes, he admits in his autobiography to have adopted reading very early on as a true inner home. Two involvements singularize the young professor of philosophy in the 'non-conformist' mood of the 1930s: one from the side of Protestantism and the other from the side of the left (a card-carrying member of the *SFIO* [the French Social Democratic Party]) and even the extreme left (his participation in the journal *Terre Nouvelle*, which had anarcho-communist leanings).

Despite the interruption of his university career during the Second World War (mobilized as a reserve officer, he was quickly taken prisoner in Pomerania following a 'debacle'), Ricoeur was first known as one of the introducers of Husserl in France (notably for his translation of *Ideas*), as a phenomenologist (for his thesis on the philosophy of the will, *The Voluntary and the Involuntary*), and as an existentialist influenced by Jaspers, Marcel, and Heidegger. After his selection at the University of Strasburg, then as a Professor at the Sorbonne, Ricoeur then chose the young University of Nanterre, in which he would be elected to serve as dean, prior to the 'events of May' (he would then resign from his functions as dean following the intervention of the police on to the campus in 1968). It is at that time that he enriched his phenomenological method with the hermeneutic tradition (Dilthey, Heidegger, Gadamer) and engaged a confrontation, not without its obstacles, with structuralism (*The Conflict of Interpretations*) and the 'masters of suspicion' (*Freud and Philosophy*).

After the failure of his candidacy at the *Collège de France* (in competition with Michel Foucault), he left to teach at the University of Chicago, where he discovered currents of analytic philosophy that he helped to introduce in France (*The Rule of Metaphor*). As an exemplary passer between philosophical traditions, Ricoeur also continued to dialogue with the human and social sciences (*Ideology and Utopia*, *From Text to Action*), with the construction of a philosophical anthropology as the framework of all his work. It is undeniable that historical science was the object of most of his epistemological attention, especially in the three volumes of *Time and Narrative* (a trilogy that contributed to his international reputation) and later in *Memory, History, Forgetting*. As an observer who was involved in his century, a companion of the journal *Esprit*, Ricoeur remained faithful politically to strong convictions about the left (the 'anti-totalitarian left'), though against the revolutionary Marxism of his youth.

REFERENCE

Dosse, François. 1997. *Paul Ricoeur: Les sens d'une vie (1913–2005)*. Paris: La Découverte.

CORNELIUS CASTORIADIS (1922–1997)

Cornelius Castoriadis was born in Greece (Constantinople) in 1922. Very young, 'unreasonably young' he admits, he was passionate about politics and philosophy. He maintained these two passions his whole life – and the 'project of autonomy' would be one of its results. In 1937, the young militant revolutionary joined the Young Communists and quickly turned to Trotskyism in order to join the organization led by Spiros Stinas, under the German occupation. During the civil war, threatened with death both from the Greek police and by the Stalinists, he went into exile in France in 1945.

Castoriadis joined the *Parti Communiste International* (PCI) in 1946, a French section of the Fourth International. With Claude Lefort and some other comrades, he created a critical movement. They would leave the PCI in 1949 and this would be the birth of the group *Socialisme ou Barbarie*. The first issue of the journal appeared the same year. Over the course of fifteen years, forty issues of *Socialisme ou Barbarie* would develop a virulent and stubborn critique of all forms of bureaucratic totalitarianism, whether Stalinist or capitalist. Castoriadis played a considerable role in this. But he would also apply all the force of his conviction and his exceptional ability of synthesis to the elaboration of a set of anti-hierarchical recommendations concerning the notion of direct democracy. These themes resurface several years later, but are considerably diluted, if not distorted, in the term 'self-management' (*auto-gestation*).

At the same time, he worked as an economist at the European Organization of Economic Cooperation (OECE), began training as a psychoanalyst, attended Jacques Lacan's seminar, and elaborated the philosophical themes that would become his 'mother-ideas'. In 1970, his naturalization allows him to abandon his pseudonyms (Chaulieu, Cardan, Barjot, etc.) in order to use his own name in his writings. He then published his major work, *The Imaginary Institution of Society* [1975]. In the first part, he attempts to show that in order to remain revolutionary, it is necessary to abandon Marxism. In the second part, he shows that the project of an autonomous society implies a rupture with the inherited philosophy, the conception of being as perpetual creation, of the human subject as radical imagination and of society as a radical imaginary. This work, at the crossroads of many disciplines, including philosophy, epistemology, psychoanalysis, economics, philosophy of history, and so forth, will be pursued and deepened in the series 'Crossroads of the Labyrinth' (a total of six volumes, one of which is posthumous), as well as in seminars at the EHESS (*École des hautes études en sciences sociales*; 1980–1997), of which five years of teaching have been published after his death in 1997.

REFERENCE

Dosse, François. 2014. *Castoriadis: Une vie*. Paris: La Découverte.

Index

Abel, Olivier, 82
action, xix, xxii, xxiv, xxvii, xl, xli,
    xliv, 17, 24, 33, 55, 57, 81,
    94–95, 97–98, 117–18, 125, 127,
    128, 139–40, 143–47, 162, 164;
    autonomous, xxiv;
    historical, xxxviii, xli, 126;
    human, xxiv, xxvii, xxxvii, xlv, 17,
    25, 78, 81, 94, 97–99, 124, 126,
    140, 146;
    philosophy of, xxvii;
    political, xvi, xlvi, 125;
    social, 115;
    theories of, 70.
    See also doing; *praxis*
Adorno, Theodor, 17
after-effect [*après-coup*], 14.
alienation, xxxix, xliii, 54, 100, 159
Althusser, Louis, 59, 150, 154
ancients, 11
Anheim, Etienne, 155–56
anthropology, 56, 79, 81, 120–21,
    159, 163;
    anthropological, xxiv, xxvi–xxvii,
    xxxv, xl–xli, 54, 57, 85, 120,
    126, 157;

cultural, xli, 80, 100;
philosophical, xxvi, 96, 117, 121,
    124–25, 162, 172;
structural, xxv, 90
antinomy, 65
Apples, 10
Arc, L', 143, 155
Arendt, Hannah, xxxvii–xxxviii, xlv,
    17, 89, 120
Arnason, Johann, xvi, 51, 121
Asia Minor, 62–63
Assmann, Jan, 133
Athenians, 17, 161
Athens, Greece, 68
Auschwitz, 17
autonomy, xv–xlv, 5, 27, 30,
    54, 58, 65, 67, 71, 93,
    102, 113, 129, 131,
    150, 161;
    Project of, xliv, 67, 86, 102, 113,
    120–23, 132, 173.
    See also heteronomy
autopoiesis, 104, 147
Axial Age, 60, 67;
    Chinese, 67;
    Indian, 67;

Azoulay, Vincent, 155
Aztecs, 8, 17

Babylonians, 6
Bachelard, Gaston, 142, 160
Barel, Yves, 161–62
basso continuo, xxxv, 7, 32.
being, xxvii–xxviii, xxx–xxxvi,
    xliv, 5, 11–12, 16, 23, 28,
    31, 37, 41, 52, 61, 67, 79,
    84–85, 92–94, 97–98, 101, 104,
    116–17, 141–42, 144–46, 152,
    160–62;
  human, xxiv, xxvi, xxx, xl, 7, 11,
    27, 52, 56, 93, 124, 163;
  mode of, xxvii, 10, 40, 92,
    94, 130;
  social, xxii;
  social-historical, xxv, xxvii;
  social-imaginary, 87
Benveniste, Émile, 60
Bible, 9
Bielefeld school, 12
biology, 7, 12
Blumenberg, Hans, 65, 131
Bon Plaisir, Le, xiii, xxxiv, 3, 165
Budapest, Hungary, xxxviii

Canguilhem, Georges, 11
Cézanne, Paul, 10
Changeux, Jean-Pierre, xxxiii, 85–86
chaos, xxxvi, 65, 86, 93, 98, 112,
    116–18, 128, 130, 158, 160.
  See also formless
Chicago, University of, 35, 83,
    172, 176
Christianity, xvii–xviii, 69
Cochin, Augustin, 4
collective, xxv, xxx, xxxiv, xxxix,
    xliii, 55, 60, 93–94, 97, 102,
    129, 131–33, 139, 143, 157
  effervescence, 60

Columbus, Christopher, 8, 69
configuration, xxxvi, 4, 6, 8–9, 13,
    30–34, 38, 52–53, 56, 61–62,
    64–65, 84, 97, 99, 119, 128,
    151, 165;
consciousness, 37, 80, 88,
    124–25, 127–28, 141, 148,
    151, 160;
  false, xlii;
  of the mass of individuals, xliii;
  proletarian, xvi;
  social, xxii
continuity, 6–12, 14–16, 28, 32, 34,
    38, 57, 64–69, 77, 90, 99–102,
    111, 115, 118–21, 124–27,
    130–131, 162;
  historical, 7, 112, 115, 118, 124;
  of existence, xxxv, 7, 32, 65, 92,
    101–2, 118, 124, 165.
  See also discontinuity
Copernicus, Nicolaus, 6
cosmos, 65, 86
creation, xxxv–xxxvi, xlvi, 4–5,
    9–13, 27, 29–30, 32, 40–41,
    49–50, 52, 61, 69, 73, 77–78,
    82, 84–85, 91–93, 95, 99–102,
    112–14, 116–17, 120, 123, 127,
    129, 130–32, 140, 142, 146–47,
    154, 159–63, 165, 173;
  cum nihilo, 40–41, 59, 92;
  ex nihilo, 24, 28–29, 35–36, 40–41,
    59, 93, 111–16, 118, 121;
  historical, xxxv–xxxvii,
    xlvii, 3, 111–15, 120–21,
    130–31, 162;
  in nihilo, 40–41, 59, 92;
  of institutions, 7, 86, 111;
  ontological, 101, 106;
  (-ing), xxxv, 4–5, 27, 63, 85.
creativity, xxiii, 36, 38–39, 42, 50,
    59–60, 65, 81, 95, 111, 114,
    116, 124, 129, 148, 153;

in language, 37, 60;
  social-historical, xxv, xxvi, 12,
  50, 51
culture, xxv, xxviii, 16, 25, 31, 56,
  59, 63, 66, 69, 70, 77, 86, 102,
  133, 154–56;
  human, 15, 77, 87

Davidson, Donald, 16
democracy, 113, 163, 173;
  ancient Greek, 86, 112–13,
  120, 122;
  modern, 54
Derrida, Jacques, 8, 43, 59
determinacy, 79, 92, 101, 117
determination, 27–28, 54, 72, 79, 84,
  93, 97, 101, 158, 162
development, xxv, xxx, xlv, 11, 12,
  23–24, 36, 40, 43, 53, 56, 60,
  65, 70, 81, 88, 94–95, 104, 117,
  129, 131.
  See also Entwicklung
Dilthey, Wilhelm, xxi, 172
discontinuity, xxxv, xxxvii,
  6–7, 11, 14–15, 30, 32,
  57, 68–69, 77, 90, 92, 95,
  100–2, 111–13, 118–22,
  124–25, 127, 130–31,
  161–62, 165;
  historical, 34, 118–19, 124, 130;
  of meaning, xxxv, 124, 165;
  of production, 9–10, 67.
  See also continuity
discourse, xliii, xliv, 57, 60, 85–86,
  91, 95–96, 117, 128, 144–45,
  147–48, 150, 151–52;
  hermeneutical, xxii, 122, 150;
  poetic, 145–48
doing, xxiv, xxvii, 42, 81, 96, 105,
  129, 135, 140, 154;
  human, xxiv–xxvii.
  See also action; *faire*; *praxis*

Dosse, François, xviii, xlvi, 25–26,
  42, 154
Duby, Georges, 155
Durkheim, Émile, xvii, 54–56, 60

Egyptians, 6, 14–15, 63
eidolon, 156
Eliade, Mircea, xix, xx, xxii, 50
Elias, Norbert, 62, 70–71
England, Victorian, 9
Entwicklung, 12
Eratosthenes, of Cyrene, 6
Euclid, of Alexandria, 11
Eudoxus, of Cnidus, 6
existentialism:
  Christian, xviii
Eynde, Laurent Van, 162–63

faire, xxiv–xxvii.
  See also doing; action; *praxis*
fantasy, 12, 151
Fauconnet, Paul, 55
Fermat, Pierre de, 11
Ferry, Jean-Marc, 16
Fichte, Johann G., xxviii, 3, 18,
  52–54, 79, 84, 89, 103
fiction, 36–38, 43, 106, 129,
  151–52.
figuration, 32–33, 62, 114;
  historical, xxxiv;
  social, xlv;
  Foessel, Michaël, 26, 45, 82, 139
formless, xxxvi, xlvii, 5–6, 32, 38,
  97, 116–18.
  See also chaos
forms: new, xxxvii, xlvii, 28, 84,
  93, 112
Foucault, Michel, xxxv, 6–7, 9, 59,
  118, 125–26, 165, 172
foundationalism, xxix, xxxi
freedom, xxiv, 84–85, 98, 100, 102,
  105–6, 141, 146, 159, 162

Freud, Sigmund, xxi, xxii, xl,
    xlii–xliii, 11–12, 14, 80, 149,
    151, 154, 156–57, 160
functionalism, 62
Furet, François, 4

Gadamer, Hans-Georg, xxi, 122–27,
    148, 172
Gauchet, Marcel, 54
Geertz, Clifford, xli, 26, 80, 100
Gladstone, William E., 9
Greece, xvii, 9–10, 15, 65, 86,
    123, 161;
    ancient, xxx, xxxvii, 10, 50, 64,
    111, 119, 122–23;
    classical, 33
Greek(s), xvii, xxvii, xxx, xliv, 4,
    6, 8–9, 15, 40, 50, 60, 62–65,
    67, 70–71, 86, 112–13, 119–21,
    123, 129, 131, 163
Greisch, Jean, xix
Gulag, the, 17

Habermas, Jürgen, xliii, xliv, xlvii,
    17, 125–27
Hegel, Georg W. F., xvi, xviii,
    xxxvii–xxxviii, 53, 99, 127.
Hegelian-Marxist, 8
Heidegger, Martin, xxi, xxvii, 3, 8, 12,
    43, 52–53, 97, 144, 160, 171–72
hermeneutic circle, 112, 122–23,
    125–126, 128–29, 131, 146.
hermeneutic spiral, 118, 125,
    128–31
hermeneutics, xviii, xix, xx–xxii,
    xxviii, xxxvi, xlii, 16, 31, 50,
    98, 122–24, 127, 131, 146;
    depth, xliii
Herodotus, 11
heteronomy, xvii, xxi, xliii, 67,
    98, 102
    See also autonomy

history:
    and the imaginary, xxxvii;
    as project, 112, 123, 128–30, 132;
    as recounted, 112, 123, 128–29,
    131, 133;
    European, 8, 15, 67;
    Greek, 9, 63, 121, 123;
    Hebrew, 9;
    historical understanding, 150;
    human, xxxvii, 27, 31, 33–34, 57,
    100, 119;
    intellectual, 59;
    literary and artistic, xxxiv;
    of science, xxxiv, 77;
    of religions, 56;
    of thought, 140;
    our own, 8;
    singularity of, 14, 34, 121, 123,
    129, 131;
    social, 154–55;
    social and political, xxxiv;
    theory of, xxiii, xxxiv, 93;
    Western Greek, 8;
    Western thought, 30, 36, 43
Hitler, Adolf, 17
Homeric poems, 8, 119
Homo faber, xl
Homo laborans, xl
Homo loquax, xl
Homo sapiens sapiens, 66
horizon:
    of expectation, xlv, 12, 126, 149.
    See also world
human condition, xxi, xxiv, 28, 89,
    119–21, 124–26, 130–31

idealism, German, xix, 53.
ideology, xxii, xxv, xxxiv, xli–xliv,
    xlv, xlvii, 24, 72, 81, 83, 87,
    100, 102, 114, 118, 129, 145,
    149–50, 155
Iliad, 9

image(s), xvii, xxiv, xxv, xxvi, xxx,
  30, 37, 40, 56, 62, 65, 80, 86,
  96, 117, 129, 140–42, 144, 149,
  155–56
imaginary, xxvii, xxx, xxxiv,
  xxxvii, xli–xlii, 3, 16, 25–29,
  51, 55, 57–58, 61, 63–64,
  68–69, 71–73, 78–79, 84,
  87, 89, 92–95, 98–99, 113, 115,
  118, 127, 139–44, 146, 151,
  153–66;
  creative, 28;
  cultural, 81, 86;
  instituted, 87, 100, 102;
  instituting, xxxvi, 79, 82, 87,
    94, 100;
  institution, 55, 61;
  meaning, 25;
  production of the society,
    xxxiv, 3, 51;
  radical, 27–28, 42, 81, 154, 156;
  social and political, xli.
  See also social imaginary
  significations
Imagination, xxi, xxiii, xxx,
  xxxiv, xl, xli, xliv, 3–4, 12,
  16, 24, 26, 30–31, 34, 36–37,
  50–54, 57, 60, 72–73, 77–84,
  87–89, 92–102, 111–12, 114,
  116–17, 127, 139–46, 153,
  156, 163;
  creative, 4, 23–24, 26–31, 33–39,
    41, 43, 49, 68, 78, 81, 111, 116,
    154, 159;
  epistemological, 37;
  function of, 36, 81, 100;
  Kantian, 12;
  practical, 16, 146;
  productive, 26, 28, 30–31, 34–37,
    41, 43, 51–53, 77–79, 81–83,
    89–92, 94–102, 114, 128, 130,
    141, 144;

radical, 29, 79, 86, 92, 106, 117,
    139, 163;
  religious, 64;
  reproductive, 30, 36, 90, 96;
  social, xiii, 37, 139;
  Social-historical, xxxiv;
  symbolic, 88;
  transcendental, 97, 140
indeterminacy, 117, 158
Indo-European, 62
Indology, 56
innovation, xxiii, xxv, xxxv, xxxviii,
  6, 12–13, 16, 31–32, 40, 43,
  55, 57–62, 64, 67, 99, 101, 114,
  142, 162;
  semantic, 50, 96, 142, 145.
institution, xvii, xix, xxv, xxviii,
  xli, xlv, 3, 5, 7, 11–13, 28,
  33–34, 41–43, 54–58, 60–61,
  63, 65–67, 77–78, 82, 84,
  86–88, 90, 111, 113–14, 121,
  123–24, 133, 156–62;
  pre-instituted, 13, 31;
  Self-institution, 5, 27
interpretation, xix, xx, xxi, xxii,
  xxiii, xxiv, xxv, xxvi, xxxvi,
  9–10, 31, 50–53, 55, 57–59,
  61–62, 64–65, 69, 71, 94, 97,
  100–2, 113, 115, 121–23,
  128–31, 133, 146, 150
invisible, 141, 144

Jakobson, Roman, 9, 56
Jerusalem, Israel, 68
Juda, Kingdom of, 67

Kant, Immanuel, xviii, xix, xxviii,
  3, 28, 36, 51–54, 79, 96–97,
  140, 142
Kearney, Richard, 24, 39, 82
Kepler, Johannes, 6
Khomeini, Ayatollah, 7, 17, 119

knowledge, xix, xxv, xxxviii, 9, 14,
66, 90, 133, 150, 163;
Theory of, 80–81, 145
Koran, 16

Lacan, Jacques, xxxvi, xli, 14, 59,
154, 156–57
language, xxi, xxii, xxxvii, xli, xliii,
4–6, 8–9, 12–14, 28–29, 31,
33–34, 36–40, 42–43, 50, 56,
58–61, 66, 73, 90–91, 96–97,
111–12, 116, 127, 142, 145,
147–48
Langue, 60
Lao Tzu, 16
Law, xxxvii, xli, xlii, xliii, 6–7, 14,
16, 152, 158;
international, 16
Leibniz, Gottfried W., 11
Lévi-Strauss, Claude, 90, 114
linguistics, 56, 60, 157
logic, xxiii, 166;
ensidic, 161;
Fregean, 80;
identitarian, 62, 91–92
Logon didonai, 14, 123, 133
Logos, xxx;
palaios logos, 15
longue durée, 70
Lorenzer, Alfred, xliii
Luhmann, Niklas, 70

magma, 14, 28, 41, 43, 86, 158, 161
Malebranche, Nicolas, 79
Malraux, André, 5, 60
Mann, Michael, 62
Marx, Karl, xxii, xxiv, xxxvii, xxxviii,
xl, xli, xlii, xliii, xliv, xlvi, xlvii,
3, 24–25, 52–53, 79, 88–89, 93,
149–50, 154, 157, 159
marxism, xvi, xxiii, xxiv, xxv,
xxxvii, xxxviii, xxxix, xli, xlii,

xliv, xlv, xlvi, xlvii, 54, 88–89,
150, 153–54
master-signifier, 156
mathematics, xxxvii, 6–7
Mauss, Marcel, 50, 55–57, 61, 90, 114
meaning, xix, xx, xxi, xxii, xxiii,
xxiv, xxvi, xxviii, xxix, xxx,
xxxv, xxxvi, xl, xlv, 4, 8–10, 12,
14–16, 25–27, 40–42, 51–52,
55–58, 61–62, 64–66, 68–72,
77–78, 82, 84, 86–87, 91–93,
95, 98–100, 111–13, 115–16,
118–19, 121, 123–24, 126–30,
132–33, 135, 139, 142, 147–49,
157–59, 161–63, 165.
See also sense
Melians, 17
memory, 15, 67, 99, 124–25,
133, 144;
cultural, 10, 66, 99, 132–33;
Human, 10
Merleau-Ponty, Maurice, xxix, 87–88,
115, 118, 142–44, 160–62
metaphor, xx, xxi, xxiii, xxxviii,
4, 25, 31, 37–39, 41, 43, 60,
90, 96, 99, 112, 116–17, 130,
145–48, 152
metaphysics, 43, 52;
Heideggerian critique of, 79;
Kantian critique of, 85, 94
Michel, Johann, xxix, 51–52, 58,
83, 116
mimesis, 99, 120, 125, 127–29, 147,
151–52;
mimesis1, 127–28;
mimesis2, 128;
mimesis3, 128–29
mirror stage, the, xliii
modernity, 113, 124–26, 131–32,
148, 159
Monet, Claude, 10, 99
monotheism, Jewish, 67

Mouzakitis, Angelos, 26
Mycenaeans, 62
myth(s), xxx, xl, 4, 15, 25, 38, 86, 95, 116–17, 129, 140
mythology, xxx, 40, 56, 64–65; comparative, 56
mythos, xxx

narrative, xxi, 4, 8, 32, 70, 84, 90, 96–97, 99, 115, 128, 151–52
natural sciences, xxviii, xxxvii
Nietzsche, Friedrich, xlii, 15

Old Testament, 9, 67
ontological, xxv, xxvii, xxviii, 36–37, 40, 59, 64, 68, 85, 92–93, 98, 100, 102, 112–13, 117, 140, 142, 145, 147–48
ontology, xvii, xxv, xxvii, xxviii, 37, 51, 64, 68, 78–80, 86, 89, 92–94, 98, 100–2, 119, 143, 146, 148, 154, 156, 160, 163
order: institutional, 4, 30–31
Orphism, 64

Paris Commune, xxxvii, xliv, xlvi
parole, 60
Pascal, Blaise, 79
phenomenology, xvi, xviii–xix, xxviii, xxix; genetic, 87; Husserlian, 80; of creative imagination, 36; of individual imagination, 81; of the will, 84–85, 98–99
philosophy, xvi, xvii, xviii, xix, xxi, xxvi, xxvii, xxviii, xxix, xxxiii, xxxiv, xxxvii, xli, xlvi, 4, 50, 53, 65, 68, 78, 80, 83–85, 88, 94, 96, 101–2, 113, 120–22, 131, 139, 141, 143–44, 146, 149, 151, 160, 162–63;

Christian, xviii; continental, xviii, 43; Hegelian, xxxvii, 99; History of, xxxiv, 53, 79, 96; of imagination, 78, 80, 82–83, 95–96, 140
Phoenicians, 63
physis, xxvii, 59, 104
Plato, xxxviii, 6, 15, 79
plot, 4–5, 97, 99, 115
poetic, xix, xxi, 37, 85, 95, 100, 139, 142, 144–48, 152
poiesis, xxiv
polis, xliv, 4, 40, 50, 60, 63, 65, 70–71, 120–21, 123
Popper, Karl, xxxvii, xxxviii
postmodernism, xxix, xxxi
poststructuralism, 58
potential, xx, xxxvi, xliii, 11, 35, 37, 54–55, 61–62, 67, 80–81, 101, 117, 121, 132, 141, 146–48
potentiality, xxviii, 11, 27–28, 41, 117, 131, 141
power, xxii, xxxix, xli, xlii, 12, 30, 36, 37–38, 61–63, 65, 67, 70–72, 78–82, 87–88, 96, 98, 101–2, 115–16, 125, 139, 141–42, 145–46, 151, 162–63.
praxis, xxiv, xxxvii, 81, 88–89, 95, 100, 102, 139, 149, 161
prefiguration, 31, 84, 97, 99, 128, 151;
production, xxxiv, xxxv, xxxvi, xxxix, 3–5, 9–10, 18, 24, 30, 51–53, 57, 60, 67, 77–78, 84, 86, 88–92, 96, 100–1, 111–12, 114–15, 118, 123, 127, 131, 140, 142, 154; determinism, of, xlvi; human, xxxiv, xxxv, 52; means of, xxxix; of radically new meaning, xlv;

produce, 84;
producing, 4, 52, 97, 133;
productive forces, xxxix, xlvi, 88;
relations of, xxxix
Produzieren, 89;
Fichtean, 3, 84
Proust, Marcel, 151–52
psyche, xxviii, xxx, xxxi, 40, 60, 64,
117, 142, 156–57, 160, 164
psychoanalysis, xxiv, xliii, 79, 156;
Freudian, xl, xlii, 80
psychologism, 80

Radio France Culture, xiii,
xxxiv, 165
rationalism: Hegelian, xxxviii.
rationality, xxiii, xliii, 6, 81, 86, 91,
97–98, 154, 158–59
Rawls, John, xlvii
reality, xxv, xxviii, xl, xliv, 17, 30,
36–38, 43, 80, 87, 92, 118,
129, 142, 147, 149–51, 153,
157, 159
reason: practical, xix, 16, 52
reconfiguration, 13, 32, 61–65, 115,
128, 153
refiguration, 99, 129, 151–52
Reich, Wilhelm, 157
Reinhart, Koselleck, 12
religion, xvi, xvii, xviii, xix, xx, xxv,
xxvi, xxx, xli, 7, 49–50, 64–66,
68, 119, 123, 125;
sociology of, 56
representation, xix, xxx, 6, 29, 55,
96, 98, 141, 143–44, 154,
156–57, 160
retroaction, xxxvi, xliii, 11–12,
14, 32, 34, 39, 101, 125,
132–33, 165
revolution, French, xxxvi, 4, 13, 115,
118, 125, 128
Ryle, Gilbert, 80

sacred:
symbolism of, xxii;
the foundational, 49
Sartre, Jean-Paul, 141–42, 160, 162
Saussure, Ferdinand de, 56, 60
Schleiermacher, Friedrich, xxi
scientific historicism: determinism
of, xlvi
Second Temple, 67
sedimentation, xxxv, 6, 31, 43, 93,
99, 114
sense, xxiii, xxxv, xxxvii, xliv, 7,
10, 12, 16–17, 27–28, 30,
32–33, 65, 71, 85–86, 88, 92,
115–19, 123–24, 133, 139–40,
147, 165.
See also meaning
Sinngebung, 8
social change, xxiv, xxxiv, 72,
111, 131
Social imaginary, xxx, xlv, 12,
23–28, 30–31, 33–34, 40,
42–43, 77–78, 81–83, 87,
90–94, 97, 111–16, 128–31,
139, 143, 145, 149, 156,
158, 162;
significations, xxx, 40, 81, 87, 91,
112–13, 115, 131, 135, 162
Social, the, 39, 41–42, 90, 144.
Social-historical, xvii, xxii–xxiii,
xxv–xxvi, xxxi, xxxiv, xliii, 40,
51, 54–55, 59, 60, 64, 66,
72–73, 77, 79, 91–92, 112,
113–114, 119–21, 139, 146,
154, 157, 162, 164
Socialisme ou Barbarie, xvi, xxxix,
xlv–xlvi
Society, xvii, xxiii–xxviii, xxx–xxxi,
xxxix, xliv, xlvii, 5, 7, 8, 27–28,
42, 52, 55–57, 92–94, 112,
121–22, 155, 158–64;
autonomous, 61;

causalistic and deterministic
theories of, 88;
imaginary production of,
xxxiv, 3, 51;
instituting, 113;
instituted, 56, 113;
practical transformation of, 100;
radical transformation of, xlv;
self-creation of, 12;
self-institution(-ing), xvii, 5, 54;
self-projection of, xvii
socius, 156
Soviet Union, xxxix
Spinoza, Baruch 8, 79, 85
Stalinists, 17
structuralism, xxxvi, 11, 24, 25, 31,
56–57, 58, 78, 89–90, 146–47,
159–60, 165–66;
Critique of, 84;
French, 56
Structure(s), xl, 5, 11, 24–25, 37–38,
42, 56, 59, 70, 90, 91–92, 127,
153, 157;
of communication, 127;
creation of, 91;
power, 61, 72;
pre-structure, 5, 31, 92–93;
of reality, 43
sublated [*relevés*], 8
superstructure(s), xl, xlii–xliii, 25,
139, 154;
basis-superstructure, 54, 58
symbol(s), xix–xx, xl, 25, 56–57, 86,
94–95, 98, 104, 128, 140–42
symbolic, the, xx, xxxiv, xl, xli,
12, 24–25, 29, 33, 50, 56–57,
86, 88, 90, 113, 114, 128, 150,
156–59;
creative productivity of, 100;
Lacanian schema of, 156;
non-symbolic, xl;
pre-symbolic, xl

Symbolism(s), xx, xli, 25, 56, 90–91,
157, 159;
creative productivity of, 142;
functional, 157–58;
institution of, 90;
poetic, xix;
rational, 157–58;
transcultural, xxii
System(s), 25, 85–86, 90–91, 160,
165–66;
capitalist, xlvi;
of law, xli;
oligarchic, 161;
philosophical, xxi, xxix;
symbolic, xli, 159;
theory(-ies), 62, 70

Tarot, Camille, xvi
Taylor, George H., 82–83
temporality, 5, 97–98, 126, 161
Terre Nouvelle, xlvi
text, xl, 9, 15, 52, 55, 72, 86, 94,
98, 122, 123, 127, 146, 147,
151, 155;
canonical, 9;
hermeneutic theory of, xxxvi;
Homeric, 113;
literary, 9–10;
religious, xxvi;
sacred, 123
Thales, of Miletus, 13–14.
Thomasset, Alain, 82–83
Tocqueville, Alexis de, 4
totalitarianism xxxviii, xli, xlv, 17
totemism, Australian, 56
Touraine, Alain, 51
Tradition(s), xxi, xxv, xxvii,
xxix, xxxi, 10–11, 16, 40,
72, 121–23, 125–33, 143,
148, 149;
Authority of, 100;
Biblical, xxx;

Critical, 100;
Cultural, 61;
Democratic, 122–23;
Durkheimian, 54, 56;
Greek, 67;
Greco-European, 119;
hermeneutic, xxxvi, xl,
 xlv, 123;
historical, 120;
Marxist, xxii, xxiv, 52;
Marxist-Leninist, xxiii;
phenomenological, 149, 160;
philosophical, xix, xxi, 34, 53, 57,
 78–81, 90, 96, 101, 120–21,
 140–41;
religious, xviii, xxvi, 50, 64, 68;
revolutionary, 122–23
transfiguration, xvii, 33, 38–39

Upanishad, 16

Utopia, xxii, xxv, xliii–xlv, xlvii, 24,
 37, 38, 43, 72–73, 83, 87, 102,
 118, 129, 133, 145, 149.
 See also social imaginary

Verdun, Battle of, 9
Visible, 119–20, 141, 144.
 See also invisible

Wagner, Wilhelm R., 6
Water Lilies, The, 10
Weber, Max, xv, xvi, xli–xlii,
 24–25
World, the, xvii, xxvii, xxviii, xxx,
 xxxix, 8, 31, 37, 51–52, 55–56,
 60, 64–65, 72, 86, 91, 97, 99,
 114, 116–18, 121–22, 129, 139,
 141, 145–46, 152, 154, 157–58,
 160–61.
 See also horizon

About the Contributors

Suzi Adams is senior lecturer in sociology at Flinders University (Australia), a permanent external fellow at the Central European Institute of Philosophy at Charles University (Czech Republic), and a coordinator editor for the *Social Imaginaries* journal and book series. Her research focuses on a hermeneutic of modernity, social creativity, sociopolitical change, and social imaginaries. She has written extensively on Castoriadis's thought, and is the author of *Castoriadis's Ontology: Being and Creation* (2011). Recent publications include 'The Significance of the Ancient Greek *Polis* for Patočka and Castoriadis: Philosophy, Politics, History', in Tava, F., and Meacham, D. (Eds), *Thinking After Europe: Jan Patočka and Politics* (2016); 'On Ricoeur's Shift from a Hermeneutics of Culture to a Cultural Hermeneutics', *Études Ricoeuriennes/Ricoeur Studies* (2015); and 'Interpreting the World as a Shared Horizon: The Intercultural Element', in Xie, Ming (Ed.), *Critical Intercultural Hermeneutics* (2014).

Jean-Luc Amalric is Agrégé and doctor of philosophy from the University of Paris 1, Panthéon-Sorbonne. He is a member of the research center Centre de Recherches Interdisciplinaires en Sciences humaines et Sociales (CRISES) of the University Montpellier 3. Together with Professor Eileen Brennan, he is the general editor of *Etudes Ricoeuriennes/Ricoeur Studies* (*ERRS*). A member of the Scientific Board of Councillors of the Fonds Ricoeur, he is currently editing and translating, in collaboration with Professor George Taylor, the *Lectures* *on Imagination* (a course taught by Paul Ricoeur at the University of Chicago in 1975). He is also the author of *Ricoeur, Derrida. L'enjeu de la métaphore* (2006) and *Paul Ricoeur, l'imagination vive: Une genèse de la philosophie ricoeurienne de l'imagination* (2013).

Johann P. Arnason is emeritus professor of sociology at La Trobe University, Melbourne, and professor at the Faculty of Human Studies, Charles University, Prague. His research interests focus on historical sociology, with particular emphasis on the comparative analysis of civilisations. Recent publications include *Nordic Paths to Modernity* (co-edited with Björn Wittrock, 2014) and *Religion and Politics: European and Global Perspectives* (co-edited with Ireneusz Pawel Karolewski, 2014).

François Dosse is an historian and epistemologist, who specializes in the history of thought. He is the founder of the journal *Espace Temps*. He has written intellectual biographies of Paul Ricoeur, Cornelius Castoriadis, Michel de Certeau, Gilles Deleuze, Félix Guattari, Pierre Nora, and others.

Johann Michel is a university professor at the University of Poitiers and is affiliated with the *École des hautes études en sciences sociales* (*Institut Marcel Mauss*) [EHESS (IMM)] in Paris. He is a member of the scientific council of the Fonds Ricoeur and is a co-founder of the international journal *Ricoeur Studies*. He is also a member of the Institut Universitaire de France. He has published widely on Ricoeur. His most recent book was translated into English as *Ricoeur and the Post-Structuralists: Bourdieu, Derrida, Deleuze, Foucault, Castoriadis* (2014) and *Quand le social vient au sens* (2015).

George H. Taylor is a professor of law in the United States at the University of Pittsburgh. He specialises in legal hermeneutics and hermeneutics more generally. He studied as a graduate student under Paul Ricoeur, and he is the editor of Ricoeur's *Lectures on Ideology and Utopia* (1986) and co-editor of Ricoeur's *Lectures on Imagination* (forthcoming). He has written on Ricoeur extensively. He was the founding President of the Society for Ricoeur Studies and a co-founder of the online, bilingual journal *Études Ricoeuriennes/Ricoeur Studies*.